HUEY P. NEWTON

THE RADICAL THEORIST

D0583734

Judson L. Jeffries

University Press of Mississippi   *Jackson*

HUEY P. NEWTON

THE RADICAL THEORIST

www.upress.state.ms.us

Copyright © 2002 by University Press of Mississippi
All rights reserved
Manufactured in the United States of America

10   09   08   07   06   05   04   03   02   4   3   2   1
∞
Library of Congress Cataloging-in-Publication Data

Jeffries, J. L. (Judson L.).
    Huey P. Newton : the radical theorist / Judson L. Jeffries.
      p.   cm.
    Includes bibliographical references and index.
    ISBN 1-57806-432-5 (alk. paper)
    1. Newton, Huey P.   2. Black Panther Party—Biography.
3. African Americans—Biography.   4. Radicals—United States—
Biography.   5. Newton, Huey P.—Political and social views.
6. Black power—United States.   7. African Americans—Politics
and government—20th century.   I. Title.

E185.97.N48 J44   2002
322.4'2'092—dc21
[B]   2001046780

British Library Cataloging-in-Publication Data available

This book is dedicated to my brother, the late Roger J. Jeffries, a fifth-degree black belt who began teaching me the art of self-defense at a very young age, thereby instilling in me confidence, courage, determination, and a sense of honor that has made me what I am today.

CONTENTS

The 1960s represent one of the great epochs in American history. That period involved widespread social upheaval and continued protest on the part of those Americans who considered themselves disenfranchised from the American mainstream. Through it all, black Americans emerged as the principal actors for political, social, and economic change. The ethic of resistance to oppression as the basis of making strong appeals for justice has always been a part of the black protest tradition.

Unlike in the 1950s though, there emerged out of the black community a number of militant groups that turned their backs on the philosophy of nonviolence that so permeated the previous decade. Leaders of those earlier organizations tended to think of racism as some type of moral defect in the conscience of white America. For them, America needed a cleansing of its conscience, a moral reform. Charles Evers, Mississippi field director for the National Association for the Advancement of Colored People (NAACP), once said: "White Americans are sick and their minds are twisted. We've got to straighten them out and heal them."[1] Conversely, according to these newly founded militant groups, white America had no conscience, hence it was fruitless to talk about moral reform. "What morality? This country ain't got no morality!" was a common theme in the speeches of Stokely Carmichael (later Kwame Ture). In the minds of these militants, what was needed was power to bring about the redistribution of wealth. Among these groups were the Congress of African Peoples, Us, the Revolutionary Action Movement, the Deacons for Defense and Justice, and the Republic of New Africa. But none of these groups commanded the attention and captured the imagination of the American people as did the Black Panther Party.

The Black Panther Party for Self-Defense, as it was originally called, was established in Oakland, California, in October 1966 by Huey P. Newton and Bobby G. Seale. The Panthers adopted the name and symbol, Black Panther, from the Lowndes County Freedom Organization, which used a black panther as its symbol. (The Lowndes County party was founded in Alabama in the early 1960s by southern civil rights activists to encourage blacks to register to vote and run for office.)[2]

In some sense the Black Panther Party considered itself the heir apparent to Malcolm X's short-lived Organization of Afro-American Unity, calling for armed self-defense and black self-reliance. Newton maintained that "the Black Panther Party exists in the spirit of Malcolm."[3] Even though the organization was cofounded by Seale and Newton, Newton was and is recognized as the unquestioned leader of the Black Panther Party. Newton was the group's minister of defense and chief ideologist. Approximately thirty books have been written about the Black Panther Party since its founding. However, none of them presents or examines the ideas of its leader in an expansive or systematic fashion. This book attempts to fill that void. It is not a biography but rather a work that presents and to some extent analyzes the political thought of Huey P. Newton. Although some of the ideas expressed throughout the Party's existence came about as a result of a collective effort on the part of Black Panther leaders like Seale, Eldridge Cleaver, David Hilliard, Kathleen Cleaver, Elaine Brown, and others, Newton wrote many of the organization's theoretical treatises and presented them to the general public. Party members credit Newton with advancing many of the ideas discussed in this book.

In terms of literary quality, Newton's pronouncements lack the rhetorical eloquence of Dr. Martin Luther King Jr.'s, are devoid of the fire and intensity present in the writings of Malcolm X, and lack the academic rigor that distinguish W. E. B. DuBois's works. However, as political scientist John McCartney has noted, "Newton was, without a doubt, the most forceful, best-known and most ambitious theorist-practitioner of the Black Power Movement."[4] "The most important thinker on the left American Left" is the way *Politiken*, a Swedish newspaper, described Newton in 1973.[5] Because of these characterizations of Newton, a book-length study of his ideas is merited. Critical to understanding Newton the thinker is to understand the roots of his political awakening. An introduction to political philosophy piqued his intellectual curiosity and in turn sparked a never-ending search for answers and solutions to many of America's long-standing societal problems. Dr. Mary Aguilar, a physician at the hospital where Newton was admitted after suffering a gunshot wound to the stomach (as a result of the 1967 altercation with police officer John Frey), had this to say about Newton's intellectual acumen: "I have marveled that a young man of twenty-five years can interpret in such scholarly fashion, the historic, socio-economic, and political implications of the trend of modern society, while I, on the other hand, after forty-five years—seventeen of them spent in study at college and in postdoctoral education—discover I learned very little of human value and must begin again."[6]

In 1989, Newton was shot and killed, allegedly over a drug deal gone bad. It was well known that Newton had developed an addiction to drugs years before his death. The irony is that Newton was well aware of the perils of drugs and the adverse impact drugs were having on the black community. In a 1978 interview, Newton, talking about heroin, said, "The trafficking of heroin is one of the greatest dissipating factors in the black community. . . . It is an evil that has to be driven out of our community."[7] In the end the temptation must have proved to be too great. Sadly, Newton's addiction to drugs parallels the unfortunate ills that have befallen many African American males. Indeed, one writer argues that, in a way, Newton succumbed to "reactionary suicide"—something he steadfastly cautioned others against.[8] Some have argued that Newton's drug addiction contributed in part to the Black Panther Party's demise. Exactly when Newton developed his drug habit is still a subject of much debate. However, by the early 1980s, the Black Panther Party was, for all intents and purposes, defunct, and Newton was a mere shell of his former self, given to violent outbursts and repeated scrapes with the law that had little or nothing to do with matters of racial equality. Some hinted of a conspiracy that, while in prison, Newton was the victim of a gruesome mind-altering medical experiment—a "clockwork orange" type of treatment.[9] At any rate, for some in the African American community, black leaders are expected to approach perfection in their heroism, and the more nearly they do so the more their other failings are overlooked. Consequently, some in the black community were willing to overlook many of Newton's later transgressions that may or may not have been induced by his drug addiction or some macabre behavior-modifying experiment.[10]

One could argue that Newton's later acts of imprudence provide his critics with a convenient excuse to disregard him as a scholar and author and an important political thinker. After all, whenever one picks up a mainstream textbook that discusses the great thinkers of various times, black intellectuals and scholars are almost always conspicuously absent. When white political theorists convene at their annual meetings to present papers, scholars and intellectuals such as Anna Julia Cooper, W. E. B. DuBois, Oliver Cromwell Cox, Maria Stewart, Edward Blyden, CLR James, or even Martin L. King Jr. are seldom the subject of these essays. When blacks are the subject of scholarly endeavors, their work is oftentimes belittled for lack of originality and rigor. Francis S. Broderick wrote of DuBois: "none of his books except *The Philadelphia Negro* is first-class. His writings on African culture, history, and politics all possess some information, but nothing which indicates the mind or hand of an original scholar." This seemingly racially motivated critique has a long-standing tradition within the white scholarly community. Is it because many whites believe that there are no black theorists worthy of recognition or study? Scholars of the Enlightenment period put forth the theory that the ability to reason is what separated humans from animals. As far as they were concerned, blacks showed no signs of being able to think rationally; therefore, they must be animals or, at most, some form of primitive creature. The rationalization that blacks were subhuman was practical, for to acknowledge blacks as men and women would be tantamount to admitting that whites did not behave as Christians. Georg Wilhem Friedrich Hegel, one of the most important political philosophers of the modern era, denied that Africa has any history because blacks could not write and suggested that blacks were morally improved by being enslaved.[11] He spoke about the African American as "natural man in his wild and untamed nature" and argued that there is "nothing remotely humanized in the Negro's character."[12] In a major essay, "Of National Characters" (1748), the esteemed David Hume discusses the "Characteristics" of the world's major divisions of human beings. In a footnote added in 1753 to his original text, Hume posited with authority the fundamental identity of complexion, character, and intellectual capacity:

> I am apt to suspect the negroes, and in general all the other species of men to be naturally inferior to the whites. There never was a civilized nation of any other complexion than white, nor even any individual eminent either in action or speculation. No ingenious manufactures amongst them, no arts, no sciences. . . . Such a uniform and constant difference could not happen, in so many countries and ages, if nature had not made an original distinction betwixt these breeds of men. Not to mention our colonies, there are Negroe Slaves dispersed all over Europe, of which none ever discovered any symptoms of ingenuity". In Jamaica indeed they talk of one negroe as a man of parts and learning [Francis Williams, the Cambridge-educated poet who wrote verse in Latin]; but 'tis likely he is admired for very slender accomplishments, like a parrot, who speaks a few words plainly.[13]

Immanuel Kant, considered the most important moral theorist of the modern period, was one of the earliest major European philosophers to equate color with intelligence. For Kant, one must be white to be fully human, for "humanity exists in its greatest perfection in the white race."[14] Around the turn of the twentieth century, Robert Bennett Bean, a professor of anatomy at the University of Virginia Medical School, offered scientific support for the theory that blacks were innately stupid. The "Negro Brain," while normal in perception, memory, and motor responses, was deficient in logical critical thinking and in grasping abstract ideas due to its arrested development, said Bean.[15] More recently, the late

Richard Herrnstein of Harvard University and Charles Murray published their controversial book, *The Bell Curve*, which demeaned black status in American eyes by insisting on the low intelligence levels of blacks. Indeed, *The Bell Curve* is striking in its insistent focus on the centrality and inferiority of African Americans in this regard.[16] The book discusses the intelligence levels of immigrants, Latinos, and Asian Americans, but those discussions are not extensive and are not as central to the book's main arguments.

Given the sentiments of these highly learned individuals, is it fair to expect more from Newton's critics who have less in the way of academic letters, who have accomplished little professionally, and who are seemingly far less cerebral than their predecessors? The answer to this question is probably a resounding "No." Philosopher Charles W. Mills suggests that whites have entered into a racial contract where they have agreed not to recognize blacks as equal persons.[17] This reality was not lost on Newton, as he exclaimed upon receiving his doctorate: "I've been called many things, but at least now they will have to call me Dr. Nigger."[18]

This book attempts to do what Newton's critics and other scholars have not done and that is to take an objective and to some extent critical look at a number of ideas, issues, and theories that Newton raised and grappled with in his quest to combat racial, gender, and class oppression. In order to write this book, I have drawn from a number of sources, many of them previously untapped. Among the rich sources consulted are essays, articles, and unpublished position papers written by Newton, including the five books Newton authored. I was also privy to transcripts of interviews of Newton, other Party members and activists. In addition, I read every article that Newton wrote and published in the Black Panther newspaper and conducted several personal interviews with former Black Panther Party members and other activists.

This book has benefited from several people who took the time to read and critique parts or all of the manuscript as well as those who have engaged me in conversation about it over the past three years. A special thanks goes to Floyd W. Hayes III of North Carolina State University, Renford R. Reese of California State Polytechnic University, and Michael Weinstein of Purdue University, who read the book in its entirety and provided valuable advice and comments along the way. Others who contributed to the writing of this book by way of intellectual discourse include Charles E. Jones and Regina L. Cody. This book has also been enhanced by J. P. Herubel and Carol Black of Purdue University, two librarians whose assistance proved to be invaluable. I would like to give thanks to all of the older black men and women from Baltimore and New York City who implored me to "keep on keeping on" and not make the same mistakes that they made during their youth. This schooling was immensely valuable as I made the transition from youth to adulthood. Additionally, I need to thank my classmates at P.S. 36 and P.S. 99 wherever they are. I also need to thank the education specialists who worked hard to help me overcome my learning disability during my youth; without them, I probably would not have the necessary tools to write this or any book. Appreciation is also extended to the late Frank L. Wilson of Purdue University, who granted me a one-semester research leave in spring 1999 in order to get started on this book. Betty Hartman and Michelle Conwell of Purdue provided much needed typing assistance during this period. And Craig Gill of the University Press of Mississippi and Robert Burchfield of Doghouse Editing and Research Services helped mold the book into the polished product it has become. Finally, I should give thanks to all the "brothers" that wear the illustrious royal purple and old gold who supported me during this endeavor, especially those of Upsilon Kappa Kappa.

*Our Black heroes are important to us because of
the way they lived their lives, not the fashion in
which they met their death.*

—Stokely Carmichael

Huey Percy Newton was one of the most
widely known and controversial activists of
the twentieth century. It has been more than
ten years since he was killed, yet few scholarly attempts have been made to put him in
his rightful place among those considered
champions of human rights. Newton was the
cofounder of the Black Panther Party, arguably the most effective black revolutionary
organization born in this country. Some supporters of the Black Panther Party have called
them the first genuine revolutionaries since
1776. Indeed, the Black Panther Party has written a chapter in
the history of American radicalism that ranks with the International Workers of the World (Wobblies) or ahead of them for
grit and élan. So much has been written about the Black Panther Party that one might get the impression that most people
know what the organization stood for and what it sought to
achieve. However, this is not entirely the case.

In point of fact, little of substance is known about this
much maligned and often misunderstood organization, and
even less is known about its leader, Huey P. Newton. James
Baldwin said it best when he asserted: "Huey Newton is one
of the most important people to have been produced by the
American chaos. His fate is very important. And not one person in white America, if they read the mass media, knows
anything about Huey, what produced him or what produced
the Black Panther Party."[1] Many of those who followed or
were frightened by Newton knew him from that famous
poster (beret, black leather jacket, spear in one hand, rifle in
the other, seated in a wicker chair) that decorated people's
walls, especially those of students all over the world. Given
that, Newton could no more escape being misunderstood
than so many of those whose imagination he captured could

escape the consequences of their misunderstanding. This book, though, is not about the Black Panther Party per se but about its leader.

Huey P. Newton was a complex figure. He had an international reputation forged as much from his passionate defense of black liberation as from his highly publicized confrontations with police. His courage to address police brutality won him admirers in minority communities, on college campuses, in select Hollywood circles, as well as in some foreign countries. He gave Black Power a compelling urgency and played a vital role in the politics of black America during the 1960s and 1970s. In the early 1970s, *Ebony* magazine rated Newton as one of the hundred most influential blacks in America. Not surprisingly, his death attracted worldwide media attention.

For the most part, journalists, politicians, and, to some extent, scholars have denigrated Newton, dismissing his accomplishments and portraying his life as one violent episode after another. Shortly after his death, a number of disparaging newspaper articles appeared commenting on the so-called tragic life of Huey P. Newton. In the *San Francisco Chronicle*, Tom Orloff, the district attorney who failed on a number of occasions to obtain convictions of Newton, called Newton "a thug," a man who "lived by violence and outside the law," and "nothing but a gangster."[2] Likewise in the *Oakland Tribune*, an unidentified police sergeant said Newton "finally got what he deserved. He died like the thug he was."[3] In an unflattering yet typical editorial, the *New York Times* stated that the Black Panther Party leader was a self-destructive "prisoner of the Oakland ghetto where he grew up."[4] In other words, other Panther leaders had successfully made the transition to the mainstream and black middle-class life but not the troubled Newton.

Newton suffered the same fate in literary and scholarly circles. Stanley Crouch, a noted black critic, had this to say about Newton: "The charismatic criminal falls, stripped of all romance, and dies in some scum-sticky situation, like a fly caught on the documentation of his own disorder and degradation."[5] In a mostly accurate and sensationalistic book on the Black Panther Party, *Shadow of a Panther*, Hugh Pearson demonized Newton, reducing him to a common hoodlum with an expensive drug habit.[6]

Few can deny that Newton's life was strewn with incidents of violence and that his police record was long. Indeed, Newton saw the inside of a jail cell long before he cofounded the Black Panther Party and several times thereafter. In 1964, he was convicted of assault with a deadly weapon, for which he served eight months in jail. However, Newton's struggles with police took place in a complex and troubled setting that included urban unrest, police brutality, government repression, and an intense debate over civil rights tactics. Stripped of context and interpretation, the violence of Newton's life was made into an emphatic indictment of him. Suffice it to say that the above accounts provide little insight into Huey Newton—the freedom fighter, intellectual, and revolutionary.

There is evidence that suggests that, early on, Newton was not unaware of the tendency of some to view him as a thug and nonintellectual. Bob Avakian, a member of the Revolutionary Communist Party, remembered: "There was a CORE convention in the San Francisco Bay Area and they had all these nationalist figures who came to speak. And they didn't invite the Panthers to speak as a political organization or party . . . but they invited them to do security! But Huey told them to get fucked! The Panthers weren't going to act as thugs for a bunch of reformists. . . . They weren't going to be reduced to being the 'armed goons' for a bunch of reformist assholes basically."[7] Avakian observes correctly that this was very significant in that Newton was making a statement that the Black Panther Party was a political party with ideas, theories, and a political program that should and would be taken seriously. This book should be seen, in part, as an attempt to correct many of the misunderstandings that surrounded Newton and provide a more complete and nuanced picture of him—the intellectual and theoretician.

Huey P. Newton, the son of a Baptist minister and the youngest of seven children, was born on February 17, 1942, in Monroe, Louisiana. His parents, Walter and Armelia, named him after Huey P. Long Jr., Louisiana's former governor and

U.S. senator. Governor Long impressed the elder Newton with his propensity for bringing about programs that were beneficial to blacks: free books to schools in black areas, free goods for the poor, road and bridge construction projects that provided blacks with jobs. T. Harry Williams has written, "Huey Long was the first Southern mass leader to leave aside race-baiting and appeals to the gold-misted past and address himself to the social and economic ills of his people."[8]

After the Civil War was over and the era of Reconstruction had come to a close, Louisiana politics became the special possession of a privileged group of wealthy planters and lumber, railroad, sugar, and oil tycoons. Long decided to try to upset the control of the privileged few and provide for the needs of the masses. His intention was to build a machine of his own, using the same tactics against his wealthy political foes that they had used against the working-class and poor people of Louisiana. Said Long, "I'm fighting a crooked machine in the Old Regulars and have to fight fire with fire."[9] Long's Share the Wealth program spoke of a fair distribution of wealth, of closing the gap between the haves and the have-nots, and of making government more responsive to the needs of the common folk. Consequently, the elder Newton believed that Huey P. Long Jr. had been a great man, and he wanted to name a son after him.

Nevertheless, Louisiana, like most of the Deep South states, maintained a comprehensive tripartite system of domination whereby blacks were oppressed politically, economically, and socially.[10] In response, some blacks opted to migrate to other areas of the country in search of a better life. Such was the case with the elder Newton. Two years after Huey was born, his father went to California in search of wartime employment and landed a job at the Oakland Naval Supply Depot. As large numbers of men were taken into the military, World War II created a severe shortage of labor in northern and western industries while it led simultaneously to an increased demand for war production and an increased demand for consumer goods. The initial reluctance to use blacks on production jobs was soon overcome by necessity. The promise of economic prosperity had its impact. An estimated quarter of a million black workers and their families migrated during the war years, substantially increasing the populations of the black communities situated mostly in the industrial areas east of the Mississippi as well as in California. The elder Newton was part of the surge of fifty thousand black migrants who headed west to work in shipyards and other industries. Eventually, the entire Newton family moved from Louisiana and settled in Oakland.

As young Huey got older, he took to the big city and found it difficult to resist the allure of Oakland's seductive streets. He enjoyed pitching pennies, shooting dice, playing the dozens, and committing small-time crimes like dislodging coins from parking meters. While in junior high school, Newton and another schoolmate formed a gang called the Brotherhood. Newton claimed that they started the gang to combat racist students, faculty, and administrators at school. According to Newton, white staff and students called blacks "niggers" on a regular basis, hence tension was always high. Newton would often get kicked out of class because he refused to knuckle under. He spent almost as much time on the street as he did in school. His high school experience was very much like his elementary and junior high school years. By his accounts, he was suspended from high school anywhere from thirty to forty times.[11] An incident during Newton's high school days would have a profound impact on the way he viewed the world. Hurrying to get the students into the shower at the end of the class period, the teacher thoughtlessly shouted, "Last one into the shower is a nigger baby!" Black and white students alike ran for the shower, except Newton. Newton, seemingly shocked, stopped in his tracks momentarily, fighting to compose himself, then walked slowly to the shower. Newton held his temper, but he never forgot the incident, which, he says, opened his eyes to a widespread pattern of racism in society.

Consciously or unconsciously, Newton's instructors succeeded in instilling in him a feeling of inferiority and incompetence that would stymie his ability to learn. The feeling that black children were not capable of learning what the white students could learn was the prevailing sentiment among whites and blacks. On one occasion, when one of

Newton's elementary school teachers thought that he was not paying attention, the teacher called him to the front of the room and told the class that he was misbehaving because he was stupid. Handing him a piece of chalk, she told Newton to write the word "business" on the chalkboard. However, when Newton walked to the board and tried to write he froze, unable to form even the first letter. Feeling humiliated, Newton hurried out of the classroom. Newton admitted, "I didn't get involved in school at all. It was a matter of fear that if I got into it and I didn't do well, it might magnify what the whites thought about my inferiority."[12] Newton confessed years later that when given homework, he would coerce the white students into doing his work, especially math and spelling assignments, by threatening to take their lunch money. Newton admitted that by the time he entered his senior year he was a functional illiterate. Newton's older brother Melvin convinced him to leave the streets alone temporarily and devote his time to learning to read. Newton recalled that Melvin seemed shocked and disgusted when he learned that his brother could not pronounce some of the easiest of words. That hurt Newton. "I had been hurt many times in fights, but nothing equaled the pain I felt at not being able to read," exclaimed Newton. "The pain from fighting went away in time. But the shame I felt from not being able to read would not go away." Years later Newton would say, "I actually learned to read—really read, more than just dog and cat, which was about all I could do when I left high school—by listening to records by Vincent Price reading great poetry, and then looking up the poems while he read them to see how the words looked."[13]

According to Newton, the first real book he ever read was Plato's *Republic*. He read it about five times. Newton worked through the book word by word with the help of a dictionary. The process was laborious and painstaking. "By the fifth time, I could read it and understand it," said Newton. "The only thing I still had trouble with was all those Greek names. I would give them my own nicknames, so I could tell the characters apart."[14] At Newton's murder trial, though, in 1968, Melvin testified that "it wasn't literally true that Huey could not read or write, but he clearly could not read at the level of a high-school graduate."[15] Later Newton would become a voracious reader. He remembered: "When I began to read, a whole new world opened up to me. Although I could still not read very well, each book made it easier. By this time I did not mind spending many hours reading because reading was enjoyment, rather than work. When I reached this point, I accumulated books and read one after another."[16] Newton developed a keen interest in the works on the black experience, particularly those of W. E. B. DuBois, Ralph Ellison, James Baldwin, and Malcolm X. While Newton was especially fond of books by black writers, his intellectual pursuits were eclectic, prompting him to read such authors as James Joyce, B. F. Skinner, and Mao Zedong.[17] In his autobiography, Newton tells how his undetected illiteracy may have been a blessing in disguise, in that when he began to read, his mind was not cluttered and locked by the programming of the system; therefore he could view matters in an entirely different light. In his words, "What I discovered in books led me to think, to question, to explore and finally to redirect my life."[18] Newton's exposure to books and reading is similar to what Malcolm X said of his experience: "I knew right there in prison that reading had changed forever the course of my life. As I see it today, the ability to read awoke inside me some long dormant craving to be mentally alive.... My homemade education gave me, with every additional book that I read, a little bit more sensitivity to the deafness, dumbness, and blindness that was afflicting the black race in America."[19]

Newton explained that he wanted to read for several reasons. First, he associated reading with being a grown-up. "It was a skill that people naturally acquired in the process of maturation," said Newton. Second, he wanted to read so that he could go to college, and he wanted to go to college "because my counselor at high school always told me it was out of the question." The counselor's advice was based on the seventy-four that Newton scored on an IQ test, extremely low by any standard. "I mean, I had a D minus average, but I just wanted to prove him wrong."[20] In addition, according to Melvin, the Newton family emphasized education as a tool "for dealing with the problems of black people." If you want to help the community, get an education—be a lawyer or something like that, Melvin remembers his parents saying. While Newton's counselors provided him with some incentive to get a college education, his family may have been perhaps his main motivation. Newton admitted, "My high school diploma was a farce."[21] He acknowledged that when he graduated he was ill equipped to function in society, except at the most elementary level, even though the system declared him educated. Newton asserts, "Maybe they knew what they were doing, preparing me for the trash heap of society, where I would have to work long hours for low wages."[22]

Newton would overcome his learning disability and the inadequate preparation he received and earn an Associate of Arts degree at Oakland City College (now Merritt Junior College) in 1966. It took Newton approximately six years to earn that degree because he only enrolled for two or three courses a semester. Mindful of his earlier difficulties with reading, Newton kept his course load manageable as a way of dealing with his learning problems. He also found writing in cursive challenging. Nevertheless, at Oakland City College Newton displayed flashes of being a budding intellectual. Not only did he do the assigned readings, he also noted the references cited in the bibliographies of those books and read some of them as well.

That Newton was able to perform well in college is either a testament to his desire to work hard to overcome his ineptness or additional proof that so-called intelligence tests do not accurately measure one's aptitude to do well scholastically. Upon graduating from Oakland City College, Newton enrolled in San Francisco Law School for a short time. There, he registered for law enforcement courses to help him better understand how to deal with the police. "Before I took Criminal Evidence, I had no idea what my rights really were," said Newton.[23] Convinced that he did not want to become a lawyer, Newton left San Francisco Law School and entered the University of California at Santa Cruz, earning a bachelor of arts degree in 1974. Shortly thereafter, Newton would be admitted into graduate school there. While at Santa Cruz, he enrolled in a course titled "The Principles of Underlying Social Evolution." Newton's professor remarked: "Huey read the stuff and he would point out subtleties in animal literature that had even escaped me. And I'm no slouch in animal literature."[24] In 1980, Newton received a Ph.D. in the History of Consciousness program, an accomplishment often downplayed or unknown by his critics.

Although Newton's life was prematurely cut short, he enjoyed a relatively prolific career as an essayist and intellectual. His portfolio includes scores of articles, essays, poetry, and position papers. Several of Newton's works are especially intriguing because they illustrate that Newton appeared to be ahead of other activists in his thinking on a number of matters. For instance, early on Newton expressed concern with the preservation of the environment, an issue that received very little attention from other leaders of the black movement. In an unpublished paper entitled "The Dialectics of Nature," Newton talks about the impending ecological crisis and its stresses on the ocean, wildlife, and humankind. Concerning the ocean, Newton says that "no other natural phenomenon on this Planet—not Mountains, sprawling rivers or redwood forests—evokes such reverence as the sea. Yet this same all-powerful ocean now proves as slavishly subservient to man-made laws like a moth caught by candlelight or a rose seed blown into the Atlantic."[25] Newton saw this ecological crisis as a war against nature, against the race, even against the unborn. As far as he was concerned, the depletion of the world's natural wonders was driven by the profit motive. When Newton spoke of the ecological crisis as a war against the race, one wonders if he foresaw the present and increasing problem of environmental racism that has plagued many minority communities throughout the United States. Other essays Newton wrote support McCartney's characterization of Newton as the most ambitious theoretician of the Black Power movement. In another unpublished essay entitled "The Historical Origins of Existentialism and the Common Denominations of Existential Philosophy," Newton wrestles with and attempts to master the sophisticated and intricate writings of Søren Kierkegaard, Martin Heidegger, and F. W. J. Schelling in an effort to fully comprehend existentialism.[26] Newton saw existentialism as a philosophy of thought functioning as a broad-based critique of bourgeois culture and industrial society.

In addition to the many articles and papers that Newton wrote, he is also the author of five informative and thought-provoking books. Newton's first book, *To Die For the People*, is a collection of essays, retorts, and speeches beginning with the founding of the Party to 1971. Among some of the topics discussed are U.S. foreign policy, the importance of coalition politics, and the defection of Eldridge Cleaver from the Black Panther Party and the Black Panther Party from the black community. His second book, *Revolutionary Suicide*, is a gripping autobiographical account of a young man who comes of age (politically and personally) in the midst of the struggle for black equality. He describes his efforts at self-education, his political awakening, and the founding of the Black Panther Party. Newton's attempt at self-learning is similar to that of Malcolm X, who read the entire dictionary as a way to get command of the English language. *Revolutionary Suicide* lacks the poetic flair and literary pen of Cleaver's *Soul on Ice*; however, it is a more substantive presentation of the ideas and sentiment of the Black Power era. *In Search of Common Ground*, coauthored with Erik Erikson, the noted Harvard psychologist, is a dialogue between Newton and Erikson and a group of Yale students wherein they discuss such matters as Western imperialism, Intercommunalism, and the impact of technology on the state of world affairs. Initially, each man states his fundamental position on the role and plight of blacks in America. Newton discusses his theory of Intercommunalism; in turn, Erikson articulates his notion of identity crisis and its relationship to the Black Power movement. Both arguments are somewhat convoluted. Newton's opening remarks (which lasted over an hour) are reduced to ten pages. The result is an inadequate presentation of the principles of Intercommunalism and Marxist methodology. Hence, the reader is given little more than an assertion that the revolutionary class of the future will not be the proletariat, as Marx claimed, but the underclass called the lumpenproletariat. Newton's fourth book, *Insights and Poems*, coauthored with

Erika Huggins, is a compilation of poems and proverbs by the authors and several others. Through artistic prose the authors crystallize the plight and frustration of black Americans and the revolutionary intentions of those considered as the vanguard of the black movement. This work is an indication of Newton's intellectual versatility.

Newton's final book, *War Against the Panthers*, a dissertation published posthumously, is a scholarly analysis of the various ways that governmental repression caused the demise of the Black Panther Party. Newton describes how the Federal Bureau of Investigation (FBI) worked to annihilate the Black Panther Party. He also examines the repressive tactics engineered against the Party by the Central Intelligence Agency (CIA), thereby undermining the myth that the CIA does not involve itself in domestic affairs. This work is essential to understanding the nature of the repression to which the Panthers in the Oakland Bay Area were subjected. However, Newton does not go into great detail about the organization's other chapters. Moreover, Newton fails to examine the more routine acts of repression involving the local police and the rank-and-file members of the organization. Although Newton's study is not objective, it is the first attempt to analyze systematically the repressive tactics levied against the Black Panther Party, which makes it a valuable and pioneering effort.

In this book, I argue that, contrary to the white media's pejorative portrayal of Newton, he was one of the most important political thinkers and practitioners in the struggle for black equality during the 1960s and 1970s. Given the inaccurate and defamatory accounts of Newton's life's work and the misrepresentation of his theories, a scholarly and in-depth study of his ideas is crucial to understanding the Black Panther Party and Newton's place in American political and cultural history.

It is quite easy to shout slogans, to sign manifestos, but it is quite a different matter to build, manage, command, spend days and nights seeking the solution of problems.

—Patrice Lumumba

OUT OF THE ASHES OF DESPAIR RISES A MILITANT PHOENIX: THE BIRTH OF THE BLACK PANTHER PARTY

While at Oakland City College, Newton became a student leader on campus. Because of his ardent support of socialism and his concern for oppressed peoples all over the world, he became a well-known figure. During the United States blockade of Cuba, Newton often lectured to anyone who would listen, urging them to refrain from supporting the blockade because Cuba had done exactly what black people should do—revolt against United States capitalism. Newton's sidewalk lectures occurred during the hey-day of the Berkeley Free Speech Movement. The movement, led by Bay Area white radicals, insisted on the right to hold noonday soap-box rallies on campus. They denounced the war in Vietnam, the draft, and capitalism. They also accused universities of neglecting their responsibility to truly educate undergraduates, preparing students instead to become cogs in the industry of means and production. When Bobby G. Seale heard Newton speak at a rally, he was impressed with Newton's knowledge of black history.[1] The two would eventually become friends and join the student Afro-American Association at the University of California at Berkeley and later the Soul Students Advisory Council. The major purpose of these organizations was to generate pride in things black and push for the introduction of black history courses at the college and the hiring of additional black faculty. Newton believed that the Afro-American Association's leader's message was ineffective. A lawyer named Donald Warden created the organization. Newton noted that people came to listen to Warden because "they were bored and wanted some entertainment, not because Warden's words were relevant to their lives."[2] Furthermore, Newton grew irritated with Warden when he realized that Warden espoused militant rhetoric in the presence of blacks yet blamed blacks for their problems when speaking before white audiences. Newton eventually resigned from these groups, citing their failure to recognize the link between capitalism and racism and the relationship between them and the local black community. In Newton's opinion, all these organizations cared about was bringing about campus reform. While the efforts of these organizations benefited the students on campus, they did nothing for the larger community. In addition to these organizations, Bobby Seale became involved with the Revolutionary Action Movement (RAM), which had a chapter on the campus of Oakland City College.[3] Ironically, Newton was refused membership in the local RAM chapter because he was seen as being too "bourgeois." Newton says:

> Bobby Seale tried to get me into the RAM chapter, but the members refused to accept me. They said I lived in the Oakland Hills and was too bourgeois, which was an absolute lie. All my life I have lived in the flatlands. Actually, I think I threatened them, because I could use my head but could also 'get down' like the street brothers. They claimed to be dedicated to the armed overthrow of the government, when, in reality, most of them were headed for professional occupations within the system. Freeman and the other RAM members eventually excluded Bobby because he lacked bourgeois skills.[4]

Disappointed with the organizations on campus, Newton stated:

> Nothing we had done on the campus related to the conditions of the brother on the block. Nothing helped them to gain a better understanding of those conditions. As I saw so many of my friends on their way to becoming dropouts from the human family, I wanted to see something good happen to them. . . . The Oakland brothers worked hard and brought in a salary, but they were still in perpetual debt to the stores that provided them with the necessities of life.[5]

Fed up, Newton flirted with the Nation of Islam, after hearing Malcolm X and Muhammad Ali (then Cassius Clay) speak at a local high school. Soon after, Newton started frequenting mosques in Oakland and San Francisco. He recalled that he was very impressed with the objectives and overall program of the organization but admitted that he could not bring himself to join because of their heavy emphasis on religion. Coming from a very religious family where his father was a preacher, Newton had had his fill of religion. Said Newton, "By this time, I had had enough of religion and could not bring myself to adopt another one. I needed a more concrete understanding of social conditions. References to God or Allah did not satisfy my stubborn thirst for answers."[6]

By the mid 1960s, Newton had become disillusioned with the Civil Rights movement, not to mention the various student groups in the Bay area. Newton argued that these groups and the traditional civil rights organizations such as the NAACP, the Congress On Racial Equality (CORE), and the Southern Christian Leadership Conference (SCLC) were not protecting African Americans from the heinous crimes inflicted upon them by white racists. Newton also argued that these organizations did little to create a better livelihood for the majority of people of African descent.[7] Eldridge Cleaver recalled that Newton and Seale were so dispirited over the inaction of so-called black-oriented revolutionary groups that they began planning a gigantic bank robbery. They put their minds to work on that because they recognized that they needed money for the revolution. Newton's and Seale's plan had a historic precedent: Joseph Stalin had once robbed banks in tsarist Russia to get money for the Russian Revolution. However, as Newton and Seale mulled over their plan, they considered the implications. Then one day Newton jumped up and said, "Later for a bank. What we're talking about is politics. What we're talking about essentially is the liberation of our people. So later for one jive bank. Let's organize the brothers and put this together. Let's arm them for defense of the black community, and it will be like walking up to the White House and saying, 'Stick 'em up, motherfucker. We want what's ours.'"[8]

In October of 1966, Newton and Seale cofounded the Black Panther Party for Self-Defense. As the organization evolved, the word "self-defense" was dropped from the title. The emergence of the Black Panther Party was the culmination of a year that saw many segments of the black community exert themselves in a way that had not been previously witnessed. Indeed, the emergence of the organization seemed to coincide with the mood of times. In the spring of 1966, Muhammad Ali would petition the Selective Service for an exemption from military service and subsequently refuse induction into the United States Army. As a result of his position, Ali was stripped of the heavyweight title. That same year, for the first time a college basketball team that started five blacks players, Texas Western University (now University of Texas at El Paso), would defeat an all-white University of Kentucky squad and their bigoted coach, Adolph Rupp, for the National Collegiate Athletic Association (NCAA) championship. That fall, Howard University students elected as homecoming queen a woman who ran on a Black Power platform and wore the emerging Afro hairstyle in defiance of the school's prevailing white American look and worldview.[9] Even the black music industry, with its roots in gospel and rhythm and blues, became nationalist in an extraordinary way. Songs such as James Brown's "I'm Black and I'm Proud" and the Temptations' "Message to a Black Man" established a distinctive sound that became the preferred expression for a generation of politically conscious blacks. CORE leader Floyd McKissick put it best when he said, "The year 1966 shall be remembered as the year we left our imposed status as Negroes and became Black men."[10]

The founding of the Black Panther Party came at a critical juncture in the life of many black Americans. In the summer of 1966, civil rights activist James Meredith was shot by whites while he was on a one-man "March Against Fear" in Mississippi, thereby reinforcing what blacks had already known—that many whites had a total disregard for black life. A year earlier, numerous cities across the United States experienced massive violent turmoil—the most publicized being the Watts rebellion in Los Angeles, where blacks took to the streets to avenge the treatment of a black motorist by white police. The Los Angeles police department was notorious for police brutality. As early as 1961, Roy Wilkins, the executive director of the NAACP, made headlines when he said that the Los Angeles police were "next to those in Birmingham, Alabama, in the treatment of Black citizens."[11] During a speech at a rally in October 1961, Wilkins noted that he was appalled at the recurring beatings and cold-blooded killings by Los Angeles police officers. As he explained, "The Negro citizens have great difficulty in getting at this evil because the system in Los Angeles makes the Chief of Police almost completely independent of the Mayor and elected officials."[12] Wilkins concluded that this system allows the police department to be the judge and jury of its own personnel without having to pay attention to public outcry.[13] The Watts rebellion resulted in the destruction of neighborhoods and businesses, not to mention the loss of black lives.

Between 1964 and 1968, there were 329 uprisings in 257 cities, resulting in 52,629 arrests, 8,371 persons injured, and 220 killed.[14] The number of these incidents and the manner in which they unfolded are significant in two ways. The number spoke to the increasing frustration that permeated many black communities. The way the violence was carried out to some degree spoke to the message the participants were sending to those whites who were directly responsible for exploiting them and those whites who, while not personally responsible for keeping blacks subjugated, nevertheless had the power to help alleviate that oppression. For the most part, the unrest was focused against property rather than against people. There were relatively few cases of injury to persons, and the vast majority of the insurrectionists were not involved in attacking people. The much publicized "death toll" and the many injuries that marked the rebellions were predominantly inflicted on the participants by the National Guard and the police. A close look at the Kerner Commission report on riots revealed an unmistakable pattern: a handful of blacks used gunfire mainly to intimidate, not to kill, and other participants had a different target—property.[15] The focus on property was not accidental. If hostility toward whites was ever going to dominate

an African American's psyche and reach murderous proportions, an uprising would provide such an opportunity. Why did
the aggrieved avoid personal attacks on whites? The explana-
tion could not be fear of reprisal, because the physical risks in-
curred in the attacks on property were no less harsh than for
personal attacks. The answer lies in the fact that property represented the white power structure. The violence was directed
against symbols of exploitation, and it was designed to express
the depth of anger in the community.

Equally as important, Malcolm X had been assassinated,
thus robbing many urban blacks of their spokesperson for
black militancy. Malcolm's death created a void that could not
be filled by traditional civil rights leaders. Furthermore, many
blacks had become disenchanted with the direction in which
the Civil Rights movement was headed. Nonviolent protest
had earned blacks the right to vote in the South, as long as
they were willing to do so at their own peril; it had earned
blacks the right to eat in previously segregated restaurants
where most blacks could not afford a meal and to hold public
offices that were for the most part devoid of any real power.
Suffice it to say, these enactments did little to substantially
enhance the majority of black people's livelihood. In fact,
black unemployment rose; black income, while it did increase, never caught up with white income; and the number of
blacks considered to be poor swelled. The moderate success of
the Civil Rights movement resulted in raised expectations and
growing dissatisfaction. Dissatisfaction with the rate of
change increased concomitantly with the growing belief that
change was possible. As a result, large numbers of less patient
activists demanded more and faster change; they, in turn, reduced their commitment to nonviolence and turned to more
militant tactics. Indeed, by the mid 1960s, the results of a
Gallup public opinion poll indicated that Martin L. King Jr.'s
status as the undisputed leader of black America had begun to
wane.[16] In the words of King, "For many people nonviolence as
a strategy for social change had been cremated in the flames of
the urban riots of the 1960s."[17]

On a local level, oppressive conditions for Bay Area blacks
reached unbearable proportions. Oakland's Mayor John Read-

ing, former U.S. Senator and publisher of the *Oakland Tribune* William F. Knowland, and Police Chief Charles R. Gain were the oligarchy behind maintaining this system of domination over blacks. Mayor Reading stated on numerous occasions that he believed that black militants were not interested in civil rights, jobs, or better housing and that their covert aim was political and economic control of the nation. Equally as absurd, Knowland once referred to a picket demonstration by the Panthers as "a form of extortion."[18] Along the same lines, when Black Panther leaders suggested that black police should patrol communities in West Oakland, a predominantly black community, Police Chief Gain reported to the press that the Black Panther Party had "no practical program to offer the police." He added that the idea of his meeting or negotiating with the Black Panther Party was "the most ridiculous suggestion" he had ever heard.[19]

Given the conditions black Americans faced, the stage was set for a new and more aggressive organization—the Black Panther Party. In forming the organization, Newton's first task was to ascertain the concerns and needs of the black community. Conducting door-to-door surveys, Newton and Seale found police brutality to be the dominant concern among black residents. Police departments have had a long-standing history of brutality against and hatred of blacks in America. Historically, white police officers have dispensed arbitrary justice in black neighborhoods and have later been exonerated on the grounds of justifiable homicide. An eye-opening study found that, between 1960 and 1968, 51 percent of the people killed by police were black, even though blacks made up less than 10 percent of the total population.[20] In Newton's mind, the police were universally disliked by the black community. According to him, the police were quick to kill blacks for minor offenses, such as youth stealing automobiles.[21] Los Angeles Black Panther Earl Anthony remembers that Newton used the following analogy to explain the police presence in the black community: "The police in America, are like the Marines in Vietnam. They are in the ghetto to protect the interests of the multinational corporations, and the military/industrial complex that dominates people of color and poor people in America and around the world."[22] Hence, for liberation to occur, the power of the police had to be neutralized by a countervailing force. Newton was not alone in his assessment of the Oakland police. An Oakland bookstore owner declared that "the police force of Oakland considers itself an arm of the military. The police have declared war on the black community, and their assaults should be recognized for what they are—actual war atrocities, complete with ambush, entrapment, and execution, either in the courtroom or outside it."[23]

Some years earlier the California state legislature investigated the Oakland police department and, not surprisingly, discovered corruption so pervasive that the police chief was forced to resign and one officer was convicted and sentenced to jail. Because few people had the nerve to confront the police, Newton was faced with the challenge of recruiting individuals with the courage and fortitude to confront the Oakland police and demand to be treated fairly. Newton visited bars, pool halls, and other nightspots where street-corner blacks hung out, hoping to interest them in his newly founded organization. Thus, Newton recruited those blacks whose backgrounds were similar to a young Malcolm X: the unemployables, gangsters, hustlers, and convicts. Malcolm X said in his autobiography, "The most dangerous man in America is the ghetto hustler . . . the hustler out there in the ghetto jungles has less respect for the white power structure than any other group."[24] Ex-military personnel were also targeted by the Panthers for membership.

In some ways, the makeup and organizational structure of the Black Panther Party was Leninist in nature. The recruitment of former military personnel followed a Leninist maxim; Lenin had argued that revolutionary organizations should target for membership those who have been professionally trained in the art of combat in order to make it difficult for the oppressor to neutralize that organization.[25] In addition, like Lenin, Newton realized that no organization could be effective without a stable cadre of leaders to maintain continuity. In the Panthers' case, that unit was the "Central Committee," a term traditionally used by the communist movement. This group of leaders functioned as the governing body for the entire organization. The committee consisted of eleven offices: minister of defense, chairman, minister of information, chief of staff, minister of education, prime minister, minister of justice, minister of foreign affairs, minister of culture, minister of finance, and communications secretary. Decisions affecting the organization were made by this set of officers and sent down. The notion that the top position should reside with the military commander who simultaneously fulfills the role of chief theoretician and strategist derives directly from Régis Debray, the Latin American theorist.[26]

Organizationally, the Party displayed many of the characteristic features of the classic cadre party. For information purposes, there was an official organ of party opinion, the *Black Panther* newspaper. Newton believed that blacks were being duped by the U.S. government and were being misinformed by the mass media. Hence, the Black Panther Party Intercommunal News Service "was created to present factual and reliable information to the people." As Newton said, "The newspaper is the alternative to the government approved stories presented in the mass media and the product of an effort to present the facts, not stories as dictated by the oppressor, but as seen from the other end of a gun."[27] Emory Douglas, Panther minister of culture, recounted that Huey compared the Party's need for a publication with the armed struggle of the Vietnamese. He said that "the Vietnamese carried mimeograph machines wherever they went to produce flyers and other literature to spread the word about their fight to free their country. The Party needed to have a newspaper so we could tell our own story."[28]

There also was an official Ten-Point Party Platform/Program that was similar in form to *The Communist Manifesto* and the Nation of Islam's program. The program benefited from suggestions made by Bobby Seale, but it was actually written by Newton. Newton divided the program into two specific components. The first component was philosophical in nature and expressed the ideas and goals that the Black Panther Party aspired to accomplish. It was titled "What We Believe." The second enumerated organizational demands that would bring these ideas into fruition. This component was titled "What We Want." Summarized, the ten-point program demanded: land, bread, housing, clothing, education, justice, peace, and "the power to determine our own destiny of our black community."[29] Furthermore, the Party established a list of some twenty-six rules, which members of the organization were to learn and abide by. Some of these rules define the relations of command between the Central Committee and local chapters and branches, some govern behavior, while others are basic Maoist-like exhortations to improvement. Organizational structure below the level of the national governing body was composed of local deputy ministers, local program coordinators, area captains, section leaders, subsection leaders, and rank-and-file members. The system of organization at the local level was called the "10-10-10."[30] First, a city was divided into ten sections, and each of the ten sections was assigned a section leader. Next, each major section was divided into ten subsections and assigned subsection leaders. The subsections were then divided, and each rank-and-file member was given the responsibility of organizing a certain number of people in a given community. The chain of command was centralized. Decisions affecting the organization were made by the Central Committee in Oakland and passed down to the local central staffs, who were responsible for carrying them out using the "10-10-10" system. The key actor in this process was the area captain, who was the link between the local central staffs and the section leaders. According to one Panther, "In the event of police harassment of a black motorist/pedestrian you were to call your block leader who would get some type of defense to the individual being harassed. . . . The bigger the problem got the higher you went into subsections and sections. Such as a mass thing, like a riot, all 10 sections would be dispatched."[31]

Needless to say, Newton's work with the black underclass defied the claim by sociologists that attempts at organizing and sustaining a mass organization among the lower rung of society was fruitless due to the individualism of "lower class people."[32] The notion that blacks are members of a "lower race" and do not have the "same inherent abilities" as European groups has been a part of the sociological literature since 1896, when F. H. Giddings published his *Principles of Sociology*.[33] Later, the premise that blacks are inferior and less culturally advanced than whites appeared in the writings of the founders of the "Chicago school" of sociology and urban studies. Two major figures of this school, Robert Ezra Park and Ernest W. Burgess, in their *Introduction to the Science of Sociology*, written in 1921, viewed the temperament of African Americans as infantile.[34] A review of the more contemporary literature on urban blacks sees black culture and life as deficient in institutional forms, anemic, and culturally pathological. According to Lee Rainwater: "One can assume that except when lower-class people feel trapped in their neighborhood by low income and unemployment or by discrimination they will not be available for neighborhood organizations. Even when there is this sense of being trapped, the preferred route for mobility is individual: Lower-class people will often have difficulty in seeing a strategy of organized groups as really relevant to their own needs and values."[35]

Earlier, Karl Marx offered a similar prognosis but for different reasons. Marx called this segment of society the lumpenproletariat. He argued that the lumpenproletariat was the most undisciplined and untrustworthy segment of society, and that, because of these characteristics, it was ill equipped to contribute significantly to the revolution. Marx claimed that this group was more likely to be co-opted and converted into informants: "The dangerous class, the social scum, that passively rotting mass thrown off by the lowest layers of old society, may here and there, be swept into the movement by a proletarian revolution; its conditions of life, however, prepare it far more for the part of a bribed tool of reactionary intrigue."[36]

One could argue that a careful analysis of black ghetto life reveals a viable and cohesive culture that may be more politically and socially unified than comparable white communities. This reality was not lost on Newton, as he maintained that the most viable black strategy was to organize the black lumpenproletariat into a guerilla-type movement in order to challenge the oppressor as a collective. History had taught Newton that the lumpenproletariat were full of enormous potential. Mao Zedong did not hesitate to use such so-called unreliable types in the Chinese Revolution. Mao noted, "The lumpenproletariat are brave fighters but apt to be destructive, they can become a revolutionary force if given proper guidance."[37] CLR James commented on the revolutionary potential of blacks in general over fifty years ago when he wrote:

> Let us not forget that in the Negro people, there sleep and are now awakening, passions of a violence exceeding, perhaps, as far as these things can be compared, anything among the tremendous forces that capitalism has created. Anyone who knows them, who knows their history, is able to talk to them intimately, watches them at their own theatres, watches them at their dances, watches them in their churches, reads their press with a discerning eye, must recognize that although their social force may not be able to compare with the social force of a corresponding number of organized workers, the hatred of bourgeois society and the readiness to destroy it when the opportunity should present itself, rests among them to a degree greater than in any other section of the population in the United States.[38]

Newton envisioned an omnipresent force, made up of the most revolutionary and marginalized subgroups in society, ripping the vitals out of the American Empire and dragging the rotting corpse to some fiery Armageddon.[39] Drawing from Frantz Fanon's *Wretched of the Earth*, Newton maintained that scores of blacks had been forced out of the urban labor market and onto the street corners of the ghetto. He understood that advances in technology had eliminated the jobs of unskilled black labor. As a result, Newton argued that it would not be long before only a small percentage of the workforce would be necessary to run the industries. The working class would be scaled down and the class of unemployables would grow because it would take more and more skills to operate machines. According to Newton, this would result in the disappearance of the minimum-wage worker. Consequently, the majority of those considered proletarian would become the lumpenproletariat. And as these people became part of the lumpenproletariat, the more alienated they would feel. Given these developments, Newton theorized that blacks were quickly becoming valueless to the American capitalist economy. He argued that the black ghetto in America should be considered as analogous to the exploited and dependent Third World colonies abroad, that white institutions and their representatives hamper black advancement and cast costly aspersions on black life. Sociologists Everett C. Hughes and Helen M. Hughes suggested that the major difference between the colonial situation and that typically found in the United States was in the degree of openness of the system of racial and ethnic oppression.[40] The United States exhibited a high degree of racial and ethnic exploitation but ringed it with mystification and obfuscating details that made it more difficult to discern. That which is more difficult to recognize is also more difficult to oppose.

The Black Panther Party's position was that American blacks suffered more than any group in the United States. Poverty, homelessness, and hunger could not be destroyed, Newton argued, unless the oppressed seized the reins of power.[41] The lumpenproletariat, then, seemed a likely audience for Newton's ideas. Newton believed that the lumpenproletariat had the most revolutionary potential because they possessed qualities such as bravery, courage, and a nothing-to-lose attitude, whereas the proletariat was composed of working-class individuals with families and jobs and thus had much more to lose by waging a revolution. And with increasing automation, the lumpenproletariat would eventually be in the majority. Newton pointed out that when Rome fell, 80 percent of its people were unemployed. Privately, Marx himself feared that the proletariat would accept reformist policies and lose sight of their real interest, which was to make a revolution and socialize the means of production.[42]

Once Newton was able to develop a rapport with "the brothers off the block," he faced the challenge of getting them interested in the politics of black liberation. Through months of discussions with the lumpenproletariat and by relating to them in a way they could understand, Newton was able to raise their level of consciousness and convince many of them to join the Black Panther Party. Said Oakland County Supervisor John George, "Huey could take street-gang types and give them a social consciousness."[43] As political scientist Floyd W. Hayes noted some thirty years ago, the first step in effecting the realization of black liberation is the achievement of black consciousness.[44]

Influenced by the speeches and writings of Malcolm X, by Robert F. Williams's book *Negroes with Guns*, and by the example set by the Deacons for Defense and Justice, Newton thought that if the Black Panther Party were to confront and patrol the police, it would be necessary to do so with gun in hand.[45] Newton was a firm believer in the Second Amendment to the U.S. Constitution, which states that "the right of the people to keep and bear arms shall not be infringed." He thought that armed resistance would have two effects: the Black Panther Party would put fear in the hearts of the police, making them apprehensive about brutalizing African Americans, and it would earn the respect and admiration of the African American community. Before receiving weapons, all Party members were required to go through a period of political education and training. During this period, Newton and Seale were able to indoctrinate Party members with Panther ideology. The two also provided new members with instruction on the proper care and use of firearms. Drawing from his law school training, Newton insisted that each Panther patrol take along a law book, entitled *Legal First Aid*, which included a list of thirteen basic legal and constitutional rights.[46] Until Newton armed the Black Panther Party, most people did not know that, according to California law, every citizen had the right to carry openly a gun for self-defense. Newton wanted the African American community to see the virtues of a disciplined change agent as an alternative to the outbreaks and riots in which some blacks participated during the 1960s. Newton insisted that the Black Panther Party press the system for better treatment of blacks. Part of this included ensuring that police not be allowed to violate the rights of motorists and pedestrians. Prior to *Miranda v. Arizona* police enjoyed a great deal of latitude when dealing with suspects. Even after *Miranda* was implemented, many hard-line police officers ignored the new ruling, claiming that it interfered with their ability to do their jobs. By patrolling the police, the Panthers gave the police an added incentive to comply with the new statute.

Although preventing police brutality was a central concern to Newton, he thought it was equally significant to address the many other concerns of the community. In the past, there had been those who studied the African American community from afar to determine its problems and provide solutions. Newton thought this to be a mistake, referring to this approach as armchair intellectualizing. He believed that the only way to find out what the community's problems were and what solutions would best remedy these problems would be to go to the community and ask the neighborhood residents. As noted earlier, Newton went door-to-door to find out what the residents needed to sustain a better standard of living. After gathering this information, Newton oriented the Black Panther Party's goals to address the concerns conveyed to him by the people in the community. In response, the Black Panther Party instituted a free breakfast program for schoolchildren; a clothing and shoe outlet, an elementary school, a free medical clinic, and a number of other survival programs, including some that catered to senior citizens. Consequently, Newton and other Panther leaders recruited individuals with expertise that matched the needs of the organization. One of the most lauded endeavors included hiring teenagers to take senior citizens on errands and protect them from muggings ("Hire the mugger to protect the muggee," as one Panther put it).[48] Also, the first broad public awareness of sickle-cell anemia as a disease that disproportionately plagued blacks was for the most part due to the efforts of the Black Panther Party. At its peak, the breakfast program fed seventy thousand children annually throughout the United States. In addition, the Party estimated that it gave away a thousand bags of groceries and a thousand pairs of shoes each month to the needy.[49] While the well-intentioned efforts of the Black Panther Party did not go unnoticed by many in the general public, criticism of the organization by the Establishment and the media was in no short supply.

Falsehood is in itself mean and culpable, and truth noble and full of virtue.

—Aristotle

Despite the substantive impact that the Black Panther Party had on oppressed communities throughout the nation, several misperceptions about Newton and the Party persist. Again, this is due in part to a misinformed press and an intolerant power structure. Among these incorrect views are that the Black Panther Party was racist, that it perpetuated violence, and that it was a reformist rather than a revolutionary organization. These three misperceptions cloud and diminish the contribution that the organization made to the struggle for human equality. Newton's response to these ill-informed judgments would provide critics, intellectuals, and activists with a glimpse of his ability to analyze and disentangle important issues.

DISTORTIONS, MISREPRESENTATIONS, AND OUTRIGHT LIES: SETTING THE RECORD STRAIGHT

The misperception that Newton and the Black Panther Party were racist befuddled most black militants. After all, racism involved not only exclusion on the basis of race but exclusion with the intent of instituting and preserving a system of widespread subjugation. Throughout American history, whites, not blacks, had been the main supporters of this supremacist ideology. Blacks had not lynched whites, killed their leaders, bombed their churches, or possessed the power to manipulate the nation's laws to maintain racial hegemony. William L. Van DeBurg notes that for African Americans to adopt the ways of the white racist as their own would be counterproductive.[1] Bobby Seale put the issue into perspective in a 1968 speech:

> When a man walks up and says that we are anti-white I scratch my head. . . . I say, 'Wait a minute man-let's back up a little bit. That's your game, that's the Ku Klux Klan's game." To hate me and murder me because of the color of my skin. I

wouldn't murder a person or brutalize him because of the color of his skin. Yeah we hate something alright. We hate oppression that we live in. . . . If you got enough energy to sit down and hate a white person just because of the color of his skin, you're wasting a lot of energy. You'd better take some of that same energy and put it in some motion and start dealing with those oppressive conditions.[2]

One of the reasons for the misconception that the Panthers were racist is that most whites and some blacks misconstrued the notion of Black Power, the prevailing sentiment among many black militants at that time. Although made popular by Stokely Carmichael, the slogan has been traced back to the 1950s to black icons like Richard Wright, Paul Robeson, and Adam Clayton Powell Jr. At the first Black Power conference convened by Powell in September 1966 in Washington, D.C., Powell called Black Power "a working philosophy for a new breed of cats-tough, proud young Negroes who categorically refuse to compromise or negotiate any longer for their rights . . . who reject the old-line established white-financed, white-controlled, white washed Negro leadership."[3] Powell said the phrase, which meant only a "dynamic process of continuous change toward a society of true equals," had been "deliberately distorted" by "self-righteous, old fashioned leaders" out of touch with the masses of black Americans.[4] According to sociologist Robert Blauner, "there seemed to be a paranoid fear in the white psyche of black dominance; the belief that black autonomy would mean unbridled license is so ingrained that such reasonable outcomes as all-black institutions and organizations brings about bitter resentment."[5] A 1967 survey of 850 Detroit residents conducted by University of Michigan scholars revealed that almost 60 percent of the whites interviewed thought Black Power was synonymous with violence, black racism, and black domination.[6] According to one respondent, "the Negro wants to enslave the white man like he was enslaved 100 years ago." "Blacks won't be satisfied until they get complete control of our country by force if necessary," said another.[7] In reality, Black Power spoke of the need for black unity, self-determination, empowerment, and control of black communities. The intention of Black Power was not to subjugate anyone to slavery or oppression. Black Power was but the culmination of a journey that began with blacks singing "We Shall Overcome Someday" to cries of "Freedom Now" to shouts of "Black Power," with each exasperated pronouncement representing a maturation in the ideological development of the struggle for black equality. Indeed, Julian Bond wrote that Black Power must be seen as a natural extension of the work of the Civil Rights movement.[8]

From its inception, the Black Panther Party declared publicly that it was not a racist organization, that it aimed to eradicate racism. Never in the Party's history did it call for reverse slavery. Unlike some Black Power activists at that time, Newton did not make a blanket condemnation of whites. For instance, a major tenet of the Nation of Islam's doctrine is that all whites are devils. Newton admitted that it was hard for him to accept the doctrine that all whites were evil.[9] Newton said he tried to develop a hatred for white people but would feel a sense of guilt for harboring those feelings. "I never thought color should be the way to tell people apart, the cue was always the way white people treated me," said Newton.[10] The Black Panther Party's policy to exclude whites may have erroneously contributed to the misperception that the Party was antiwhite. Whites were often members of and sometimes held leadership and advisory positions in such organizations as the NAACP, CORE, SCLC, and the Student Nonviolent Coordinating Committee (SNCC). In contrast, the Black Panther Party would have none of that. The reason for this policy, Newton asserted, was that black people's problems had to be dealt with within the black community. "After these problems are resolved the Black Panther Party would be willing to accept assistance from the white radical as long as they realize that we have, as Eldridge Cleaver says in *Soul On Ice*, a mind of our own," stated Newton.[11] Newton's and Cleaver's position on the role of whites ran counter to the argument put forth by some others. Noted black sociologist Oliver C. Cox, asserted that not only did blacks need white allies if significant gains were to be made, but that blacks also needed white leadership. According to Cox, a white leader could take advantage of favorable features of the existing accommodative order. He argues that blacks are accustomed to doing what whites tell them and that a white radical should take advantage of this to help blacks and others free themselves.[12] Bernardine Dohrn of the Weather Underground seemed to know where Newton and the Party were coming from when she said: "The best thing that we (whites) can be doing for ourselves, as well as for the Panthers and the revolutionary black liberation struggle, is to build a fucking white revolutionary movement."[13] In addition to the Party's membership policy, its inflammatory rhetoric directed at the white power structure may have erroneously contributed to the perception that the Party was a black supremacist organization.

When Newton was asked of his feelings about whites at a Yale University symposium, he said he needed something else other than color by which to judge people. "I often open doors for people without even noticing that they are white or giving it a thought; but I can be very, very hostile toward someone if he gives any indication whatsoever of feeling superior. Now most white people have a kind of opposition to me just because I am black, you see, so they have their cue, but I do not have mine," said Newton.[14] Newton urged the Party to oppose all forms of racism. On another occasion Newton said, "We don't suffer in the hang-up of skin color."[15] Huey, says his brother Melvin, never had any pronounced antiwhite feelings, even though some antiwhite sentiment did run through the Afro-American Association of which Newton was a member. Even during high school Newton always had some white friends. Todd Gitlin, a prominent member of the Students for a Democratic Society (SDS), recalls, "At a time when most other black militants donned dashikis and glowered at whites, the Black Panther Party welcomed white allies."[16] At a 1967 forum where Newton spoke on "The Future of the Black Liberation Movement," he was heavily criticized for working with whites. He explained his position by saying:

> While the viewpoint (of working strictly with blacks) was understandable to me, it failed to take into consideration the

limitations of our power. We needed allies, and we believed that alliance with you whites—students and workers—was worth the risk. . . . In a few years' time, almost half of the American population would be composed of young people; if we developed strong and meaningful alliances with white youth, they would support our goals and work against the Establishment.

Everywhere I went in 1967 I was vehemently attacked by black students for this position; few could present opposing objective evidence to support their criticisms. The reaction was emotional: all white people were devils; they wanted nothing to do with them. I agreed that some white people could act like devils, but we could not blind ourselves to common humanity.[17]

Newton understood black people's plight in relation to working-class whites. He argued correctly that blacks were at the bottom rung of society because blacks were exploited not only by a white elite but were oppressed and repressed by working-class whites as well. The reason for this, Newton concluded, was that the white ruling class used the Roman policy of divide and conquer. "In other words, the white working class is used as pawns or tools of the ruling class, but they too are enslaved."[18] Newton's point is well-founded. In fact, after the Civil War, poor whites and poor blacks joined forces in opposition to the plantation owners, but only for a short time because racism was used as a tool to destroy that potential alliance. "So it's with that historical thing of dividing and ruling, that the ruling class can effectively and successfully keep the majority of people in an oppressed position," said Newton.[19]

In 1968, the Black Panther Party announced a merger with SNCC, appointing Stokely Carmichael as field marshal, James Forman as minister of foreign affairs, and H. Rap Brown as minister of justice. By the late 1960s, SNCC leaders could no longer rationalize the feasibility of the philosophy of non-violence in the face of intense oppression. Even Ralph Abernathy of the Southern Christian Leadership Conference exclaimed that "there is a calculated design of genocide in this country. . . . America is doing everything in her power to destroy black people."[20] Thus as Eldridge Cleaver put it, the activists from the Bible Belt joined the brothers and sisters from the gun belt.[21]

Such a merger between the two groups seemed like a good idea at the time, since the Black Panther Party lacked the administrative skills and material resources of SNCC, and SNCC lacked the northern and urban base of the Party. In addition, several key party members (Kathleen Cleaver, Bobby Rush, Connie Matthews) had, at one time, been members of SNCC.[22] However, the merger was short-lived, mainly because of egos and mistrust and misunderstanding between Panthers and the newly inducted SNCC members.[23] There were also points of disagreement that led to the disintegration of the coalition. One point of disagreement was the Black Panther Party's willingness to form alliances with white groups.[24] Carmichael pointed out that it was illogical to form an alliance with such groups as the Peace and Freedom Party, which represented the bourgeoisie, the economically secure. "It is totally un-Marxist for the economically insecure, because the economically secure are not going to fight, they have much to lose," argued Carmichael. "Workers of the world unite, you have nothing to lose but your chains."[25] This is precisely what Marx was talking about: only those who have nothing to lose will fight, and Carmichael's argument was that the Peace and Freedom Party had everything to lose. Carmichael's point is not without merit. In retrospect, that Carmichael resigned is not surprising because he and Newton always seemed to hold positions that were polar opposites of one another on a number of issues. For instance, when Newton was optimistic that one day a socialist system would prevail in the United States, Carmichael at a 1974 conference on racism and imperialism stated that "building socialism in the U.S. could not be the main objective for African people in the U.S."[26] In addition, when Newton began to move in the direction of electoral politics in 1972, Carmichael openly repudiated conventional politics as a viable avenue for black empowerment. Ironically, it was Carmichael who, as a young SNCC organizer, marched with Martin Luther King Jr. to get the right to vote; moreover, he had helped organize the Lowndes County Freedom Organization and the Mississippi Freedom Democratic Party, organizations that prominently featured an electoral politics orientation. On the other hand, in his early years, Newton dismissed conventional politics because he saw black politicians as puppets and black voters as poker players without chips.

In the end, SNCC members resigned because of, among other reasons, ideological differences over the role that white leftists should play in the black liberation struggle.[27] Carmichael and political scientist Charles V. Hamilton in their book, *Black Power*, provided a more elaborate discussion on the issue of black-white alliances, arguing that blacks should eschew alliances with other groups, specifically white liberals, and organize on their own.[28] First, the interests of blacks are never identical to those of labor groups, white liberals, and other reform groups. Second, all too often black participation in coalitions has been under terms dictated by the more powerful white participants in the coalition. Third, lacking their own base of political power, blacks have tended to rely on moral persuasion and "friendship" to influence their allies, with poor results. Until blacks act independently of whites and build their own separate political organizations, their interests will always be subjugated to the interests of the more powerful group. Carmichael and Hamilton asserted that the ideological liberalism of whites is simply not enough to sustain a biracial political coalition when the racial or economic interests of whites clash with the policy interests of blacks.

Despite these words of caution, the Black Panther Party increasingly emphasized coalitions with whites, particularly against the Vietnam War—"one of the most important movements that's going on at this time," according to Newton.[29] Bobby Seale stressed the nonracist character of the Black Panther Party, saying that the Panthers would work with anyone who was serious about fighting to end racism, social and political injustice, and police brutality. Overtures to white groups were made as early as 1967. An ad hoc group of white leftists called Stop the Draft Week (SDW), which was primarily interested in obstructing the American military, was drawn into the struggle for black liberation.[30] By 1968, SDW's literature carried demands to "Free Huey!"—who was in jail for allegedly killing a police officer—and get the "Cops Out of the Ghetto!" However, these campus radicals kept their major focus on the Asian war. Another group, the Friends of the Panthers, engaged in fund-raising activities, staged rallies, and helped with the establishment of a Panther-run clinic. Founded by author Donald Freed and Shirley Douglas Sutherland in 1967, this Los Angeles-based group consisted largely of upper-middle-class whites, including actors Burt Lancaster, Vanessa Redgrave, Elizabeth Taylor, Jane Fonda, and Elliot Gould.[31] This group also served as a conduit to the Hollywood Left.

Perhaps the most productive alliance was with the California Peace and Freedom Party. This coalition began in the interest of seeking Newton's release from jail. Although support for Newton came from many sectors of the white community, not all whites were advocates of Newton. To no one's surprise, the Hells' Angels, a long-haired motorcycle gang, called for Newton's execution. They sported "Fry Huey" buttons—an obvious play on the "Free Huey" campaign.[32] By contrast, the Peace and Freedom Party leaders agreed to donate $3,000 to Newton's defense fund.[33] Floyd W. Hayes III and Francis A. Kiene III maintain that it is unlikely that the Black Panther Party would have been able to make the Free Huey movement a cause cèlébre throughout the country without the support and resources of the Peace and Freedom Party.[34] In addition, Black Panther Party members were invited to fill slots on the Peace and Freedom Party's electoral slate in 1968. Eldridge Cleaver was tapped as the presidential candidate, Newton was nominated for a congressional seat, and Seale and Kathleen Cleaver made a run for state assembly seats. Eldridge Cleaver's bid for the presidency was largely symbolic because he was too young (thirty-three years old) to hold the office. Two years after the Black Panther Party joined forces with the California Peace and Freedom Party to free Newton, whites at Yale University formed a Black Panther Party Defense Committee. In a 1997 lecture at the University of Southern California, essayist David Horowitz mentioned that Hillary Rodham (now Hillary Rodham Clinton) was a principal organizer of the rally on behalf of Party members charged with the murder of a suspected Panther informant in Connecticut.[35]

Other white organizations with which the Party formed coalitions included SDS, groups from the women's liberation movement, and the Gay Liberation Front. In 1969, SDS passed a resolution at its national council meeting stating that "within the black liberation movement, the vanguard force is the Black Panther Party."[36] In the resolution, SDS declared its support for the Black Panther Party's program for the liberation of the black colony; its commitment to defend the Black Panther Party against the vicious attacks of the racist "pig" power structure; its commitment to join the Black Panther Party in the fight against white national chauvinism and white supremacy; and its commitment to the fight for liberation of all oppressed people in the United States. Richard Parker of SDS would say years later that SDS joined forces with the Panthers because "we believed that both groups had a number of things in common, namely the fight against capitalism and racism."[37] That same year, the Panthers issued a call for a conference to form a united front against fascism in America. The Panthers also invited the Yippies, a white left-wing group headed by Abbie Hoffman and Jerry Rubin, to this conference. Out of this developed the predominantly white National Committee to Combat Fascism. This group established chapters throughout the nation, which served as subsidiary groups to the Black Panther Party.[38] These chapters, or National Committees, were designed to involve whites, especially those who, as Seale put it, had been asking why they could not join the Black Panther Party. "We see the National Committees as the political organizing bureaus of the Black Panther Party," Seale declared.[39]

The Black Panther Party also recognized the potential political clout of organized women and gays and openly supported alliances with such groups. Allen Young, who analyzed the role of gays in SDS, lamented that he felt "totally alienated."[40] Lawrence Lader noted that gays and lesbians were always isolated in the 1960s, even among radicals.[41] Lader went on to say that the traditional Left, both the Old Left and the New Left, had been as oppressive to gays and lesbians as had been establishment America. In addition, by 1970, the National Organization for Women (NOW) emerged as a political force, boasting seven hundred chapters and over forty thousand members throughout the United States. When twenty-five thousand women marched down New York's Fifth Avenue to mark the fiftieth anniversary of women's suffrage (with thousands more marching in other cities), the women's movement came of age. George Katsiaficas notes that, as thousands of autonomous women's groups formed in the United States, the women's movement rapidly became an international phenomenon.[42] When Newton was asked for his take on the struggles of women and gays and lesbians, he replied:

> We [the Black Panther Party] think it is very important to relate to and understand the causes of the oppression of women and gay people. We see that there are contradictions between the sexes and between homosexuals and heterosexuals, but we believe that these contradictions should be resolved within the community. Too often, so-called revolutionary vanguards have tried to resolve these contradictions by isolating women and gay people, and of course, this only means that the revolutionary groups have cut themselves off from one of the most powerful and important forces among the people. We do not believe that the oppression of women or gays will end by the creation of separate communities for either group. We see that as an incorrect idea, just like the idea of a separate nation.[43]

Newton's response implied that he recognized the justness and expediency of forming coalitions with these groups. He reasoned that these groups shared some of the same concerns that were of interest to blacks, namely discrimination, harassment by the police, and opposition to the Vietnam War. These commonalities enabled the Black Panther Party to tap into a segment of the population that had never before been reached by radicals.[44] Excerpts from a press release from Newton to the woman's liberation movement and gay liberation groups show that he encouraged the formation of an alliance. To those who opposed the participation of these groups, Newton said:

Whatever your personal opinions and your insecurities about homosexuality and the various liberation movements among homosexuals and women (and I speak of homosexuals and women as oppressed groups), we should try to unite with them in a revolutionary fashion. . . . We must gain security in ourselves and therefore have respect and feelings for all oppressed people. . . .

We should deal with the factions just as we deal with any other party that claims to be revolutionary. We should try to judge, somehow, whether they are operating in a sincere revolutionary fashion and from a really oppressed situation. . . . [T]he women's liberation front and gay liberation front are our friends, they are potential allies, and we need as many allies as possible.[45]

At the plenary session of the Panther-sponsored Revolutionary Constitutional Convention in Philadelphia, there were workshops that dealt with self-determination for women and sexual self-determination, in which the participants themselves were given responsibility for drafting specific items for a new constitution for the United States.[46] Lader notes that the Black Panther Party always had more defined radical objectives than did the New Left.[47]

Many white activists held the Party in such high esteem that several white organizations modeled themselves after the Black Panther Party. White radicals at the University of Michigan named their group the White Panther Party (WPP). The WPP even adopted a ten-point program that included support of women's issues as well as the struggle against racism, capitalism, and institutional repression. The head of the WPP wrote in the Panther paper that his group had been organized in the summer of 1968 as part of the duty of "white mother country revolutionaries" to join the Panthers in "liberating America."[48] The Black Panther Party also inspired the Patriot Party, a revolutionary organization that grew out of the poor white community of Chicago. In its programs and goals, the Patriot Party paralleled the Black Panther Party, and its leaders worked closely with the Panthers.[49] In sum, as Newton proclaimed many times, the Black Panther Party was anti-exploitation, antidegradation, and anti-oppression. "If the white man doesn't want us to be anti-him, then let him stop oppressing, degrading and exploiting us."[50] Newton argued that no fundamental change could occur without the help of poor whites. He asserted that poor whites also experienced oppression at the hands of the white ruling class.

A second misunderstanding is that the Panthers were violent terrorists much like the Irish Republican Army; Al Fatah, which declared a holy war on Israel; and the Ku Klux Klan and White Citizens Council, which for decades has engaged in harassment, torture, and murder. Vice President Spiro Agnew declared, "The Panthers are a completely irresponsible anarchist group of criminals."[51] Even so-called liberals like Daniel P. Moynihan (later U.S. Senator from New York) had harsh words for the Party. In his "benign neglect" memorandum to President Richard Nixon, he undoubtedly had the Panthers in mind when he referred to "black extremists" who used "lower class" blacks to threaten white society with the prospect of mass arson and pillage.[52] Agnew's and Moynihan's attempts to portray the Panthers as terrorists are unconvincing. If terrorism is the use or threatened use of violence for political purposes to create a state of fear that will aid in extorting, coercing, intimidating, or otherwise causing individuals and groups to alter their behavior, then perhaps the Panthers can be considered terrorists. Under this definition, however, the eighteenth-century revolutionary insurgency that led to the creation of the United States could be considered terrorism.[53]

Gilbert Moore, a reporter for *Life* magazine, offered a more sympathetic view of the Panthers when he wrote that the myth of the fearsome black man was perpetuated by a nearsighted press that could not see past Newton's bandoliers.[54] Newton formulated a very sound and reflective position on the issue of violence. He did not advocate violence: "My position is that I'm absolutely against violence, I advocate nonviolence."[55] Newton exclaimed, "Everybody looks at that famous poster of me sitting in the wicker chair with a spear in one hand and a rifle in the other. But no one sees the shield there next to me. The shield explains the Black Panther Party best: we intend to shield our people from the brutalities visited upon them by the police and other racist institutions in society."[56] The Black Panther Party is against

violence and works for the day when it will no longer be necessary, said Newton. In fact, Newton stated the Black Panther
Party chose the panther as its symbol because it was reputed
to be an animal that never makes an unprovoked attack but
will defend itself vehemently when attacked.[57]

While Newton laid much of the blame on the media for
the distorted image of the Black Panther Party as a cop-hating
group of violent rogues, he admitted that some of the blame
rested on his shoulders. In a 1973 interview with *Christian
Century*, Newton acknowledged that it was he who coined
the term "pigs"; he who caused a stir by dispatching twenty-
six Panthers armed with shotguns to the California state legislature to protest an antigun measure; and he who fostered
the Panthers' bold practice of following the police around
town to monitor the treatment of citizens the police stopped,
a practice regarded by some sectors of the public as cop-bait-
ing. Newton explained, though: "In order to understand me
and the Black Panther Party, you have to understand that we
were always motivated solely by a determination to protect
the people—the black people of Oakland."[58]

Given Newton's position, it is not surprising that when
Bay Area blacks took to the streets in 1968 to avenge King's
assassination, the Black Panther Party served as a calming influence, imploring the black community to abstain from such
counterproductive behavior. In his report for the National
Commission on the Causes and Prevention of Violence,
Jerome H. Skolnick acknowledged that the Black Panther
Party had to be "given credit for keeping Oakland cool after
the assassination of Dr. King."[59] He noted, however, that this
did not stem from any desire on their part to suppress black
protest. Rather, it stemmed from a sense that the police were
waiting for a chance to shoot down blacks in the street. In any
event, the Black Panther Party viewed riots as acts of violence
that lack direction and purpose. At the same time though,
Newton believed that the uprisings of the 1960s were a prelude to the revolution.[60]

Nevertheless, Newton repudiated violence of any kind, including that of a verbal nature. When David Hilliard (chief of
staff) threatened President Richard Nixon in a profanity-laced

tirade at a 1969 peace rally in San Francisco's Golden Gate Park, Newton later chastised him. "People won't relate to that kind of talk," Newton told Hilliard. But Hilliard protested that he had used the language of the street. "Maybe so," said Newton "but would you use it in front of your mother?" Hilliard said that he "wouldn't use those words anymore," and swearing in public came to a halt. When the Symbionese Liberation Army (SLA), a group of mainly white extremists whose claim to fame was the kidnapping of heiress Patty Hearst, announced it was responsible for the murder of Marcus Foster, the superintendent of Oakland's schools, the Black Panther Party publicly denounced the group. The Party also rejected overtures from the bomb-happy Weathermen to partake in their penchant for undisciplined and nonproductive violence.[61] Unlike Hannah Arendt, however, who argued that all violence is indiscriminate and unpredictable, the Black Panther Party thought that violence, if harnessed properly, could serve productive revolutionary ends.[62] In their concept of a disciplined party, the Panthers were strict Leninists. Newton argued that force would come in handy but mainly to enhance the ideological awareness and preparedness of the masses. For Newton, revolution was a matter of the mind—the transformation of the ideology held by the people. Newton argued that violence can be inflicted in many ways. The epitome of violence is the vicious service revolver of the police and the rifle of the military. To deprive children of food is a manifestation of violence; to deprive people of decent housing is another; and to deprive individuals of full employment is a violent act.[63] Newton asserted that the Black Panther Party was for self-defense, and self-defense is a declaration against violence.

In keeping with that position, Newton advocated the abolition of war. The Black Panther Party maintained that the purpose of picking up the gun was to get rid of war. Newton argued that most people pick up the gun for the purpose of waging war; consequently, they do not understand that someone else might pick it up in order to abolish war.[64] The Panthers wanted to abolish all guns and all wars because "we believe it is better for people to resolve their differences without violence. However, until the actual conditions exist where defense with a gun is not necessary, we have to act appropriately. For instance, it is insane to ask the Vietnamese to lay down their guns when the American ruling class is napalming them."[65]

Newton made a distinction between the violence of the aggressor and self-defense of the people. During the years of slavery, for example, the slave master kidnapped people, forced them to labor for no compensation, and tortured and killed those who rebelled or outlived their usefulness. This was the material condition of those held as slaves. So when the slaves revolted, they were defending themselves against murder. This is what Frederick Douglass meant when he said: "The slave is fully justified in helping himself to the gold and silver, and the best apparel of his master. . . . Such taking is not stealing in any sense of the word. . . . Slave holders had made it almost impossible for the slave to commit any crime known to the laws of God or to the laws of man. If he steals, he takes his own; if he kills, he imitates only the heroes of the Revolution."[66] The Black Panther Party interpreted Douglass to mean that the oppressor has no rights that the oppressed are bound to respect.

Frederick Douglass's personality was transformed when, as a slave, he fought back against his master. After having been whipped daily until he was broken in body, soul, and spirit, he found the courage to turn on his master one day, seizing him by the throat until the master relented. The result was that the slave master abandoned the whip and ignored Douglass for the four remaining months of enslavement. Douglass defines this fight as the turning point in his life:

> It rekindled the few expiring embers of freedom and revived within me a sense of my own manhood. It recalled the departed self-confidence, and inspired me again with a determination to be free. The gratification afforded by the triumph was a full compensation for whatever else might follow, even death itself. He only can understand the deep satisfaction which I experienced, who has himself repelled by force the bloody arm of slavery. I felt as I never felt before. It was a glorious resurrection, from the tomb of slavery, to the heaven of freedom. My long-crushed spirit rose, cowardice departed, bold defiance took its

place; and I now resolved that, however long I might remain a slave in form, the day had passed forever when I could be a slave in fact.[67]

Newton always maintained that the Black Panther Party had great compassion for people and that the Black Panther Party believed that the death of any person diminishes us as a whole because we are involved in humankind. In Newton's autobiography, the compassion he had for people is evident when he says, "Officer Frey's death bothers me, and the things that caused his death bother me."[68] According to Newton, the revolutionary program of the Black Panther Party was guided by a feeling of love.[69] Although Newton does not go into detail here, the love that he speaks of was probably derived from Che Guevara, whom Newton held in high esteem. Guevara said, "The true revolutionary is guided by strong feelings of love. It is impossible to think of an authentic revolutionary without this quality. The revolutionary's love involves doing away with human pettiness and it is both higher and more persistent than love that exists under normal circumstances."[70] While Newton's love of humankind was profound, he readily added that neither he nor the Black Panther Party would hesitate to use whatever force was necessary so that sanity might prevail and allow people to keep their dignity; that is why members of the Black Panther Party armed themselves openly.[71] Newton maintained that they took that risk because they believed that the people had to be educated about the potential power of an armed black community. After the example had been set, Newton and the Black Panther Party then concentrated on helping the people with projects such as the survival programs mentioned earlier.

Newton pointed out that Mao's quote that "political power grows out of the barrel of the gun" is misunderstood. Most people interpreted that statement to mean that political power is a gun, but that is not the point.[72] According to Newton, political power culminates in the people's ownership and control of the land and the institutions thereon. Mao's own practice shows this. He was not interested in spreading the Communists' influence through mobile guerrilla units, but he believed deeply in establishing political power. Newton, as noted previously, believed that in order to get rid of the gun it was necessary to pick up the gun. According to Newton, material conditions produce the violence of the aggressor and the self-defense of the victim, and the people have a right and an obligation to resist attack upon their attempts to change the material conditions of their lives. Newton understood that the existing institutions of American society were brought about by violent means and that violence would probably be necessary to overthrow them. Herbert Marcuse said it best when he declared that violence used to uphold domination is bad, but "violence used against the established order is another matter. In terms of historical function, there is a difference between revolutionary and reactionary violence, between violence practiced by the oppressed and the oppressors. In terms of ethics, both forms of violence are inhuman and evil—but since when is history made in accordance with ethical standards?"[73]

Another factor that undoubtedly contributed to the misperception that the Black Panther Party was violent was the organization's call for revolution. People usually believe that all revolutions are violent. But this is not so. Violence is not inherent in revolution. Many revolutions are accompanied by violence, but some are not. The term "revolution" means a profound or fundamental change in a social, economic, cultural, or political system that occurs in a relatively short period of time. Hence, while the American, French, and Russian revolutions were violent transformations of the political order of those countries, the Renaissance, the Industrial Revolution, the Jacksonian Revolution, and the revolution in India all represented fundamental changes in society. Thus they qualify as revolutions, even though they were almost entirely peaceful.

The third misconception is the impression that the Black Panther Party was a reformist organization and not a revolutionary one, in some sense implying that its leadership possessed a shallow understanding of revolutionary ideology. Newton himself was well grounded in the theories of revolution; he studied the works of Mikhail Bakunin, Fidel Castro, Régis Debray, Frantz Fanon, José Martí, Carlos Marighella, Vo Nguyen Giap, Che Guevara, Abraham Guillen, and others.

Said Newton: "We read these men's works because we saw them as kinsmen; the oppressor who had controlled them was controlling us both directly and indirectly."[74] Particularly important was Fanon's *Wretched of the Earth*, a book on the psychology and sociology of colonialism, written by a black psychiatrist about the Algerian revolution. Newton and many others found it to have practical applications to the plight of blacks in America. Newton considered this work to be a blueprint for revolutionary action.

While Newton maintained that the Black Panther Party was a revolutionary organization, some critics point specifically to the Party's Ten-Point Program as evidence that the Party was reformist in nature (see appendix for more detail).[75]

What We Want/What We Believe

1. We want freedom. We want power to determine the destiny of our Black Community.

2. We want full employment for our people.

3. We want an end to the robbery by the capitalist of our Black Community.[76]

4. We want decent housing, fit for shelter of human beings.

5. We want education for our people that exposes the true nature of this decadent American society. We want education that teaches us our true history and our role in the present-day society.

6. We want all Black men to be exempt from military service.

7. We want an immediate end to police Brutality and Murder of Black people.

8. We want freedom for all Black men held in federal, state, county and city prisons and jails.

9. We want all Black people when brought to trial to be tried in court by a jury of their own peer group or people from their Black communities, as defined by the constitution of the United States.

10. We want land, bread, housing, education, clothing, justice and peace.

Political theorist Harold Cruse wrote that "for all its revolutionary rhetoric, the Black Panther Party worked for essentially reformist demands." While most of the ten planks could be considered reformist, points one, six, and eight hardly qualify as such. Hugh Pearson, author of *The Shadow of a Panther*, probably had these points in mind when he stated that several of the Panthers demands were nothing more than mere idealistic pronouncements rather than anything the Black Panther Party actively worked to implement. Pearson added that Newton acted as if being brutalized by the police was a problem that most black people faced on a daily basis.[77] Pearson's words reek of naïveté. The irony in his statement is that Pearson is African American.

The fact that some of the Panthers' demands were reformist was not lost on Newton. He argued that reforms were good as long as they did not serve as an obstacle to the final revolutionary objective. He believed that in some instances reforms helped the revolutionary vanguard to mobilize the people against the oppressor.[78] In that vein, Newton saw reforms as useful steps in the pursuit of revolution. Newton admitted that most of the survival programs were reformist in nature but submitted that they were integrated into the revolutionary program of the Black Panther Party.[79] From time to time, Newton would use the analogy of the raft to describe the Party's survival programs. He pointed out that a raft put into service in the midst of a disaster is not meant to change conditions but to help people get through a difficult time. "During a flood the raft is a life-saving mechanism, it is only a means of getting to safer ground."[80] Furthermore, Newton argued that the Black Panther Party was a revolutionary party because it didn't support the system.[81] Newton submitted that revolution is a process, not a particular action or a conclusion. More specifically, revolution is a contradiction between old and new in the process of development. Newton submitted that the Ten-Point Program was formulated to serve as a basis for a structured political vehicle whose goal was to move toward revolution. Newton maintained that the Black Panthers specifically left the Ten-Point Program open-ended so that it could develop to the point where people could identify with it.[82] The Ten-Point Program was not offered to the people as a conclusion; it was offered as a vehicle with which to move the people to a higher level. Robert Allen, author of *Black Awakening in Capitalist America*, understood the context of the Ten-Point Program: "This program is of great significance because it represented the first concrete attempt to spell out the meaning of black power. It is a sweeping program, ranging from such mundane but fundamental matters as employment and education to broad issues of freedom and self-determination (with the preamble to the U.S. Declaration of Independence included as witness to the fact that the Black Panthers fall squarely within the stream of American revolutionary tradition)."[83]

Newton argued that in people's quest for freedom and in their attempts to prevent the oppressor from stripping them of the basic essentials, the people see things as moving from A to B to C; they are not able to move directly from A to Z.[84] Newton further explained that the people first have to see some basic accomplishments in order to realize that major successes are possible. The revolutionary has to educate the people by example and cannot take them from A to Z in one jump. Newton declared, "When the revolutionary begins to engage in Z, the people cannot relate to him because they lack the tools to do so. When this happens, that individual is no longer a revolutionary, if revolution is a process."[85] Hence, any action or function that does not promote the process is nonrevolutionary. According to Newton: "As revolutionaries we must recognize the difference between what the people can do and what they will do. They can do anything they desire to do, but they will only take those actions which are consistent with their level of consciousness, they will understand even more fully what they in fact can do, and they will move on the situation in a courageous manner. This is merging your theory with your practice."[86]

In the infancy stages of the Black Panther Party, the Revolutionary Action Movement (RAM) criticized the Party for openly displaying weapons and talking publicly about the necessity for the community to arm itself for self-defense. In addition, labor activist and scholar James Boggs chimed in, stating that the fanfare with which the Panthers announced their formation "reveals democratic illusions about the rights a revolutionary party contending for power can expect to enjoy in this country."[87] The Revolutionary Action Movement conducted their activities underground, claiming that this was the correct way to carry out a revolution. Newton responded by saying, "Uncle Ho [Chi Min] said that it is incorrect to publicize military strategy for military reasons, but that it is perfectly correct to publicize military strategy for political reasons."[88] Newton argued that one must establish an organization aboveground so that the masses know the group exists. If the masses are unaware of the Party, it will be impossible for the masses to follow the Party's program. Newton noted that underground parties like RAM logically could not distribute leaflets announcing underground meetings. If they did so, they would be ideologically inconsistent. If they failed to do so, they either remained unknown within the community or risked charges of cowardice. Inevitably, someone would accuse them of fearing exposure to the very dangers they were asking the community to confront.[89]

The aim of the Black Panther Party was to change black people's perception about power, to teach them the strategic method of resisting the power structure through educational programs and activities in which the Party participated. Newton believed that helplessness in the face of oppression was the first attitude that had to be changed, because slaves never expropriates power from the master until they realize that the master is not God and is not bulletproof.[90] Next, it was necessary to teach people that they do not have to accept life at the cost of the loss of their dignity. The only way to do this is to offer them examples of "people who say if they cannot be free, then they will die trying."[91] As people's attitudes evolved, the Black Panther Party no longer carried guns around openly. However, as Newton said, "If we had never offered them an example, they would have never noticed us; we would have never become their representatives and leaders."[92] Newton submitted that there are three ways of learning: reading, observation, and actual experience. He argued rather presumptuously that the black community was not a reading community. Newton claimed that the black community learned best by observing or participating in the activity rather than through actual study. "To learn through reading is good, but the actual experience is the best means of learning," said Newton. According to Newton, it was very important that the Black Panther Party engage in activities that teach the people. For the Black Panther Party, the revolution was a vast educational and organizational effort that did not necessarily need to rely on the use of force (though never excluding it) against the ruling class. At the same time, Newton made it clear that the Black Panther Party was willing to make any revolutionary sacrifice necessary in order to advance the interests of the people of the world, even if that meant using force.

Newton also argued that, when an organization goes underground before establishing a rapport with the community and before setting an example for the community, the community finds it difficult to connect with it. The Party's intention was to develop a lifeline to the community by serving its needs and defending it against the oppressors who invade the community. Besides self-defense, the strategy of carrying guns was designed to raise the consciousness of the people and gain their support. Newton referred to this stage as the prerevolutionary period.[93] In the event that the Black Panther Party was driven underground, the people would defend it because of the rapport established with Party members. "The people would know that in spite of the oppressor's interpretations, that our only desire was to serve their interests," argued Newton.[94] Newton pointed to the Cuban revolution as an example. When Castro started to resist the Batista regime, he began by speaking publicly on the University of Havana campus. He was later driven to the hills. Castro's impact upon the dispossessed people of Cuba was tremendous, and his teachings were well received. "When Castro went into hiding, the Cuban people searched him out, going to the hills to find him and his band of twelve," said Newton.[95] To a large degree, Newton's strategy was effective. A 1968 public opinion poll revealed that 25 percent of the black population had great respect for the Black Panther Party, including 43 percent of those blacks under twenty-one years of age.[96]

On the matter of guns, Newton noted that the gun is not necessarily revolutionary because the oppressor carries a gun. By all revolutionary principles, the gun is a tool to be used as a part of a particular strategy; it is not an end in itself said Newton. It should be noted that some Panthers did not join the Party until they witnessed confrontations with police in which the police were afraid to go for their guns. These individuals interpreted this as the revolution. In fact, Eldridge Cleaver's fascination with the gun would eventually create a rift between him and Newton that proved detrimental to the entire organization. Not long after joining the Party, Cleaver advocated a full-scale revolution led by the Black Panther Party. Newton, on the other hand, countered that the masses were not mentally ready; hence, he would not support such an endeavor. Again Newton's position is similar to Lenin's in that Lenin argued that the vanguard alone cannot achieve victory. "To throw the vanguard alone into battle, before the masses have taken a position of support of the vanguard would not merely be folly but a crime," Lenin wrote.[97] Instead, Newton encouraged the Party to focus its attention on survival programs.

Newton pointed out that he intentionally did not mention the gun until point seven. The right to bear arms for protection was less important than those demands that the Black Panther Party considered more vital, like freedom, employment, education, and housing. "We were trying to build a political vehicle through which the people could express their revolutionary aims. We recognized that no party or organization can make the revolution, only the people can. All we could do was act as a guide to the people," argued Newton.[98]

For Newton, all great revolutions, despite what bourgeois theorists with their elitist notions have written, have always succeeded where the leaders and cadres were the "vehicles" of the people, where they were able to translate into organized and effective action the things the people wanted.[99] In addition, Newton believed it was important for a revolutionary organization to set up a program of practical action and be a model for the community to follow and appreciate. He realized that the masses are constantly looking for a guide, a messiah, to help liberate them from the yoke of oppression. Therefore, Newton believed that it was important for the vanguard to exemplify characteristics of worthy leadership.[100] The actions in which the Black Panther Party engaged were strategic. They were designed to mobilize the community. According to Newton, any action that does not mobilize the community toward the revolutionary goal is not a revolutionary action. Newton admitted that an action might be a tremendous statement of courage, but if it did not mobilize the people toward the goal of a higher manifestation of freedom, it was not making a political statement and could even be counterrevolutionary.

*Rational is the Imagination which can become a
priori of the reconstruction and redirection of the
productive apparatus toward a pacified existence,
a life without fear. And this can never be the
Imagination of those who are possessed by the
images of domination and death.*

—Herbert Marcuse

Thomas Hobbes, John Locke, Jean-Jacques
Rousseau, and Karl Marx are considered four
of the leading theorists on the existence and
development of humankind and the state. In
order to appreciate the uniqueness of Newton's philosophical thoughts on this subject,
it will be worthwhile to compare, to some degree, the work of these theorists with Newton's. Like Hobbes, Newton believed that
people are motivated by personal desires. For Hobbes,
people's desires are completely egocentric and selfish, and
these desires push them to commit every conceivable act of
violence and trickery in order to raise their status. Newton
argues that a person's principal motivating desire is a need for
power.[1] However, a careful reading of Newton reveals that
this drive for power is not egocentric in nature. Instead,
people are consumed with a desire for power in order to free
themselves from all that controls them, be it external or internal controls. By contrast, Locke and Rousseau maintain
that a person is born free. In Locke's words, "man is born
with perfect freedom and independence."[2] Both Locke and
Newton think that people should be concerned with the
well-being of other individuals. Locke asserts that all people
are obligated to preserve themselves and not quit their stations willfully. In other words, when a person's own preservation is not imminently in danger, he or she should do as
much as possible to preserve others. Similarly, Newton believed that the state's duty was to preserve its citizens and to
ensure that every person is afforded an equal opportunity to
live a prosperous and harmonious life. Like Locke, Newton
also discouraged people from quitting their stations willfully.

As Newton saw it, those who quit their stations willfully were victims of what he called "Reactionary Suicide." The operative words in Locke's statement are "quit" and "willfully." For Newton, a person should be willing to put his or her life at risk for the good of the people. However, in Newton's view, to take one's own life or to quit one's station willfully is a cop out—the ultimate expression of Reactionary Suicide.[3]

Reactionary Suicide, as defined by Newton, is when a person commits suicide as a reaction to social conditions that the person endures and that eventually are so overwhelming that he or she is enveloped in a cocoon of helplessness and hopelessness. To illustrate his point, Newton refers to research conducted by Herbert Hendin, who found that black men who committed suicide had been deprived of human dignity, crushed by oppressive forces, and denied their right to live as proud and free human beings.[4] Newton pointed out that this development is accompanied by a feeling of "what's the use?," which sometimes ultimately ends in suicide.[5] To further illuminate his argument, Newton points to a passage in Fyodor Dostoevsky's *Crime and Punishment*, where a poor man named Marmeladov submits that poverty is not a vice. "In poverty," he says, "a man can attain the innate mobility of soul that is not possible in beggary; for while society may drive the poor man out with a stick, the beggar will be swept out with a broom."[6] Why? Newton says it is "because the beggar is totally demeaned, his dignity taken from him. At last bereft of self-respect, immobilized by fear and despair, he sinks to self-murder."[7] Revolutionary Suicide, by contrast, is premised on the belief that one's life chances will not improve without an assault on the Establishment.[8] Embedded in Revolutionary Suicide are courage, self-respect, and dignity, which arouse revolutionary enthusiasm. For Newton, it is far better to oppose the forces that could drive one to self-murder than to succumb to these forces. In addition, although a person risks the possibility of death, there is a chance of improving intolerable conditions. The possibility of changing these conditions is key, because much of human existence is based upon hope without a real understanding of the odds that lie ahead. From Newton's standpoint, Revolutionary Suicide is not a death wish but rather the exact opposite. Those who die as a result of Revolutionary Suicide had such a strong desire to live that they were willing to risk the possibility of death in their quest for a peaceful, dignified, and prosperous existence. On the other hand, those who perish by way of Reactionary Suicide are those who consign or deliver their lives to death as a way of escaping from those forces and conditions that oppress them. Mao's statement best sums up the point: "Death comes to everyone, but it varies in its significance. To die for the reactionary is as light as a feather. But to die for the revolution is heavier than Mount Tai."[9]

Rousseau claims that while people are born free and basically good, as time goes by they develop a desire to master others, which in turn makes them slaves to that end. Newton points out that a person's drive does not necessarily have to lead to the domination of others; because people lack knowledge, their natural drive for control is distorted into a desire for power over people rather than a desire for power to control their own destiny. Newton contends that this drive for power manifests itself as early as birth. He cites the Oedipus complex as a classic example of an individual's desire for power. According to Newton, the son competes for the mother's love and feels hostility toward the father because the father vies for the mother's attention. Newton explains that it is not that the father competes with the son but that in the eyes of the son the father is perceived as the controller. Therefore, Newton asserts that the Oedipus complex is not so much a sexual drive as it is a drive to eliminate the controller or wrest control away from the controller. As far as Newton was concerned, the Oedipus complex was a symbolic fight between the controlled and the controller.[10]

A close examination of Newton's thoughts on this subject shows that although a person is motivated by a desire for power, many times this desire is not acted upon because of fear. Newton argued that much of what a person is has to do with fear.[11] In *Leviathan*, it is apparent that fear is also a key concept in Hobbes's discourse, along with pride, avarice, and ambition, though not necessarily in that order.[12] Newton claims that people are constantly grappling with their desire for power and their failure to act on this desire because of fear. On the contrary, Hobbes believed that a person's fear serves as an incentive for forming a better society. Newton admitted that, as a youngster, he was consumed with fear, until his older brother Walter taught him how to confront it. By the time he was a teenager, Newton was challenging anyone and everyone to a fistfight. After his initial fights, he discovered that his opponents bled like him and, as a result, his fear dissipated.

Newton believed that fear is in part the reason why blacks have not risen up en masse and confronted the oppressor. Newton asserted that blacks had been brainwashed to believe that they were powerless, that there was nothing blacks could do for themselves to bring about the liberation of their people.[13] Furthermore, Newton argued that "blacks had been taught that they must submit to the oppressor, that because they are only ten percent of the population, they should limit their tactics to measures that do not disturb the tranquility of their tormentors."[14]

Newton was correct when he reasoned that the oppressors rule through the submission of their subjects. In light of this, Newton maintained that the first step in the process of liberation for black people is to get past fear, to see the oppressor as simply human. Newton pointed out that the Black Panther Party's use of the word "pig" was intended to strip the oppressors, namely the police, of their invincibility in the eyes of the black community: "The pig has always been associated with grotesque qualities; it likes to wallow in filth and make hideous noises."[15] Newton said that in *A Portrait of the Artist as a Young Man*, James Joyce uses swine as a destructive, devouring image when he describes Ireland as "an old sow that ate her farrow." Newton explained that "the Black Panther Party started using the word pig, a detestable image that takes away the image of omnipotence. A pig, whether running loose in the ghetto with a gun or sitting on Wall Street or in the White House, is a man who can bleed like a man and fall like a man."[16] Newton opined that use of the word "pig" was a form of psychological warfare: it raised the consciousness of the people and also inflicted a new consciousness on the ruling circle. Newton naively reasoned that if this message resonated with whites and the authorities, they might see the errors of their ways. Newton cited Nietzsche, who noted that this tactic had been implemented by the Christians against the Romans. Initially, the Christians were weak, but they understood how to make the philosophy of a weak group work for them. Newton said that "by using phrases like 'the meek shall inherit the earth,' they imposed a new idea on the Romans, one that gave rise to doubt and led to defections to the new sect. Once the Christians stated that the meek shall inherit the earth and won over members, they weakened the strength of those in power."[17]

In Newton's mind, the Black Panther Party represented a response to black people's collective fear of the oppressor—getting past the first barrier to walking free on the streets of life. He maintained that revolution was the Party's ultimate goal but readily added, "that's a hell of a thing for black people to begin to comprehend, because their fear of the oppressor has been driven down so deep, it comes out in the form of hatred and self-hatred."[18] Newton's point is insightful. Indeed, the black self-hatred that he spoke of then manifests itself today in the killing of blacks by other blacks. For most blacks that kill other blacks, the fear of reprisal from the oppressor is virtually nonexistent because the oppressor has made clear in words and action that black life has no value. Hence, the penalty for a black killing a white is much more severe than a white killing a black or a black killing another black. The murder of a white by a black may elicit the death penalty at worse and a long jail sentence at best. It seems logical, then, that fear of the oppressor and the oppressor's sanctions prevent many blacks from realizing their capabilities. Fear may prevent black people from becoming revolutionaries. A revolutionary has learned to conquer fear. In *Revolutionary Catechism*, Mikhail Bakunin said that the first lesson revolutionaries learn is that they are doomed. Unless they understand this, they cannot fully appreciate life. Using Newton's logic regarding freedom, it could be argued that one who does not appreciate the essential meaning of life is not free. Conversely, an individual who experiences total freedom is one who has fully grasped life's meaning. According to Newton, a revolutionary acknowledges that death can come at any time; if a person is unable to conquer fear, it is impossible to proceed as a revolutionary. Newton was noted for saying you can only die once, so why die a thousand times worrying about it? As far as he was concerned, life meant nothing if freedom did not accompany it.[19]

Newton pointed to the black community as a people who, because of fear, patiently wait for a messiah to emerge and lead them to the promised land. Newton saw this firsthand when he was incarcerated. While in jail both blacks and whites bellowed, "Free Huey! Free Huey!" When Newton was freed the same people exclaimed, "Huey, now free us!" Newton observantly pointed out that people would realize more and more that they are responsible for creating leadership.[20] Groups create leaders just as they create other things. Unfortunately, because of fear, people are unable to exert their will, which in turn results in their losing their awareness and causes them to believe that they must acquiesce to their leaders. Newton believed that as people confront their fear, they become more knowledgeable. He recognized that it is the leaders' responsibility to help the masses confront their fear, thereby enabling them to acquire knowledge, piecemeal. The more knowledge people acquire the less they fear. In *This Side of Glory*, David Hilliard recalled a conversation with Newton about the relationship between people and knowledge. According to Newton, a person's initial reaction to the unknown is due in large part to his or her unwillingness to think introspectively and in an abstract way. Drawing from Plato's *Republic*, Newton says:

> Imagine people living in a cave. They've been there all their lives. At the end of the cave shines a light. Now one person among them knows the light is the sun. The rest are afraid of the light. They've lived in darkness and think the light is some kind of evil. Now let's say the person who knows about the light tells them its not evil and tries to lead them out of the cave. They'll fight and probably over-power and maybe even kill him. Because all they know is darkness, and so quite logically they would be

fearful of the light. So, instead, he has to gradually lead them toward the light. Well, it's the same with knowledge. Gradually you have to lead people toward an understanding of what's happening. Remember: one never drops a flowerpot on the head of the masses.[21]

Once people are able to rid themselves of fear, they can begin to live freely and experience all the rights that life affords. As far as basic rights are concerned, Newton argues that all persons have a basic right to live and to work and that the two are inextricably linked. Indeed, one mark of citizenship in America is earning a living, a status historically defined in light of a fear of falling into the degraded state of a slave. Newton did not believe that people should have to beg for food or money in order to survive. Each person should be given the opportunity to hold a job so that "each individual can feel like a dignified person."[22] In Newton's words, "Each person has a right to live and to provide for himself, by means of employment, and to share in the wealth that he helped to produce. And if man cannot physically work, it is the state's responsibility to formulate a program for providing man with a high standard of living, regardless of his socio-economic standing or skill level."[23] This line of reasoning is different from Locke's; Locke believed that part of the government's responsibility was to foster the virtue of people, not provide for them.

Newton submitted that those who control the means of production are obligated to furnish each person with an adequate livelihood. In Newton's mind, there was virtually no such thing as an unemployable person. All people possess some skill or talent that enables them to work for a living. A person who is unemployable is a person who is totally incapable of working at any job, and that really isn't many people. Furthermore, Newton argued that there wasn't any reason why an able-bodied person should not be given the opportunity to work. He claimed that Cuba had full employment among its male population, so why not the United States—a wealthier and more powerful country.[24] "If such a person cannot find work it is because big business wants to use racism and other tactics to keep a lot of people out of work."[25] If those in power fail to provide employment for those who desire to work, Newton, like Rousseau, believed that the people have the right to replace these individuals (representatives) for failing to govern for the good of the people. Newton goes on to say that in the event these new representatives are remiss in their duty, the people should seize the means of production so that they can provide for themselves. Indeed, Marx argued that, for people to be truly free, the means of production must be publicly owned by the community as a whole. Marx cautioned, though, that people's increasing drive to have and possess more and more material items, and to obtain the money needed to acquire them, could eventually cripple them. Since all property, like money, is alienable and can be sold, lost, or stolen, the person whose identity lies mainly in his or her property is in a vulnerable position. Consequently, Marx proposed that, after the reorganization of society wherein the public owns the means of production, goods and services should be distributed solely according to one's needs.

For Newton, if people are denied the right to work, they are denied freedom and the right to live. Political theorist Judith Shklar argues similarly that to be a citizen is to be free, which includes being an independent worker.[26] Newton implored people to realize that there is no sacredness or dignity in either exploiting or being exploited. A close reading of Newton's ideas shows that his notion of the state is somewhat similar to Marx's in that the state is not an impartial policing unit but rather an agent whose primary goal is to protect the lives, rights, and property of the ruling class from the less affluent. Locke saw government as an impartial arbitrator. It would allow people to pursue their own best interests. When, however, two or more individuals came into conflict over the extent of their liberties, the government would intervene, arbitrate the dispute, and then step out again and let people go about their business without interference. Also like Marx, Newton predicts a revolution will bring an end to the stratification of classes and the death of the state. When this happens, a new society will emerge and begin anew. Newton's view of the state is not muddied with pessimistic realities, but rather it emphasizes a utopia of sorts.

Like Rousseau and Locke, Newton believed that laws and rules that govern society should be made to serve the people. People set up rules so that they would be able to interact and function with others in a civilized and harmonious way. More specifically, in order to promote and preserve the general welfare of society, people establish rules and laws. Newton argued that people should not serve laws but rather that laws should serve people.[27] At no time should people respect rules that do not operate in their best interest. Locke's influence on Newton's thinking is apparent when Newton submits that one of people's basic rights is to rewrite and reconstruct laws that do not serve their best interest. In *Two Treatises of Government*, Locke wrote that the people should remove any part of the government when they find that the agency acts contrary to the trust reposed in it. The authority of any government is conditional on its performing the functions with which it was entrusted, said Locke. In fact, Locke believed that governmental supervision of people was for the most part unnecessary. He maintained that people were most free when they were left alone by government.

Newton, Locke, and Rousseau depart from Hobbes's notion that government is most efficient in the hands of an absolute power and that people should serve the government, not the other way around. Hobbes believed that people needed an absolute power to quell chaos and implement justice where appropriate, yet he rejected the theory of the divine right of monarchs. Without an absolute power to administer justice, those who do devilish things will be prone to do them more often. Newton's idea of government did not include an absolute power because he feared that such an entity would become corrupt, as there would be no check on its power. By contrast, Hobbes's form of government placed few limits on the monarch. In exchange for order, people agreed to surrender all of their natural rights to a monarch and render to the monarch complete and unquestioned obedience. And so long as the monarch kept order, people were to obey royal laws. However, since the social contract was an agreement among ordinary people, the monarch was not a party to it and therefore not bound by it. Only the monarch could make law. And because the monarch made law, the monarch was above it. Indeed, the only restraint on the sovereign was an obligation to keep order. Only in the event that the monarch failed to keep order could the people then resist royal authority. In short, Hobbes believed that freedom, though limited, was possible only if people surrendered their liberty to a monarch—hardly a democratic point of view.

In contrast, Newton's government would be a democratic majoritarian system where participation and cooperation of the majority is crucial. Similarly, for Locke, the majority vote was the most important feature of political decision-making, which seems to contradict his notion of the importance of the individual. For Newton, an efficient government would mean that every group of people would have representatives who bring to their constituency their fair share of goods and services. These representatives would serve only at the pleasure of their constituency. In the event that a representative behaved or performed in a way that was inimical to the people's interests, that constituency would have the right to depose him or her through peaceful means. In the event that representatives passed laws that operated to the detriment of that constituency, the people would have a right to rebuke those laws by whatever means necessary.

Newton referred to the Declaration of Independence as support for the notion that the people have the right to rebuke unjust laws by any means necessary. He stated that, prior to 1776, Americans were colonized by the English. The English government instituted various laws that the colonized Americans perceived as being contrary to their general well-being. Consequently, the colonized Americans believed they had no choice but to pick up the musket in self-defense. This in turn led to the creation of laws by the colonized Americans, ensuring their protection from both external and internal repression. One such form of protection was the Declaration of Independence, which states: "whenever any Form of government becomes destructive to these ends, it is the Right of the People to alter or to abolish it, and to institute new Government, laying its foundations on such principles and organizing its powers in such form, as to them shall seem most likely to effect their Safety and Happiness."[28]

Newton notes that the dignity and beauty of people rests in the human spirit, which makes them more than simply a physical being. This spirit must never be suppressed for reasons of repression or exploitation, said Newton. As long as the people recognize the beauty of their human spirits and move against suppression and exploitation, the people will carry out one of the most beautiful ideas of all time.[29]

*People of color have always theorized—but in
forms quite different from the Western form of
abstract logic . . . our theorizing (and I intentionally use the verb rather than the noun) is often
in narrative forms, in the stories we create . . .
[in] dynamic rather than fixed ideas. . . . How
else have we managed to survive with such
spiritedness the assault on our bodies, social institutions, countries, our very humanity?*
—Barbara Christian

At the turn of the twentieth century, many
Africans were under the control of European
imperialism. People of African descent suffered
political oppression, economic exploitation,
and social degradation in the form of systematic racial apartheid. Not surprisingly, this
widespread domination fueled the perception that the emancipation of Africans was contingent upon their political unity.
From the early nineteenth century until the eruption of World
War II, a number of "pan" movements sprouted throughout the
world. Among them were Pan-Arabism, Pan-Germanism, and
Pan-Slavism. Also included in this group is Pan-Africanism.

In its comprehensive sense, Pan-Africanism advocates
the solidarity of people who are bound to each other by their
African origins. Although W. E. B. DuBois is considered the
"father of Pan-Africanism," it was Stokely Carmichael who
put the concept on the itinerary of the American Black Power
movement and forced black activists and revolutionaries
alike to grapple with its potential as an emancipatory ideology. DuBois's reputation as the father of this movement is in
part due to his role as the principal organizer of five of the six
Pan-African conferences, but the initial organizational impe-
tus came from H. Sylvester Williams, a Trinidadian lawyer.
Williams wanted a conference that would be attended by
representatives of the "African race from all parts of the
world."[1] There was a preparatory session in 1899 whose attendees included Bishop Henry McNeal Turner and Booker T.
Washington. The actual conference in 1900 had about sixty

attendees from the United States, the West Indies, Britain, and Africa. The resolutions did not deal with specific Pan-African issues as we understand them today. They dealt with slavery, forced labor, segregation, and various other violations of human rights. In an appeal "To the Nations of the World," DuBois declared: "The problem of the twentieth century is the problem of the color line, the question as to how far the differences of race . . . are going to be made, hereafter, the basis of denying to over half the world the right of sharing to their utmost ability the opportunities and privileges of modern mankind."[2] DuBois did not see racism as an American phenomenon. He clearly understood that a resolution of the color line could only occur within the international political context and that racism was intertwined with economic exploitation and domination of people of color throughout the world. Pan-Africanism, then, was simply the concrete political expression of DuBois's intellectual commitment to root out racism, colonialism, and all aspects of exploitaion.

It was the Pan-African conference of 1900 convened by Williams in London that, in DuBois's words, "put the word "Pan-African in the dictionaries for the first time."[3] And it was here that DuBois "transformed Williams' limited conception of Pan-Africanism into a movement for self-government or independence for African peoples."[4] This later found more concrete and effective organizational expression in the Pan-African Congresses (1919, 1921, 1923, 1927, and 1945) DuBois convened.[5] Robert Allen writes that "the early congresses called for recognition of the dignity and humanity of the black race, a demand which corresponded with the cultural concepts of Negritude and African personality which were evolving during this same period."[6] The early Pan-African Congresses did not call for independence but only demanded that Africans be given a voice in colonial governments. It was not until the 1945 conference that the movement began to address itself to colonial subjects as well as to the colonial oppressors and to demand political independence for the African colonies.

Political scientist Adolph Reed Jr. notes that DuBois prescribed elaborate designs for the decolonization of Africa. DuBois's program intended to prepare African colonial territories for self-determination through gradual, supervised extension of autonomy. This gradual preparation was to include participation in colonial administration by indigenous peoples as well as by West Indian and North American "civilized" and "educated" blacks.[7] DuBois stressed the view that African Americans needed to recognize their "oneness" with all Africans and further postulated that the struggle for equality in the United States was directly related to the fight for African independence. Interest in Africa, the ancestry and culture of African Americans, and the deliverance of the African continent from European powers was a recurring theme in DuBois's work. Indeed, DuBois's celebration of African primitivism and the sensuousness of its arts was in tune with the prevailing sentiment of much of the writings of the Harlem Renaissance.

Carmichael, a student of Ghana's Kwame Nkrumah, proclaimed that Pan-Africanism was the highest expression of Black Power. By contrast, Newton asserted that Pan-Africanism was an outdated concept that would not only stymie the struggle in Africa but the entire struggle for the liberation of blacks everywhere. Newton argued that Pan-Africanism advocates an all-Africanized version of capitalist economic distribution in a world where capital and its power lie tightly in the hands of the United States, "but it fails to encompass the unique situation of black Americans."[8] Moreover, Newton submitted rather presumptuously that Pan-Africanism was the highest expression of reactionary cultural nationalism.[9] From Newton's point of view, cultural nationalism was a reaction to political oppression instead of a response to political oppression. Newton, however, was unclear as to the difference between reacting versus responding to political oppression.

Newton erroneously believed that cultural nationalists thought that blacks' return to African culture would automatically bring about political freedom. Cultural nationalist and political theorist Maulana Karenga eloquently writes that "culture is the basis of all ideas, images and actions. To move is to move culturally, i.e., by a set of values given to you by your culture. We stress culture because it gives identity, purpose, and direction. It tells us who we are, what we must do, and how we can do it."[10] Newton cited François Duvalier (Papa Doc), the president of Haiti, as an example of reactionary cultural nationalism.[11] Duvalier promoted African culture while at the same time oppressing the people. He was against anything nonblack, but it was only to mislead the people. He merely kicked out the white oppressors and replaced them with himself as the oppressor.[12]

Newton's characterization of Pan-Africanism is interesting in view of the fact that Pan-Africanism did not call for a return of blacks to Africa or things African, though DuBois stated that qualified opportunity did exist in Africa for Western blacks "with capital, education, and some technical or agricultural skills, who have the courage of pioneers, good health, and are willing to rough it."[13] Pan-Africanism also did not require that blacks adopt African names, attire, or other African ways of life in the way that Maulana Karenga's Us organization did. One can only assume that Newton was thinking of cultural Pan-Africanism, which ranges from practicing African religious rituals to adopting African languages.[14] Newton acknowledged that it was important that blacks are made aware of their political and cultural heritage in order to move forward as a people, but "returning to African culture in a complete sense was unnecessary."[15] Culture in and of itself would not liberate blacks, Newton argued. Conversely, DuBois emphasized the centrality of African culture in the development of African American life. The importance (or lack thereof) that Newton places on culture is puzzling given his reverence for Frantz Fanon and Malcolm X.

In *The Wretched of the Earth*, Fanon argued that the oppressors consolidated their hold on the colonized by destroying their cultural and value system. "Deprived of their values, the colonized become manipulatable objects who can then be assimilated into the new order; what was a life-giving indigenous culture becomes a zombie which imprisons the subjugated in a stupefied traditionalism; apathy, inertia, an inferiority complex, and guilt follow."[16] For Malcolm X, culture and politics were essential components in the quest for black liberation. A principal tenet of Pan-Africanism was that one must be aggressive and intolerant toward the enemy, the essence of what Fanon, Malcolm X, and Newton were all about. The "Statement of Basic Aims and Objectives of the Organization of Afro-American Unity," presented at a rally in June 1964, made clear Malcolm's belief that black culture played an integral role in the liberation of black America. He cited the importance of developing pride in a common racial history and affirming a distinctive black culture. "We must recapture our heritage and our identity if we are ever to liberate ourselves from the bonds of white supremacy," he said. "We must launch a cultural revolution to unbrainwash an entire people."[17] From Malcolm's standpoint, this "journey to our rediscovery of ourselves" would begin as blacks started to rediscover the folkways, mores, customs, and achievements of their African ancestors. As this process unfolded, blacks were certain to reevaluate the validity of Western history. By comparing ancient glories with their current plight, blacks would eventually come to see that Western exploiters had perpetrated heinous crimes against people of African origin. Once the magnitude of these deeds was revealed and comprehended, the time-honored practice of "forgive and forget" would be discarded.[18] In the end, this series of developments would culminate in coordinated action. Infused with cultural pride and historical awareness, blacks would set out to achieve a cultural reunification with all people of African origin and begin to chart a course of their own in the global body politic.

Newton claimed that the Black Panther Party did not subscribe to Black Power as defined by Carmichael, because Carmichael's concept was similar to President Nixon's.[19] According to Newton, Carmichael's notion of Black Power was synonymous with black capitalism; it would only support the interest of a small group of black people and would do virtually nothing to enhance the lives of the vast majority of people of African origin in Africa or the Americas. As far as Newton was concerned, black capitalism would simply result in the black elite replacing the white oppressor. He insisted that "in time the black elite would take on the role of the oppressor, resulting in blacks oppressing other blacks."[20]

One could argue that Newton misunderstood Carmichael's claim that Pan-Africanism was the highest expression of Black Power. By Black Power, Carmichael meant the right of all African people to determine their own destiny wherever they might be in the world. At a conference in 1968, Carmichael spoke of Black Power in these terms: "We must consciously strive for an ideology which deals with racism first, and if we do that we recognize the necessity of hooking up with the nine hundred million [sic] black people in the world today. That's what we recognize. And if we recognize that, then it means that our political situation must become international. . . . It must be international because if we know anything, we would recognize that the honkies don't just exploit us, they exploit the whole Third World—Asia, Africa, Latin America."[21]

For Carmichael, Black Power meant expropriating colonialism and instituting black self-rule, as Kwame Nkrumah had done in Ghana in 1957. Simply put, "Black Power means that all people who are black should come together, organize themselves and form a power base to fight for their liberation."[22] Carmichael's notion of Black Power was almost identical to point number one of the Black Panther Party's Ten-Point Program, which Newton himself wrote. In addition, Pan-Africanism, as articulated by its founders, is grounded in socialist principles, not capitalism, as Newton hastily concluded. DuBois suggested that the institutional foundation for a self-determining Africa would be a "socialism founded on old African communal life."[23] Reed argues that Pan-Africanism ultimately was, for DuBois, the African form of pluralist participation in a global socialist order, which DuBois saw as the highest expression of rational social organization.[24] In Ghana, for Nkrumah, socialism meant that prices of goods would not exceed wages, house rentals would be within the means of all groups, social welfare services would be open to all, and educational and cultural amenities would be available to everyone.[25] It meant, in short, that the real income and standard of life of all farmers and workers would rise appreciably.

Newton's problems with Pan-Africanism in part also appear to stem from a belief that those African governments that subscribed to the philosophy of Pan-Africanism were aligned with United States imperialism. However, Ghana and Bissau were two examples of black-ruled countries that were free of full-scale Western influence. Indeed, the fifth Pan-African Conference inspired Nkrumah to build the powerful Convention People's Part and under his leadership the independent nation of Ghana was born. Newton unconvincingly maintained that those countries with Pan-Africanist regimes had a silent agreement with the United States that allowed them to oppress blacks in exchange for their cooperation with American imperialism.[26] Newton, however, never gave examples of such countries. He doubted that black-run African governments could prosper without the support of the United States. Newton's point may not have been totally unfounded.

The early Pan-African Congresses vacillated on the question of imperialism, with some delegates favoring a critical approach while others desired accommodation to the status quo. DuBois himself was among those who seemed unclear on how to proceed. For example, he attacked Marcus Garvey because he said Garvey alienated the British imperialists by his lack of diplomacy, and DuBois believed that Great Britain's help was needed in any international trade arrangements. By contrast, Garvey ridiculed the leaders of the Pan-African Congress because they invited white representatives of the imperialist powers to attend their meetings.[27] Nkrumah advocated Pan-Africanism as a dialectical necessity to tackle imperialism and neocolonialism: "The foreign firms who exploit our resources long ago saw the strength to be gained from acting on a Pan-African scale. By means of interlocking directorships, cross-share holdings and other devices, groups of apparently different companies have formed, in fact, one enormous capitalist monopoly. The only effective way to challenge this economic empire and to recover possession of our heritage is for us to act on a Pan-African basis through a Union Government."[28]

Newton's critique of Pan-Africanism is perplexing because one can find a number of Pan-Africanist tenets throughout the Black Panther Party's ideological development, especially in its internationalist phase. A careful reading of Pan-Africanist literature reveals four principal ideological features: a concern with the common problems of all African peoples wherever they are situated, self-determination for all people of African origin, pride in things African, and an insistence that the economic system governing African people be socialistic. Indeed, these four elements are quite similar to what Newton and the Black Panther Party enumerated in its Ten-Point Program. Newton called upon all black Americans to find strength and self-confidence in identifying with Africans.

An essay written by Newton titled "Uniting Against the Common Enemy" clearly shows that he was more in step with the philosophy of Pan-Africanism than he publicly acknowledged. He wrote:

On the continent of Africa there are people who look like us. They are Black. We are brothers because our struggle is common. We have both suffered under white racism and under oppression. This is why we should not let the reactionaries of the world be the only ones communicating across the waters and masses of land. We have common interests to serve, and therefore, we can learn from each other. What happens here affects us. The United States has seen to this. But this is good. We can learn to fight together, though separated.[29]

Many have found Pan-Africanism as an ideology and movement to be problematic, but not for the reasons Newton did. DuBois blamed the failure of Pan-Africanism on the opposition of the colonial powers, the condescending attitudes of whites toward Africa, and the indifference of American blacks to the plight of their African brothers and sisters. Horace Campbell says that, from the beginning, some of the most adamant proponents of the Pan-African movement reneged on one of the cardinal principles of Pan-Africanism: that the people of one part of Africa are responsible for the freedom and liberation of those in other parts of Africa; indeed, black people everywhere were to accept the same responsibility.[30]

Others say that Pan-Africanism was impractical. Nkrumah had Pan-Africanism in mind when he advocated a unification of all of Africa that would result in a Union of African States, much like the United States. Some contend that Nkrumah was naive in thinking that other African states would abandon their newly acquired sovereignty and concomitant national interests to become part of a Union of African States.[31] Arthur S. Gakwandi supports this argument when he says that "the vigour of Pan-Africanism's assault on oppression and privilege became vitiated by the palliative of flag independence in many African states; thus giving way to divergence in the pursuit of Pan African goals."[32]

Since 1961, Pan-Africanism has been on two sometimes parallel, sometimes divergent tracks: the one pursued by African governments, which takes the form of official cooperation; the other pursued by freethinkers who, since the 1960s, have had no well-defined agenda. On a more banal level, some have maintained that Pan-Africanism as an ideology was unsuccessful because there was no general agreement on its ideological content. For instance, Leopold Senghor's Pan-Africanist notions seem to be founded on his cultural theory of negritude. Conversely, Nkrumah wrote that negritude, the prototype of modern cultural nationalism, was "irrational, racist and nonrevolutionary."[33] Garvey's notion of Pan-Africanism differed from Nkrumah's and DuBois's version by virtue of his dreams of an "Imperial Africa" complete with an "Emperor," "Knights," "Barons," and "Earls" of the Sudan, Niger, and so forth.[34] Even Carmichael seemed to suffer from some confusion about Pan-Africanism, despite the fact that he studied under one of its most advanced spokesman, Kwame Nkrumah. As a case in point, in *Stokely Speaks: Black Power to Pan-Africanism*, Carmichael's understanding of socialism appears less grounded than one might expect. Early on he speaks of scientific socialism, but later he refers to a socialism that "has it roots in [African] communalism." The latter is the definition of "African socialism," which Nkrumah denounced as a myth that is "used to deny the class struggle, and to obscure genuine socialist commitment."[35]

It was this lack of ideological clarity and uniformity on the part of the black intellectual vanguard of this movement that played a big part in Pan-Africanism's eventual failure as a political philosophy and blue print for social action. Despite the black intelligentsia's commitment to Pan-Africanism, they were unable to convert their commitment into mass support within the black community. Rhett Jones argues that blacks living outside of the United States are far more interested in black Americans than black Americans are interested in them.[36] Consequently, Pan-Africanism never had a significant impact on the political development of Africans or African Americans. However, for all of its shortcomings, Pan-Africanism did provide a feeling of solidarity among a segment of Africans and people of African heritage. As a moral vision, Pan-Africanism centered on values rooted in the redignification of black people in response to the colonial view that black "stood for the properly servile inferiors who had not progressed beyond the primitive stages of mankind."[37]

Every ideology, then is a collection of errors, illusions, mystifications, which can be accounted for by reference to the historical reality it distorts and transposes.

> —Karl Marx

Huey Newton is a classical revolutionary figure. His imagination is constantly at work, conjuring up strategies and tactics that apply classical revolutionary principles to the situations confronting black people here in America.

> —Eldridge Cleaver

Black Nationalism 1966–68

Newton's role as the Black Panther Party's chief philosopher flourished as he took the Party through ideological metamorphoses, experimenting and wrestling with a number of theories aimed at finding solutions to problems such as poverty, racism, classism, and sexism. Openness to change was a characteristic that enabled Newton to redefine and reevaluate conditions and situations on a continual basis. An examination of Newton's writings reveals that the Black Panther Party's ideology can be broken down into four phases: black nationalism, revolutionary socialism, internationalism, and Intercommunalism.

Early in the Party's development, the organization's position was shaped by the racial crisis that permeated all of America. Black Americans possessed little power during the first half of the twentieth century. Some blacks were even fatalistic about the prospect for meaningful change. The poverty and deteriorating well-being of black Americans were the direct consequence of slavery. Unfortunately, blacks had nothing to offer to or withhold from whites other than their labor, and they were kept so close to the minimal subsistence level they were not in a position to use their labor power as an effective bargaining tool. As a result, they were forced to create black self-help organizations and experiment with a variety of different ideologies and strategies aimed at enhancing black people's lives. During the nineteenth century, blacks like Martin Delany and Bishop Henry McNeal Turner advocated black nationalism as an emancipatory strategy but were unable to galvanize strong support around it. Delany argued that since blacks are a minority in the United States, where "many and almost insurmountable obstacles present themselves, a separate black nation is necessary in the march to self-determination."[1] John McCartney suggests that in light of black nationalists' efforts to achieve this goal, the American Colonization Society (ACS) can be considered the first organized expression of black nationalism in this country.[2]

In 1816, the white-led ACS was founded with the express purpose of finding a home in Africa for freed slaves. The ACS raised funds and initiated a campaign to encourage free blacks to emigrate to Liberia. Thousands of dollars were solicited for the purchase of ships to transport blacks to Africa. The first ten years of the ACS saw it transport 1,420 blacks back to Africa. By the mid 1800s, the ACS began to lose steam. Some contend that abolitionists had begun to question the morality of the endeavor, while others say that the society came under scrutiny regarding its motives and also that the settlement in Liberia was mismanaged. One scholar argues that the ACS failed because most free blacks opposed the idea of wholesale emigration. They opposed it for four reasons:. (1) they saw it as a way to get rid of free blacks in order to better secure slavery in the United States—in other words, to ensure that they would not influence the thinking of blacks in bondage, free blacks were shipped out; (2) they considered it their duty to stay and fight for emancipation; (3) they assumed it would give credence to arguments of black inferiority and inability to cope with "civilization"; and (4) they reasoned that they were as much Americans as whites in terms of their contribution and birth.[3]

Nevertheless, while black nationalism did not experience long-term success early on, it enjoyed a resurgence in the early to mid 1960s. This resurgence could have been due in part to the emergence of "a new black man." Carlton Goodlet, publisher of the *San Francisco Sun Reporter,* spoke of this before a National Broadcast Editorial Conference: "A new black man, as opposed to the old 'Negro,' asserts that there is one duty to be done, one end to be achieved: to destroy racism—by any means in his power. Between 11 and 12 million young blacks under age 20—or half the black population—will no longer tolerate either the overt or covert acts of a racist majority which dehumanizes and robs the black nation of its birthright, freedom."[4]

This newer black nationalism placed an emphasis on the term "black" and demanded that it be substituted for "Negro" or "colored" as a general designation for the race. "Black is Beautiful" became the motto.[5] Maulana Karenga defined "Black Nationalism as a social theory and practice organized around the concept and conviction that Blacks are a distinct historical personality and they should, therefore, unite in order to gain the structural capacity to define, defend and develop their interests."[6] Perhaps the greatest factor in the resurgence of black nationalism during the 1960s was the presence of Malcolm X. Indeed, he was to become the symbol and voice of black nationalism for a new generation of blacks in America. Early on, Malcolm X argued that America was not and would never be black people's promised land but rather was a white-run prison from which blacks had to physically and psychologically escape. America was hell and whites were inherently evil, Malcolm preached. White Americans obstructed God's work by imprisoning God's black chosen people and keeping them from fulfilling their destiny. Destruction of white domination was a necessary step to achieving black nationalism.[7]

Not all blacks who rebelled against black subjugation in America chose to fight for integration. Many looked to other options. Alternatives for black nationalists in the 1960s did not mean emigration to Africa, as it did earlier for Marcus Garvey. For some, it meant the construction of a separate black institutional structure within the confines of the United States, while for others, like the Republic of New Africa, it meant carving a separate black state out of the United States. The W. E. B. DuBois Club of America, a young black Marxist organization, moved in that direction after the Watts rebellion in 1965. The group demanded, unsuccessfully, a referendum for Watts residents to vote on seceding from the city of Los Angeles. Even before the founding of the Republic of New Africa and the W. E. B. DuBois Club of America, Cyril Briggs of the African Blood Brotherhood proposed that the race problem could be solved by the establishment of a separate black nation in the western portion of the United States.

A black-controlled nation-state represents one of the more ambitious options. Early on, the idea of a separate black nation-state appealed to Newton, who said, "We [the Black Panther Party] realized the contradictions in society, some oppressed people in the past had solved some of their problems by forming into nations."[8] He maintained that if blacks wanted to protect and preserve their own subculture, indeed to be masters of their own fate, the answer was to demand a separate nation within the continental United States. Newton figured naively that if other oppressed groups throughout the world could do it, so could blacks in America. He soon came to realize that the likelihood of America relinquishing to blacks a certain number of states in a particular region of the country where blacks could form their own nation and live apart from whites was nil. Imperialism would not allow blacks to separate. Imperialism has not allowed developing countries thousands of miles away to live in peace, Newton argued. "If imperialism has prevented those countries from being free 15,000 miles away, it is unlikely that it would allow a group of people right here in North America to separate," said Newton.[9] Later Newton would say that even if blacks were afforded the opportunity to form their own nation, it would only lead to extinction. Newton's opposition to a separate black nation is understandable, but it is not clear why he thought it would result in the extinction of human beings.[10] As far as integration was concerned, that was a pipe dream. Newton asserted that whites would never allow blacks to be integrated fully into the American mainstream— "this would be economically, politically and socially inimical to white interests." On the question of emigrating to Africa, Newton thought that was impractical. He argued that American blacks were ill equipped mentally and physically to make such a move.[11] And, more important, the overwhelming majority of blacks would be unwilling to leave their home-land of many years to journey to an unfamiliar continent.

After a more thorough and critical analysis of the concept, Newton defined black nationalism to mean black community control free of outside interference, particularly of capitalists and police. Newton's brand of black nationalism stressed, among other things, race consciousness, intraracial cooperation, and the building, controlling, and maintaining of black institutions. Under the auspices of black nationalism, he argued for decent housing, jobs, education, exemption of blacks from military service, and all-black juries, but most of all for the ability of black Americans to control their own destiny. Like Malcolm X, Newton embraced black nationalism's emphasis on black pride, black self-esteem, black solidarity, and veneration for Africa, even though he rejected mass black emigration to Africa. Newton's emphasis on back nationalism at that time is understandable. He believed that in order for blacks to achieve full equality, a revolution would have to take place within the black community whereby blacks would unite on all fronts—economically, politically, culturally, and ideologically. Once this took place, blacks would be ready to lead an effort to overthrow the ruling establishment of the United States. He justified the need for black nationalism in these terms: "after imperialism is destroyed, then there won't be any need for nationalism."[12] One writer commented that the Panthers envisioned an American apocalypse in which all blacks would be forced to unite for survival against the Establishment. Newton put it this way: "At the height of the resistance they [the Establishment] are going to be slaughtering black people indiscriminately. We are sure that at that time Martin Luther King will be a member of the Black Panther Party through necessity. He and others like him will have to band together with us just to save themselves."[13]

At no time in the recent past had any black protest group went to such lengths to prepare itself for an all-out war with the established order. Some observers viewed this new development as the work of the Marxists among young blacks. The consensus among social commentators, however, was that the new development was due to "desperation as a result of the ineffectiveness of both conventional politics and nonviolent direct action to secure significant changes in the livelihood of African Americans."[14] It was true that among some of these new advocates, black nationalism was, to some extent, proposed out of a sense of desperation and disenchantment if not disillusionment, but the advocacy of a forced takeover by the movement had more specific causes. Because it arose in the South, the black protest movement, for the most part, was both nonviolent in theory and practice. One reason for that was that many blacks had been socialized to be docile and deferential in the presence of whites. When it moved North and West, nonviolence encountered the contempt of many disenfranchised blacks, particularly in the wake of the assassinations of Malcolm X and King. These urbanites decided that blacks should no longer obey the ruling whites' timetable or believe in their goodwill. To the young blacks in these urban areas, violence was attractive and virile; nonviolence was equated with cowardice. Hence, to them, Black Nationalism seemed like the most viable strategy for black liberation.

Newton believed that blacks had a moral right to control their own communities. Drawing from Fanon as well as Albert Memmi's *The Colonizer and the Colonized*, Newton saw blacks as a colonized people that America (with the help of the police) oppressed in every conceivable way, determined to keep blacks from developing any type of consciousness and prevent them from erecting structures aimed at self-sufficiency. Seemingly influenced by Newton's thinking, sociologist Robert Blauner later spoke of black people's situation in a similar fashion. In *Racial Oppression in America*, Blauner argued that a political policy of "internal colonialism" was being employed, with the police being used to enforce the culturally repressive aspects of white middle-class American values against the distinctive ethnic orientation of African Americans and other minorities. The argument goes that tendencies in the ghetto had been directed at gaining control and ownership of businesses, schools, social services, the police, and other institutions that exist within or encroach on the community. The role of the law, especially the police, was crucial in repressing those tendencies.[15]

As part of its Ten-Point Program, the Black Panther Party had as its major political objective a United Nations-supervised plebiscite to be held throughout the black colony, in which only black colonial subjects would be allowed to participate, for the purpose of determining the will of black people toward their national destiny. When Eldridge Cleaver visited New York to lay his case before the United Nations, however, he found the audience unreceptive, and aside from generating anti-American propaganda among the nations of the Eastern Bloc, the Panther initiative garnered little visible results.[16] The Black Panthers' call for a plebiscite supervised by the United Nations is reminiscent of Marcus Garvey's petitions to the old League of Nations.[17] When some argued that the black community was not a colony, as Newton suggested (that in order to be a colony you have to be a nation and the black community is not a nation but rather a dispersed collection of communities), Newton welcomed the criticism and eventually concurred with this assessment. He said, "Those critics are absolutely right we are a collection of communities just as the Korean people, the Vietnamese people and the Chinese people are a collection of communities—a dispersed collection of communities because we have no superstructure of our own."[18] Newton defined a nation as a group of people who have in common their own land or territory, economic system, culture, and language. Suffice to say, the black community lacked these requisites. Even before he acknowledged these structural boundary issues, Newton often spoke of the difference between middle-class blacks and poor blacks, indicating that he was moving away from a nationalist approach and moving toward a more class-based analysis in which race, while still important, would not be the driving force behind formulating an ideology for eradicating imperialism.

Other factors that may have contributed to the Panthers' move away from nationalism include the hiring of Charles Garry, a white attorney, to defend Newton in the 1967 murder trial and the Panthers' alliance with the Peace and Freedom Party.[19] Garry had a reputation as an attorney who was deeply concerned with the well-being of the racially oppressed, whereas the black lawyers who vied for the opportunity to defend Newton did so in search of attaining prestige and national celebrity. As was noted earlier, the coalition with the Peace and Freedom Party not only played a decisive role in helping get Newton released, but it also helped to spur support for the black liberation movement in the white community. Progressive whites made other whites aware of the legitimacy of the black liberation struggle. While some argued that the Panthers' relationship with whites was contradictory to their black nationalist position, many Panthers, including Newton, came to understand that, while one's skin color did in fact help to shape the way one approached the world, it did not have to determine one's entire outlook on society. Moreover, Newton would eventually concede that any notion of a black armed revolution was strictly romantic. He acknowledged that blacks could not do it alone. Even if every black American supported a revolution, they would still be outnumbered ten to one by American whites; hence, blacks would have to work in tandem with progressive and politically conscious whites.[20]

At the close of 1968, the Black Panther Party still considered itself a black nationalist organization. One can see, however, that Newton had begun to talk about capitalism as the enemy. While the exact relationship between capitalism and racism was not systematically spelled out, the organization had begun to reevaluate its original position as black nationalists and to move in a new direction.

Revolutionary Socialism 1969–70

By 1969, Huey Newton and the Black Panther Party made a fundamental alteration in their political ideology. After analyzing conditions more thoroughly, Newton concluded that racism was no longer the key issue. In this phase of Panther ideology, the class struggle was given equal weight with the race struggle. He now asserted that only by eliminating capitalism and replacing it with socialism would all black people be able to practice self-determination and thus achieve freedom.[21] This new position is reflected in the revision of point three of the Ten-Point Program. The new version of point three read: "We want an end to the robbery by the capitalist of our black community." The original statement had read "by the white man" as opposed to the "capitalist." Newton and the Panthers came to see that there were many whites who were genuinely concerned about the plight of African Americans. Moreover, they were willing to do something about it— equally important, they had no ulterior motive. This change in thinking seems to indicate that the Party no longer viewed white Americans, in general, as the principal oppressors of blacks; it now viewed capitalism as being the major problem facing the oppressed. For example, Newton saw little difference between black merchants who profited from the black community and refused to contribute to the Panthers' survival programs and the white capitalists like A&P or Safeway. If black businesses refuse to help the black community, they are parasites that must be forced out of business through economic boycott, argued Newton.[22]

Newton thought that the present government and its subsidiary institutions were invalid because they failed to meet the needs of the people, especially black Americans. He claimed that civil rights measures produced no change for the majority of blacks. Therefore, Newton argued that in the interest of all oppressed people, new institutions, both political and economic, should be established, while the old institutions should be discarded. According to President Richard Nixon, what blacks needed was a "piece of the pie." He devised a minority business agency intended to promote the development of black capitalism. In March 1969, Nixon announced the creation, within the Department of Commerce, of the Office of Minority Business Enterprise (OMBE). At the official ceremony, Nixon said: "I have made the point that to foster the economic status and the pride of members of our minority groups, we must seek to involve them more fully in our private enterprise system. . . . Involvement in business has always been a major route toward participation in the mainstream of American life. Our aim is to open that route to potentially successful persons who have not had access to it before."[23]

Newton argued that black capitalism would be a detriment to black liberation, not a step toward it. He believed that black capitalism would replace one master with another. A small group of blacks would control the destiny of the majority of black people if this development came to pass. Likewise, labor activist and scholar James Boggs argued that black capitalism is irrational in that it poses as a collective strategy but is in fact a class strategy to further enrich a few at the expense of the many.[24] Newton likened black capitalism to an earlier time when there was a small number of black slave masters. And just as the earlier black slaveholders failed to alleviate the suffering of their slaves, Newton argued that the black capitalists would do little to redistribute the wealth to the suffering and poor oppressed blacks.

At the Revolutionary People's Constitutional Convention in Washington, D.C., convened by the Black Panther Party in November 1970, Newton publicly called for a socialist government to bring about a more equitable distribution of income, goods, and services.[25] Newton noted that "as a revolutionary group, we see a major contradiction between capitalism in this country and our interest. We realize that this country became very rich upon slavery and that slavery is capitalism in the extreme. We have two evils to fight, capitalism and racism. We must destroy both."[26] Newton's call for socialism was not made in a vacuum and therefore should not be viewed as far-fetched or unrealistic. Countries less well off than the United States had shown that socialism could work. England socialized medicine for the poor. Scandinavia provided socialized housing. Canada and Australian offered special allowances to large families.[27] Newton maintained that a fine example of socialism came on the heels of the revolution in Algeria in 1962 when Ben Bella assumed control. "The French were deposed, but it was a people's revolution because the people ended up in power," said Newton.[28] The leaders who took over were not guided by the profit motive through which they would exploit the people and keep them in a subservient state. Algerian revolutionaries nationalized industry and distributed the profits throughout the community. In addition, the people's representatives were in office strictly through the power of the people. The people controlled the wealth of the country, and their opinions were taken into consideration whenever industrial modifications were made, according to Newton.

For those blacks who continued to argue that black separatism was the answer to black people's problems, Newton responded: even if blacks achieved a separatist independence in the United States, they would "be unable to function side by side with a capitalistic imperialistic country."[29] Thus logic dictated that black revolutionaries abandon their racial chauvinism and ally with the white Left and other oppressed groups in pursuit of a common goal. For the Black Panther Party, coalitions with whites became increasingly important. When Cleaver was nominated as the Peace and Freedom Party's presidential candidate in 1968, student groups all over the country coalesced with the Black Panther Party. SDS had provided support to black students at Cornell University who pressed for the hiring of more black faculty and students. After six thousand students, mainly organized by SDS, staged a supportive sit-in at the gym, the university agreed to cooperate with the Afro-American Student Society.[30] When the Party entered into an alliance with SDS, a spokesperson for the latter group declared: "We must keep in mind that the Black Panther Party is not fighting black people's struggles only, but is, in fact, the vanguard in our common struggles against capitalism and imperialism."[31]

It is not coincidental that the Panthers' shift in ideology coincided with strong opposition to the Vietnam War. The war made the United States seem like an evil country in the eyes of many white youth. One year prior to the founding of the Black Panther Party, SDS held a massive antiwar demonstration at the Washington Monument. The war provided the perfect entrée for the Black Panther Party to pursue white allies. After white antiwar demonstrators were beaten by police at the National Democratic Party Convention in Chicago in 1968, Eldridge Cleaver wrote: "They've been beaten, maced and tear-gassed. They themselves have now experienced what's been happening to black people for so long. . . . They never thought it could be done to them. They are turning into a revolutionary force, and that's why we believe the Black Panthers can enter into coalitions with them."[32] Also, after one million people marched against the war in November 1969, Newton would underscore the need to form alliances with whites against the Vietnam War, commenting that the movement to end "the Vietnam war is one of the most important movements that's going on at this time."[33]

On the state of affairs in America, Newton submitted that while the United States was conceived in liberty, it presently is a nation "dedicated to death, oppression and the pursuit of profits."[34] He argued that a new constitution needed to be written and enforced so that everyone would enjoy the same rights and privileges. "The Constitution set up . . . to serve the people no longer serves the people, for the people have changed," Newton said at the Revolutionary People's Constitutional Convention.[35] Newton's theme during this conference was that there is freedom for the majority and oppression for the minority, and he recited the histories of the Native Americans and blacks as evidence. "Throughout the world, the freedom struggles of oppressed people are opposed by this government because they are a threat to bureaucratic capitalism in the United States. Racism is a profitable and essential ingredient of capitalism," argued Newton.[36]

As Newton saw it, only by eliminating capitalism and substituting socialism will black people be able to practice self-determination and thus achieve freedom. A reconstructed constitution would call for such things as true proportional representation and the equal distribution of America's wealth. Newton argued that a basic tenet of revolutionary socialism is the principle that things that all people commonly use and commonly need should be commonly owned. In other words, the people should collectively decide what they need and should share in the wealth they produce. To this end, the administration of the government should be subjected to the dictates of the people. Newton stated, "It is not impossible for a form of socialism to be voted in peacefully in the United States at a later time."[37] However, at this point, Newton thought that a revolution would be necessary to destroy American imperialism and put the means of production under the control of the people. The state would then cease to exist, and there would be socialism. Newton asserted that this new objective would correspond to Lenin's withering away of the state.

Internationalism 1970–71

By the middle of 1970, Newton had once again reevaluated his thinking on global imperialism and how blacks were situated within it. Through all of this he held fast to the fundamental tenets of socialism. The new Panther ideology represented a transition to internationalism. Internationalism represents a struggle to expand democracy and end national and colonial oppression of blacks throughout the world.[38] Newton did not give specific reasons for the shift, but one can surmise that although those in the Party saw the black community as being the vanguard of the revolution, they came to the realization that blacks needed the support of other oppressed groups throughout the world. Indeed, by this time there was a fairly well developed Black Power consciousness among nonwhite minorities in Britain as well as among black Canadians and some Australian aborigines, to name but a few.[39] In order to show solidarity with these and other groups, the Party decided to call itself internationalist.

In the internationalist stage, the Panthers saw their struggle in the United States as not only necessary for the liberation of blacks and other oppressed people in America but as a struggle whose success was critical for the liberation of exploited nations worldwide, especially developing nations.[40] "We are internationalists because we are fighting an internationalist oppressor," Newton proclaimed.[41] In retrospect, it appears that Newton may have been a step or two ahead of other black activists concerning the question of internationalism, since it was not until May 1972 that the black liberation movement officially became internationalized as a mass force. The occasion was the African-American National Conference on Africa held at Howard University.[42]

Newton's internationalist perspective came from studying powerful revolutionary movements not only in Africa but also in China, Cuba, and Vietnam. Newton realized that in order to be free, the world's ruling circle had to be crushed, and that in order to do this, it was imperative to unite with other oppressed people throughout the world. After all, one could argue that black Americans and Third World peoples shared a common struggle, for they had a common enemy— "white Western imperialism." Both were victims of the same capitalist system. Third World peoples were colonized externally, whereas American blacks were colonized from within. It would require a common struggle to liberate each. The Panthers' search for international allies in the struggle for liberation spanned the globe. "We join the struggle of any and all oppressed people all over the world, as well as in this country, regardless of color, who are attempting to gain freedom and dignity," said Newton.[43]

The Panthers' international approach mirrored that of Malcolm X. Shortly before his death, Malcolm traveled extensively to Africa and the Third World and developing countries while building the Organization of Afro-American Unity. In speeches to American audiences, Malcolm urged black Americans to identify with people of color throughout the world and seek United Nations protection of rights denied by a racist U.S. government. The Panthers' search for a network of international allies was timely because it was apparent that the federal government, as well as local police, had determined to annihilate them. President Nixon's assistant attorney general, Jerris Leonard, announced in May 1969, "The Panthers are a bunch of hoodlums. We've got to get them."[44] Shortly thereafter, the FBI, in cooperation with the Chicago police, engineered the cold-blooded murders of Panther leaders Fred Hampton and Mark Clark.

On blacks and internationalism, Newton argued that because of the abduction of the Africans from their homeland, blacks had been dispersed all over the world; thus blacks were by geographical circumstance internationalists.[45] He argued further that "blacks are internationalists because their struggle must be waged on many fronts. While we feed and clothe the poor at home, we must meet and attack the oppressor wherever he may be found. Newton also added that the historical conditions of black Americans have compelled them to be progressive. "Blacks have always talked about equality, instead of believing that other people must equal us. We want to live with other people who try to distinguish or separate themselves from others based on some esoteric sense of superiority," Newton declared.[46] Because blacks have been dispersed all over the world, they have come in contact with a variety of people from different races, backgrounds, and cultures. This interaction enables blacks to identify easily with other groups. Hence, Newton argued that blacks are true internationalists.

Newton also saw the political expediency of showing solidarity with political allies who had suffered many of the same kinds of oppressive atrocities as black Americans. Newton thought that if blacks allied with colonial peoples, blacks would have greater numbers and be in a better position to overthrow imperialism. Consequently, Newton and the Black Panther Party supported all struggles where there were people fighting for freedom. Said Newton, "We also support our European brothers and sisters who are struggling to overthrow the bourgeoisie in their country."[47] Uprisings that occurred during the late 1960s gave Newton and the Black Panther Party reason to believe that alliances with groups who shared similar grievances were possible. In May of 1968 they witnessed the near overthrow of Charles de Gaulle's government in France, resulting in a rejuvenated Socialist Party and a reformed educational system. A mass student movement was offering something of the same in West Germany. Even within the Soviet bloc, a massive anti-authoritarian revolt had challenged prevailing structures in Czechoslovakia. Mexico, Poland, and Spain were also the sites of political upheaval.

The Black Panther Party not only wanted changes in everything, including the economic system, that the oppressor inflicts upon the oppressed, but the Party was also deeply concerned with other people of the world and their desire for revolution. Again, according to Newton, the Black Panther Party would support movements that proceeded toward ridding themselves of the yoke of oppression as long as these movements were international in aim. Newton's internationalism is similar to that of Marx, who argued that people of the same social class from different countries actually had more in common with each other than people of different classes within the same country. The Black Panther Party's commitment to internationalism is reflected in their slogan: "We say All Power to the People—Black Power to Black People, Brown Power to Brown People, Red Power to Red People and Yellow Power to Yellow People. We say White Power to White People."[48]

Newton argued that the monopolists fear the unity of black, white, brown, yellow, and red people. He maintained that the oppressor is most vulnerable when the oppressed of all races move in solidarity into the arena of mass struggle.[49] The Black Panther Party made an effort to put internationalism into practice. On an organizational level, the Panthers tried to broaden their scope (with mixed results) by forming an international chapter in Algiers, Algeria. They also formed alliances with several foreign organizations. While the Party extended its hand to a number of groups, those who publicly expressed their solidarity and support of the Party included the Korean Democratic Lawyers Association, the French Federation of Black African Students, the German Socialist Student's League (West Germany), and the Communist Party of Canada. In addition, Newton extended an offer of an undetermined number of troops to the National Liberation Front and Provisional Revolutionary Government of South Vietnam to assist them in their fight against American imperialism. Nguyen Thi Dinh, deputy commander of the South Vietnamese People's Liberation Armed Forces, replied, "With profound gratitude, we take notice of your enthusiastic proposal: when necessary, we shall call for your volunteers to assist us."[50] NAACP president Roy Wilkins criticized Newton's overture as a genuine lack of concern for the advancement of black life in the United States. One year later, the Black Panther Party sponsored a survival conference where the leadership continued its opposition to the war in Vietnam. Indeed, it may rank as the first black antiwar rally ever held in America. Newton saw a correlation between the enslavement and exploitation of blacks and the exploitation of the Vietnamese people as well as the people of Cambodia, Thailand, Latin America, and Africa. In Newton's words, "We intend not only to send troops to Vietnam, but we are willing to go anywhere in the world where we have comrades."[51] There were even rumors of Panther flirtation with Al Fatah and other Palestinian guerrillas, a notion that raised immediate cries of black anti-Semitism.[52]

In 1972, President Richard Nixon announced that he planned to visit the People's Republic of China. When Newton learned of this, he decided to get there first. According to Newton, the Chinese were interested in the Panthers' Marxist analysis and wanted to discuss it as well as to show Newton the concrete application of theory in their society. Newton said that "his objective was to deliver a message to the Chinese government and the Communist Party, which would be delivered to Nixon upon his arrival."[53] While in China, Newton was pleasantly surprised when he was greeted by large groups of people who applauded, waved their "Little Red Books," and carried signs that read "We Support the Black Panther Party, Down With U.S. Imperialism."[54] This visit reinforced Newton's understanding of the revolutionary process and his belief in the necessity of making a concrete analysis of real-life conditions. The visit also confirmed his conviction that an oppressed people can be liberated if their leaders persevere in raising the people's consciousness and in struggling relentlessly against the oppressor. What Newton was exposed to in China left him searching for more answers, which in turn pushed him and the Black Panther Party to move toward something called Intercommunalism.

Intercommunalism 1971–

The notion of Intercommunalism is perhaps Newton's most important theoretical contribution. It represents a higher level of revolutionary consciousness and a further development of Marxist-Leninist theory. This concept was first publicly articulated at the September 1970 Revolutionary People's Constitutional Convention in Philadelphia. It was put under close scrutiny at a symposium held at Yale University in February 1971, where Newton debated his ideas with Erik Erikson, the renowned professor of developmental psychology at Harvard, and sociologists Kai Erikson and J. Herman Blake, along with a handful of Yale students. Newton admitted that he was a bit apprehensive about presenting his ideas before such an esteemed audience; however, he realized that if he wanted to be taken seriously as a first-rate theoretician he would have to submit his theories for close inspection and scrutiny.

Intercommunalism grew out of the Panthers' fundamental ideological position on internationalism—that the United States is not a nation but an empire that dominated and exploited the world and that United States imperialism had transformed other nations into oppressed communities. Newton used Intercommunalism to describe the inner workings of the ruling elite's domination of the world. He spoke of America's dominance in this way:

> the evidence shows very clearly that the United States is not a nation for its power transcends geographical boundaries and extends into every territory of the world. Through modern technology the United States can control the institutions of other countries. Hence, so long as it can control the political forces, the cultural institutions, the economy, the resources and the military of other territories at will and for the narrow interests of a small clique then we cannot say that America is a nation any longer—it is an empire.[55]

According to Newton, the emergence and expansion of global capitalism resulted in the disintegration of the nation-state, rendering national boundaries irrelevant. He claimed that the world was a dispersed collection of communities. Newton defined a community as a small unit with a set of institutions that exists to serve a certain group of people. Therefore, Newton contended that the struggle in the world is between the small power elite that administers and profits from the empire of the United States and the people of the world within their communities who want to determine their own destinies.[56]

Newton reasoned that the plight of blacks and other subjugated people would only be resolved when the people established revolutionary Intercommunalism. Intercommunalism pushes for egalitarianism and argues for the abolition of divisive class distinctions. Newton maintained that a class that owns property dominates a class that does not. There is a class of workers and a class of owners, and because there is a basic contradiction between their interests, the two groups are in constant struggle with one another. Newton suggested that the stage of Intercommunalism will come about when the world's nonruling class seizes the means of production (presumably of the entire imperialist system) and distributes the wealth in an equitable fashion to the many communities of the world.[57] Self-centeredness on the part of disenfranchised groups would not provide a just social order. Intercommunalism refers to the relationship of one oppressed people to the worldwide oppressed community in the larger quest for a just democratic order. Therefore, self-centeredness and "rugged individualism" on the part of any single oppressed group is de-emphasized in favor of a consciousness that stresses the group's awareness of its relationship and commitment to the larger worldwide oppressed community. As a result, in Newton's mind, there would be a worldwide coalition of revolutionaries from every country who would seize power to achieve a redistribution of wealth on an intercommunal level. The notion that a global network could be established where every country participated was idealistic on Newton's part.

A central tenet of Intercommunalism is that "contradiction is the ruling principle of the universe," that everything is in a constant state of transformation.[58] Hence, Newton argued that because things do not stay the same, one can be assured that the ruler will not stay the ruler and the dominated will not stay subjugated.[59] When the intensity of the struggle is increased, a point will eventually be reached at which the balance of power will shift, causing the positions of the two actors to reverse.

In the present state of affairs, the power elite rule and exert control by using technology. Rousseau argued that technological development brings into existence a nascent society of growing divisions in wealth between rich and poor, which are then consolidated and made permanent by a deceitful "social contract."[60] The ruling elite has imposed its technology on the people under the guise that it will help enhance people's lives. Up to now, the people have not been given access to this technology. Despite this, Newton's faith in the people's ability remained strong, as is evident when he says the spirit of the people is greater than the elite's technology. Again, Newton argued that the people of the world must seize power from the power elite and expropriate the expropriators, pull them down from their pedestal and make them equals, and distribute the fruits of the labor of an oppressed people in an equitable fashion. He maintained that when the people seize the means of production and all social institutions, there will then be a qualitative leap and a reorientation in the organization of society. Newton referenced this qualitative leap in the writings of Marx, Karl Polanyi, and Mao, who argued that a series of minor quantitative changes eventually lead to a major qualitative leap—a transformation. Newton cautioned that it would take time to resolve the contradictions of racism, chauvinism, and sexism but added that because the people would control their own social institutions in postrevolutionary society, they would be free to re-create themselves and to establish communism, a stage of human development in which human values would shape the structures of society. "When this occurs the world will be ready for yet a higher level of thinking," said Newton.[61]

Newton maintained that the Black Panther Party served as the vanguard in helping the people bring about Intercommunalism. Part of the role of the Black Panther Party, as Newton saw it, was to expose imperialist antagonisms, contradictions, and motives and to raise the people's consciousness in a way that would compel them to undertake revolutionary social action.[62] More specifically, the primary responsibility of the Black Panther Party in this process was to raise the people's level of consciousness through theory and practice in a way that would enable the people to see for themselves what is controlling them and to ascertain what needs to be done. Newton likened the Black Panther Party's mission to the work of Sigmund Freud.[63] Newton noted that one of Freud's greatest contributions was to make people aware that they are controlled throughout much of their lives by their unconscious. Freud attempted to lift the veil of ignorance from the unconscious and make it conscious: that is the first step in being free, the first step in exerting control, argued Freud. Marx made a similar contribution to human freedom, pointing out the external factors that control people. In order for people to liberate themselves from external controls, they have to know what those controls are. In other words, being conscious of how the oppressor operates is necessary in order to free oneself from the yoke of oppression. Newton argued that these steps of development are necessary for the evolution of Intercommunalism; he insisted that only when Intercommunalism exists will the world become "a place where people will be happy, wars will end, the state itself will no longer exist, and we will have communism."[64] Much like Marx, Engels, and Lenin, Newton saw the future communist world as a stateless one.

What white Americans have never fully understood—but what the Negro can never forget is that white society is deeply implicated in the ghetto. White institutions created it, white institutions maintain it and white society condones it.
　　　　　　　　　—U.S. Riot Commission Report

Our cities are crime-haunted dying grounds. Huge sectors of our youth-and countless others face permanent unemployment. Those of us who work find our paychecks able to purchase less and less. Neither the courts nor the prisons contribute to anything resembling justice or reformation. The schools are unable—or unwilling—to educate our children for the real world of our struggles.
　　　　　　　　　—From the preamble, National Black Political Agenda, Gary, Indiana, 1972

WHAT DID HE DO TO BE SO BLACK AND BLUE?: BLACKS AND THE AMERICAN POLITICAL, ECONOMIC, AND SOCIAL ORDER

The United States has been referred to as a melting pot; indeed, it is a pluralistic nation that is made up of a variety of different races and ethnic and cultural groups. The United States also professes to be the most democratic nation in the free world. However, few groups get to experience the kind of democracy that many whites have enjoyed over a lifetime. From Newton's point of view, most black Americans had been subjected to blatant violations of fundamental democratic rights, constant increases in the cost of living in conjunction with massive increases in profits for the corporations, nationwide reversals of limited gains for oppressed minorities, and a wholesale breakdown in services and a dehumanized spiritless society.[1] In *Democracy in America*, published in 1835, Alexis de Tocqueville, an early French visitor to the Republic, noted that the treatment and situation of blacks in the United States contradicted the American passion for democracy.[2] Newton expressed a similar sentiment when he wrote that "the history of the United States, as distinguished from the promise of the idea of the United States, leads me to the conclusion that black sufferance is fundamental to the basic functioning of the government of the United States."[3]

One fundamental tenet of democracy is the right to adequate and proportional representation in all spheres of political, economic, and social life. However, because of racism and capitalism, oppressed groups have failed to receive substantive representation. Newton argued that in order for these groups to receive adequate representation, it is imperative to "eliminate the office of the presidency and wipe out the small ruling circle that is uninterested in the people, but is only concerned with profit."[4] Newton believed that, over the years, U.S. presidents have neglected to represent the popular interests and instead have become a captive of special interests. "Hence, what is needed is a radical restructuring of the government, that reasserts and makes manifest the power of the people consistent with the intent of the Preamble to the U.S. constitution and its Bill of Rights; that is the only path to the realization of the American Dream."[5] The "small ruling circle" that Newton referred to was composed of the presidents and CEOs of the seventy-six companies that ran the American economy. According to President Lyndon Johnson's Commission on Civil Disorders, seventy-six monopolies or oligopolies controlled the country's economy.[6] This type of dominance is somewhat similar to that found in Benito Mussolini's Italy, where the corporate state was the primary means by which the masses of people were controlled. Under the corporate state, almost every aspect of daily existence was controlled: employment, wages, fringe benefits, housing, retail goods, recreation, entertainment, and education were all part of this elaborate organization. Newton surmised that once General Motors, Standard Oil, and other corporations are wiped out, a transformation would occur in which minority groups would be in a position to demand representation. Newton did not say exactly what he meant by "wiped out," nor did he explain specifically how this transformation would result in substantive representation for minorities.

Newton maintained that of all groups, blacks were the most subjugated. He believed that the blood, sweat, and tears of black people built the foundation of American wealth and power. Newton agreed with other blacks who argued that America became very rich through slavery and that slavery was capitalism in the extreme. Additionally, Newton asserted that despite blacks' role in helping build America, the United States government does not work for the advancement or well-being of black Americans. From Newton's standpoint, in some respects black Americans were a colony that was oppressed by the government for both racist and economic reasons. Even though black Americans were widely dispersed throughout the United States rather than clumped together in territorial units, Newton asserted that they were nonetheless a subjugated "colony" because of bonds forged by psychological abuse, similarity in language patterns, high concentrations in urban areas, and low economic status.[7]

However, the increasingly high concentration of blacks in urban areas, coupled with the passage of the Voting Rights Act of 1965, brought about a sense of optimism within some segments of the black community and in certain academic circles. Some in the black community were under the impression that these two developments would result in an increase in electoral representation. James Conyers and Walter Wallace optimistically stated that the presence of black elected officials would spur the advancement of the black community.[8] Prior to 1964, there were 103 black elected officials throughout the United States. That number climbed to 1,400 with the passage of the Voting Rights Act of 1965. By 1976, blacks were mayors of Los Angeles, Atlanta, Washington, D.C., Newark, Cleveland, and Gary, Indiana. Eighteen blacks had been elected to Congress, and hundreds of others were elected to state legislatures across the nation. Blacks also held lieutenant governor posts in Colorado and California. Oscar Handlin published a study about the political prospects of blacks in the United States in which he suggested that the mass migration of blacks into urban industrial cities would encourage political parties to seek their votes and that the parties would be willing to make trades in order to get them.[9] Politicians could be forced to respond to their needs if blacks could provide sufficient votes. Perhaps the mass migration of blacks into urban areas led to the nomination of black capitalists by political parties, which in turn put them in a position to hold office.

Initially, some in the Black Panther Party supported the theory that growing black populations in metropolitan areas should and would translate into the election of more black representatives and eventually bring about a greater distribution of goods and services to black Americans.[10] Nonetheless, while the number of black elected officials increased almost five-fold from 1970 to 1993, blacks remain significantly underrepresented. This underrepresentation is especially distressing in view of the fact that W. E. B. DuBois observed ninety years ago that blacks could not expect to achieve equal social and economic opportunities without first gaining political rights. Newton saw little reason for optimism given the black politician's stature, or lack thereof, in the American body politic. Newton always maintained a healthy skepticism regarding black politicians' ability to influence public policy on behalf of their constituents. In addition to what Newton described as the racism of America's white majority, he argued that black politicians lacked the necessary clout to compete in the political arena.

As Newton evolved, the class issue would figure prominently in his analysis of the position of blacks in American society. According to Newton, there were three kinds of power: economic power, land power, and military power. He pointed out that, whereas the importance of agriculture and industry to the American economy makes government responsive to the demands of white farmers and business owners, the poor and propertyless blacks in America lack this kind of leverage.[11] As Newton saw it, when the white masses, via their representatives, do not get what they want, there is always a political consequence. For example, Newton said, when farmers are not given an adequate price for their crops the economy experiences a political consequence. Farmers will let their crops rot in the field; they will refuse to cooperate with other sectors of the economy. By contrast, when blacks send a representative to Washington or to a state capitol, the black politician's constituency owns no land, possesses no sought-after commodity, and has no stock in the control of the means of production. Consequently, the representative lacks the power to influence government policy. Newton's point about black politicians is basically true; however, the power and influence that he ascribes to farmers is exaggerated. It is well known that farming can be a precarious undertaking for a number of reasons. Consequently, farmers are just as dependent on the economy as the economy is on them. This is not to say that farmers are without influence and leverage but that they have far less than Newton credits them with.

Newton was not the first black activist to acknowledge the powerlessness of black politicians. Martin Luther King Jr. noted the ineffectiveness of black politicians as well, but for slightly different reasons than Newton. King asserted that black political leaders were ineffective in part because they "did not ascend to power on the shoulders of mass support" but through the largess of white political machines. He then continued: "Tragically, he is in too many respects not a fighter for a new life but a figurehead of the old one. Hence very few Negro political leaders are impressive or illustrious to their constituents."[12] Like Newton, King believed that black leaders were hampered in the bargaining process with white party leaders and therefore found themselves in a vacuum, unable to build leverage or sustain influence. King suggested that blacks would have to "create leaders who embody virtues we can respect . . . who are political warriors on our behalf."[13]

Years later, in his study of black elected officials and public policy, political scientist Michael B. Preston put forth a number of limitations of black elected officials, among which were: lack of permanent political machinery, little economic clout, and lack of power to implement programs. Because of these factors, in many instances the demands of black politicians are not taken seriously.[14] Thus, for Newton, in order for one to be powerful, one must be able to inflict a political consequence when one's demands are not met. Newton applied his skepticism about American federalism to most of America's so-called democratic institutions. He argued that many of America's institutions needed to be reformed, especially those that were supposed to work on behalf of the masses of the American people. Central to Newton's position was his call to revise the U.S. Constitution. Newton pointed out that many aspects of American life had changed since 1776; therefore, a new constitution should be written that reflected those changes. Indeed, there is a school of thought that proposes that constitutions should be revised or replaced every few decades or generations, as conditions and particular balances of social forces change. In fact, periodic revision is not alien to the American tradition; although the U.S. Constitution of 1787 has not been replaced, only amended, many states have had four or five constitutions in their history, for example, Jacksonian constitutions in the early nineteenth century and progressive constitutions in the early twentieth century.

As far as Newton was concerned, the Constitution does not afford all Americans (namely the poor and people of color) the freedoms that it professed to guarantee.[15] The late U.S. representative Barbara Jordan underscored this point when she wrote: "We the people: it is a very eloquent beginning. But when the constitution of the United States was completed on the 17th of September 1787, I was not included in that 'We the People.'" Moreover, to add to Jordan's point, the phrase "all men are created equal" was understood to exclude blacks. The point was so obvious that there was no need to insert the word "white" between "all" and "men." Because the U.S. Constitution has failed to afford black Americans the same rights as whites, blacks have waged a number of battles to win the freedoms that have historically been denied them. The most well known battle began at the start of the 1950s under the auspices of the Civil Rights movement. Newton called the Civil Rights movement a struggle waged by blacks to obtain rights that white people gained in 1776. He argued logically that had blacks been able to exercise the rights promised by the U.S. Constitution, there would have been no need for a Civil Rights movement.

While many consider the Civil Rights movement to be a watershed event in American history, Newton vigorously proclaimed that the Civil Rights movement was largely ineffective. In many respects, the Civil Rights movement left institutionalized discrimination against African Americans untouched. However, the Civil Rights movement constituted a period in history when blacks were able to exert influence in such a way that ushered in a host of new rights, programs, and other measures presumably intended to enhance black life-chances. In fact, were it not for the Civil Rights movement, the civil rights acts of 1957, 1960, 1964, 1968, and 1970 and the Voting Rights Act of 1965 might not have been passed. The 1964 Civil Rights Act, perhaps the most significant of these measures, prohibited discrimination in many areas. Title I set down protections for voting in state and federal elections. Title II asserted, "All persons shall be entitled to the full and equal enjoyment of the goods, services, privileges and accommodations of any place of public accommodation . . . without discrimination or segregation on the ground of race, color, religion, or national origin." Title III required the desegregation of public facilities operated by local or state governments. Title IV authorized federal action to facilitate the desegregation of public schools, and Title VI prohibited discrimination in programs receiving federal assistance. Title VII prohibited discrimination in employment. It became illegal for an employer to fire or refuse to hire anyone because of the individual's race, color, religion, sex, or national origin, and to "limit, segregate or classify his employees in any way which would deprive or tend to deprive any individual of employment opportunities or otherwise adversely affect his status as an employee, because of such individual's race, color, religion, sex or national origin." Title VIII required the collection of voter registration and voting statistics.

The Civil Rights movement had compelled the Washington Establishment to act in a manner that for the most part meshed with the interests of blacks. In Joe Feagin's words, "The Civil Rights Movement had forced the passage of one of the most strongly worded anti-discrimination laws ever established in any nation."[16] This result would seem to coincide to some extent with Newton's notion of power discussed earlier. Despite such accomplishments, however, Newton criticized the movement for its willingness to make concessions and its overall lack of effectiveness. He maintained that the Civil Rights movement "produced humiliating programs of welfare and unemployment compensation, programs with sufficient form to deceive the people but with insufficient substance to change the fundamental distribution of power and resources in the United States."[17] One can only surmise that when Newton talked of "humiliating programs of welfare and unemployment compensation," he was referring to President Lyndon Johnson's Great Society programs. Johnson's endeavor included a variety of federal programs to help improve education, job training, and small business development for people who had been historically denied opportunity.

All things considered, Newton's assessment of the Civil Rights movement seems a bit harsh. The U.S. Supreme Court's 1954 *Brown v. Board of Education of Topeka, Kansas* decision made it illegal to deny blacks equal access to educational opportunities. Also the Voting Rights Act of 1965 would significantly increase black voter registration and the number of black elected officials over the next several decades. Despite all of this, Newton's prediction that the majority of blacks would not receive a significantly greater share of goods and services was correct. Instead of improving the livelihood of black Americans as a whole, the Civil Rights movement produced a sizeable black middle class. While Newton's argument that the Civil Rights movement was ineffective was overstated, his ultimate conclusion that the movement failed to alter the distribution of power and resources in America was on point. Newton believed that the Civil Rights movement helped the more affluent blacks who already possessed the necessary education, training, and skills to improve their life-chances. For most blacks, economic gains were limited. In *Black Awakening in Capitalist America*, Robert Allen, offered his assessment of the movement: "The civil rights movement failed. . . . Even the small victories it won benefited mainly the black middle class, not the bulk of the poor blacks. Thus blacks who were "qualified" could get jobs. . . . In its heyday the integrationist Civil Rights Movement cast an aura which encompassed nearly the whole of the black population, but the black bourgeoisie was the primary beneficiary of that movement."[18]

Newton's and Allen's argument is factually supported in the areas of occupation, income, and employment. Although blacks comprise 12 percent of the total population, only 6 percent are accountants and auditors; 5 percent are computer systems analysts and scientists; 4 percent are media personnel, engineers, college professors, and physicians; and 3 percent or less are architects, lawyers, judges, realtors, and dentists. Blacks are even more underrepresented in the private sector. As of the early to mid-1990s, blacks made up only 2 percent of the lawyers in the top hundred law firms. No Fortune 500 company was headed by a black, and blacks comprised only 3 percent of the senior managers in these companies.

In terms of income, black households are more than three times as likely as white households to earn less than $5,000 annually and are more than twice as likely to earn between $5,000 and $10,000. Similarly, on the high end, whites are more than three times as likely as blacks to have incomes exceeding $100,000 and twice as likely to be earning between $50,000 and $100,000. On a more fundamental level, the median income for blacks is $19,532, $32,960 for whites, and $22,886 for Latinos.[19] A similar disparity exists between college-educated blacks and whites. College-educated whites earn an average income of $38,700, with a net worth of $74,922 and net financial assets of $19,823. By contrast, college-educated blacks earn on average only $29,440 annually, with a net worth of $17,437 and a mere $175 in net financial assets.[20]

As for employment, Floyd W. Hayes III writes that "the transition from the goods-producing economy of the industrial era to the service-producing economy of the managerial era, the increasing polarization of the labor market into low-wage and high-wage sectors, innovations in technology, the relocation of manufacturing industries out of central cities, and periodic recessions have driven up the rate of black unemployment."[21] In 1959, the year Newton graduated from high school, 55 percent of all blacks were officially poor; a growing economy and a federal War on Poverty helped reverse that trend, shrinking that figure to 32 percent by 1969.[22] By the mid 1990s, three out of every ten African Americans were classified as poor, and approximately half of all black children lived with families below the poverty line. In 1995, 33 percent of all blacks lived in poverty compared to 31 percent of Latinos, 15 percent of Asians, and 12 percent of whites. Simply put, black unemployment has been approximately three times that of whites over the past twenty years.[23]

While Newton was correct when he noted that the more well-off blacks, not the black masses, benefited most from the Civil Rights movement, some argue that despite being the primary beneficiaries of the movement, the black middle class's situation is as precarious as that of poor and working-class blacks. In *The Rage of a Privileged Class*, Ellis Cose maintains that the most disaffected people in this country are not necessarily poor blacks but rather the black middle class. He astutely points out that middle-class blacks have played by the rules and still reach a point where they cannot go any higher. "They look up and see the folks in the executive suite—knowing there's very little chance of ever getting there."[24] This is evident by the dismal number of blacks in top positions. While the Civil Rights movement did win blacks a number of benefits, Newton's position that the movement did not shift the balance of power or redistribute wealth in a radical way is not unfounded.

In terms of reforming America's institutions, Newton was particularly concerned with the educational system. Point five of the Black Panther Party's Ten-Point Program indicates that Newton found the American educational system to be grossly inadequate. For him personally, school represented another agent of repression. His experiences in school were characterized by assaults on his self-esteem that led him to believe that being black meant being "stupid," and therefore he felt ashamed. He argued that lessons taught in schools were often inaccurate and exclusionary, particularly in the areas of history and social studies.[25] He pointed out that blacks (as well as other groups) were kept from learning about their history, particularly the atrocities of the African slave trade and the accomplishments of great men and women of African origin throughout the world. Noted psychologist Kenneth B. Clark summed up the reality of inner-city schools this way: "The clash of cultures in the classroom is essentially a class war, a socio-economic and racial warfare being waged on the battleground of our schools, with middle-class aspiring teachers provided with a powerful arsenal of half-truths, prejudices, and rationalizations, arrayed against hopelessly outclassed working-class youngsters. This is an uneven balance, particularly since, like most battles, it comes under the guise of righteousness."[26]

Newton admitted that, as a youngster, he did not fully grasp the degree or seriousness of the school system's assault on black people. He remembered that he constantly felt uncomfortable and ashamed of being black. This feeling of inferiority was the result of an implicit understanding perpetuated by the system that whites were "smart" and blacks were "stupid."[27] Everything white was good, while everything black was bad. In a study of education and black self-image, psychiatrist Alvin F. Poussaint has stated that the pattern of teaching white supremacy has been part of the educational process in both "integrated" and segregated schools throughout the United States. For example, Poussaint noted that white revolutionary leaders like George Washington and Paul Revere are portrayed as glorious heroes. On the other hand, black slave revolutionaries such as Nat Turner are depicted as ignorant, misguided, and perhaps deranged ingrates, a finding that seems to support Newton's experience.[28] Newton recalled reading *Little Black Sambo* and realizing that the character Sambo was nothing like the courageous white knight who rescued Snow White in "Snow White and the Seven Dwarfs." The knight was portrayed as a symbol of purity. Sambo, on the other hand, was depicted as a coward. Looking back, Newton remembered that he found himself identifying with white heroes rather than accepting Sambo as a symbol of blackness. He was ashamed and grimaced at hearing anything black. Over time, Newton said, he and the other black students came to view themselves as inferior: "Our image of ourselves was defined for us by the teachers as well as the textbooks that we read on a daily basis."[29]

In Newton's mind, white people had good reason to ignore black history: black men and women who refuse to live under oppression are dangerous to white society because they become symbols of hope to other blacks, inspiring them to follow their example. On a cognitive level, Newton maintained that the educational system did not teach students how to think dialectically. He argued that "students are given a conglomeration of facts to memorize so that they can be used by whatever profession they enter."[30] The reason for this, Newton asserted, was that the educational system is an agent of the status quo; hence, to teach students to think analytically and critically would be counterproductive for the survival of the system of oppression.

In his autobiography, Newton recalled his days in the Oakland public school system: "During those long years in the Oakland public schools, I did not have one teacher who taught me anything, relevant to my own life or experience. Not one instructor ever awoke in me a desire to learn more or question or explore the worlds of literature, science, and history. All they did was try to rob me of the sense of my own uniqueness and worth, and in the process they nearly killed my urge to aspire."[31] In Newton's opinion, the educational system purposely refrains from equipping students with the tools necessary to think dialectically for fear that students will use these tools to expose the true nature of the decadent and racist American political and social order.[32] In addition, were these students to find inconsistencies in what they were taught and what they discovered through serious independent inquiry, some of them might begin to question the validity of Western democratic thought, which in turn could pose a threat to those who had kept them ignorant for the express purpose of perpetuating the status quo.

Newton was also concerned about the courts and the unequal treatment that blacks received from the judicial system. While blacks were noticeably underrepresented in the political arena, they were undoubtedly overrepresented in jails and prisons throughout the United States. This is still true and has been for some time. In 1926, blacks represented 9 percent of the population and 21 percent of the prison population. Over time, the proportion of the population of blacks in prison increased steadily, reaching 30 percent in the 1940s, 35 percent in 1960, 44 percent in 1980, and leveling off to around 50 percent in the 1990s. Although some nine out of ten Americans do things during the course of their lives that could land them in prison, it is not a cross section of the American population that ends up being arrested and convicted of such criminal behavior.[33] Instead, America's prisons are overflowing with low-income individuals, roughly half of whom are black. The percentage of blacks arrested for robbery, burglary, larceny, and aggravated assault actually decreased from 1988 to 1992. Yet during that time, the percentage of blacks admitted to state and federal prisons grew from 39 percent to 54 percent.[34] In 1998, for every 100,000 African Americans, 1,860 were in jail or in prison; for whites the ratio was 289 out of every 100,000.[35] The class and racial biases of the judicial system, along with the higher crime rates in poverty areas, explain why this country's prison population is disproportionately African American. In 1993, the incarceration rate of black males in the United States was more than four times the rate of black males in South Africa at the height of the antiapartheid struggle. More specifically, the incarceration rate for African American males was 3,822 per 100,000 compared to the rate of 815 per 100,000 for South African black males.[36] To compound matters, African Americans are less often allowed to plea bargain their way out of mandatory prison sentences and are more likely to get longer prison terms than whites convicted of the same crimes, even when they are first-time offenders and the whites are second- or third-time offenders.[37]

The discrepancy with regard to how punishment is meted out to blacks vis-à-vis whites has a long history. John Roberts writes that in the nineteenth century, although many whites were guilty of committing the same crimes as blacks, few whites were ever sentenced to the two most common forms of punishment imposed on the majority of blacks: the chain-gang and convict-lease system.[38] Both forms of punishment were characterized by forced labor, inhuman living and working conditions, and an extremely high mortality rate. The chain-gang system in Texas was a classic example. In *A Social History of the American Negro*, Benjamin Brawley notes that from 1875 to 1880, the total number of prisoners discharged in Texas was 1,651, while the number of deaths and escapes for the same period totaled 1,608.[39]

Sociologist Anthony J. Lemelle Jr. argues straightforwardly that race, and not the crime rate, predicts the number of inmates in U.S. prisons.[40] According to Lemelle, states with high black populations have high prison rates. Manning Marable is equally blunt when he states that "all racist states have a black prison population that far exceeds the proportion of black people in that state as a whole."[41] A good example of Marable's point is the state of Washington. There, blacks make up less than 4 percent of the state's population but make up almost 40 percent of the state's prison population.[42]

Newton was one of the first black activists to bring attention to the disproportionate number of black women in America's prisons. In a 1974 letter to the governor of Georgia, Newton wrote: "It is our conviction that not only are women who have committed minor offenses being held unjustly in Georgia prisons but that a prison system in which 70 percent of the women being held are Black clearly demonstrates that cruel injustice has been done to Black women in the course of apprehension, juridical and sentencing procedures in the state of Georgia."[43] Newton had reason to be concerned about such matters. A study by the Southern Regional Council five years later revealed that more than half of the federal district judges in the South (including Georgia) were members of all-white country clubs. Said its executive director, "It is difficult to understand how litigants could be expected to maintain faith in a court where the judge decides the evidence of race discrimination in the morning and lunches in all-white clubs at midday."[44] Newton's observation of Georgia's prison population is still applicable today. Just over half of the female prison population is African American, with just under half identified as white.[45]

Not only was Newton concerned with the disproportionate number of blacks incarcerated in the United States, but he also stated that blacks were more likely to be victims of capital punishment than any other group. This is particularly true when the victim is white. Charles W. Mills points out that "killing whites has always been morally and juridically singled out as the crime of crimes, a heinous deviation from the natural order, not merely because of the greater value that whites place on their lives but because of its deeper meaning as a challenge to the racial polity."[43] In the history of U.S. capital punishment, seldom has a white been executed for killing a black. According to the NAACP Legal Defense and Educational Fund in New York, of the 380 people executed since the reinstatement of capital punishment, only 5 were whites convicted of killing a black. The racial disparity in the application of capital punishment was written about in a poignant way by Guy Johnson. In 1941 he said:

> If cost values and attitudes mean anything at all, they mean that offenses by or against Negroes will be defined not so much in terms of their intrinsic seriousness as in terms of their importance in the eyes of the dominant group. Obviously, the murder of a white person by a Negro and the murder of a Negro by a Negro are not at all the same kind of murder from the standpoint of the upper caste's scale of values . . . instead of two categories of offenders, Negro and white, we really need four offender-victim categories, and they would probably rank in seriousness from high to low as follows: 1) Negro versus white, 2) white versus white, 3) Negro versus Negro, and 4) white versus Negro.[47]

Newton viewed capital punishment as cruel and unusual punishment, making it a violation of the Eighth Amendment, and therefore he believed that it should be abolished. For Newton, the central question regarding capital punishment was, does the state have the right to take a person's life? He argued that under the laws of nature no death penalty can be legal.[48] Furthermore, he submitted that once the state takes a person's life, it negates and invalidates itself, it becomes illegitimate, because it robs that individual of all possible means of recourse—something to which all citizens have a right.[49] Newton also believed that capital punishment was reserved mainly for minorities and poor people. He recognized early on that the majority of people on death row have historically been blacks, Latinos, and poor whites. With regard to blacks this is still true. Forty percent of all death-row inmates are African American. Some have suggested that this condition could in part be explained by the fact that black defendants are often denied their constitutional right to be tried by a jury of their own peers; that is, historically, most juries have consisted of white males. It is widely known that when black defendants go before white juries, they are often convicted even when the evidence points to the defendants' innocence. This is especially true when the victim is white. Because of this situation, many blacks have argued that a jury of one's peers should consist of people of the same race. In other words, black defendants should face juries consisting of other blacks.

While Newton agreed that blacks should be tried by a jury of their own peers, he did not agree that being black automatically qualified an individual to be his peer. When the jury trying Newton for murder of a white police officer was being selected, he surprised many by making it clear that he did not object to whites serving on the jury and could in fact imagine an all-white jury conceding him justice provided they were from his peer group.[50] He argued that being black was not a prerequisite for belonging to his peer group. Black people could certainly be his peers, but not in all cases. He argued that whites could also be peers, even in an adversarial setting like a courtroom. An example of a white peer would be someone who lived in West Oakland or a comparable community with similar socioeconomic status and analogous language habits. Newton considered whites with characteristics such as these, along with blacks who were similarly situated, to be among his peer group.[51] Blacks who were well off and perhaps did not encounter many of the same instances of racism that most blacks are confronted with on a daily basis could not be his peers. In other words, they could not be his peers because they did not live the same reality as poor blacks and thus were probably out of touch with many of the things that most blacks deal with every day. Consequently, a jury consisting of only those kinds of individuals would be incapable of judging Newton because they would not fully comprehend the circumstances that brought on his actions or produced the trial. The fact that a jury consisting of four black jurors recently acquitted four white New York City police officers after they fired nineteen bullets into the body of an unarmed black man speaks to Newton's point.

It appears, then, that for Newton, the lack of black jurors did not fully explain why blacks were disproportionately represented in correctional facilities throughout the nation. He contended that the judicial system was dedicated to preserving the status and property of the bourgeoisie by repressing those whom the bourgeoisie consider a threat to their existence. Some have even argued that part of preserving the status of the bourgeoisie includes profiting from those considered a threat. Not only is it necessary to remove the threat from society at large, but it is also essential to profit from the threat if at all possible. The prison system offers this possibility; indeed, many see it as a more modern system of chattel slavery, superceding the chain-gang labor and peonage camps of the 1930s. Few can deny that prisons are a profitable industry. The federal prison industry has been one of the most profitable lines of business in the United States for years. In 1970, the year that Newton was released from prison, prison industry profits on sales were 17 percent, whereas the average profit for all U.S. industries was 4.5 percent. At that time, prisons constituted the fifth largest industry in California. According to official California data for 1968—the last year California released this information—some prisoners produced well over $14,000 revenue per capita. By 1974, the year Newton fled to Cuba to avoid standing trial, the highest prison wage for a Californian was $3.40 a week; using a conservative estimate of inflation for California, this prisoner must have been bringing in about $20,000 annually.[52] According to the 1975 *Sourcebook of Criminal Justice Statistics*, approximately 90 percent of those serving time in jails and prisons had not had a trial or had not been convicted of a crime.[53]

Is it any wonder that Newton equated prison with modern slavery? Both systems operated on oppression, exploitation, and repression. Newton pointed out that slaves were given no compensation for the goods they produced and that prisoners produced goods for a substandard wage or nothing. He also maintained that both systems restrained the movement of their subjects to a confined space—a plantation of sorts. In addition, those in charge have absolute power and demand deference from those under their rule. And just as under slavery, surveillance is part of prison existence; if inmates forge friendships with one another, these ties are broken by institutional transfers in the same way the slave master broke up families. Furthermore, like slavery, the prison experience is degrading both for the overseer and the prisoner alike. Newton stated, "The atmosphere of fear has a distorting effect on the lives of everyone there, from commissioners and superintendents to prisoners in solitary confinement." Newton believed that this is most evident among the prison guards. He argued that the guards have a "limited and very crude kind of power that tends to corrupt them." They never missed an opportunity to ransack his cell or to try to provoke him into a confrontation. Another way that the guards tried to compensate for their pathetic lives was by promoting racial animosity in order to foster disunity among blacks and whites. Newton stated that while the guards do not want racial hostility to erupt into wholesale violence, they do want hostility high enough to keep inmates divided. Newton argued that "many white prisoners are not outright racists when they get to prison, but the staff soon turns them in that direction." In this type of atmosphere, the prison experience becomes even more unbearable for black inmates, for they are subjected to the petty oppressive actions of the guards and constant racial agitation from the white prisoners. In many instances, black inmates lash out at these instigators and as a result receive longer jail sentences or transfers to harsher correctional facilities. From Newton's perspective, making prisoners' lives miserable, especially black prisoners, was what made the guards' jobs worth doing and their lives worth living. This state of affairs gave them a false sense of empowerment. Unfortunately, these oppressive conditions kept black prisoners from focusing their attention and energies on important matters, such as introspective thinking, which is the key to developing political consciousness. Although the criminal justice system has managed to imprison a disproportionate number of blacks and other people of color, thereby robbing the liberation movement of potential revolutionaries, Newton maintained that "the ideas that can and will sustain the movement for total freedom and dignity cannot be imprisoned. As long as the people live by the ideas of freedom and dignity there will be no prison that can hold the movement down."[54]

Despite the gloomy reality, Newton continued to push for reforms, arguing for the decentralization of police departments in the hope of revamping an inherently corrupt criminal justice system. He suggested that the police be decentralized into three departments: one for students, one for blacks, and one for whites.[55] According to Newton's unorthodox plan, the local community would elect a board to supervise and monitor police behavior and to review complaints submitted by community residents. Each community or neighborhood would be patrolled by police officers who resided in that particular community. Newton seemed to be on sound footing when he theorized that when police represent the communities in which they live, the likelihood of injurious or fatal conflict between the officer and the community has the potential to decrease because the police have a vested interest in that community and the people of that community are familiar with the officers. Newton tried to put this plan into practice when the Black Panther Party, along with the Peace and Freedom Party and others, collected signatures to get such a measure placed in the form of a referendum in Berkeley, California, in 1970–71. Newton thought that this measure, if passed, would significantly reduce incidents of police brutality and police-related deaths.

The principles behind the proposed amendment to the city charter included the creation of new centers of power, decentralization of government decision-making, and a reduction of the powers of the state machinery. Not surprisingly, only a small percentage of the electorate voted for community control of the police. While a majority of the community agreed that there was a serious "police problem," the overwhelming majority rejected a solution calling for both a radical restructuring of local government and a drastic reordering of police priorities and functions. As to be expected, strongest support came from the student community, where the proposal won by two to one; in the affluent hill section of Berkeley, it lost by nearly five to one; and ironically in predominantly black west Berkeley, it was defeated by more than three to one.[56] Although the measure was defeated, its impact could be seen in a variety of ways. The strength of the proposal lay in its ability to use the electoral process to articulate a concrete, alternative vision of popular control. It offered a class and racial perspective on the police that fundamentally differed from typical liberal reforms. Many people were politicized and educated by the campaign; the police, usually immune to outside pressure, were put on the defensive; and the university and business community, which benefit from the police, were identified and exposed by their opposition to community control.[57]

Newton realized early on that blacks received an unequal portion of every aspect of America's bounty: fewer and lower-paying jobs, inferior housing, inadequate education, and less political power to make and enforce laws. For this reason, Newton implied that blacks were not obligated to be loyal to America since America had shown no loyalty to blacks. It was not surprising, then, that the Black Panther Party argued that black men should be exempt from military service. The way Newton saw it, why should blacks fight for a country that failed to provide them with the basic essentials with which to sustain a living above the poverty line? And who could blame Newton for taking this position? It is well known that blacks were more likely to serve as cannon fodder in time of war. For example, 23 percent of the soldiers killed in the Vietnam War were black, nearly double the percentage of blacks in the total population.[58]

While the Black Panther Party did not believe that blacks should serve in the armed services, it supported those who did. The Panthers saw revolutionary potential in the disgruntled service personnel. Consequently, they helped Andy Stapp form a black organization called the American Servicemen's Union (ASU), which demanded an end to racism in the army and offered free legal service to soldiers in conflict with the armed forces. With the Black Panther Party and SDS, the ASU led five thousand demonstrators to Fort Dix, New Jersey, to demand the release of prisoners in stockade charged with rebellion. "Whoever can command the allegiance of the rank-and-file troops—that command is going to be decisive in revolution and counterrevolution," Stapp declared in July 1969, "and right now the American Serviceman's Union is building an army within an army, a worker's militia inside the U.S. Army . . . to make that revolution."[59] Three months later, in October 1969, Eldridge Cleaver went to Hanoi, where he made a radio broadcast urging black soldiers to desert and sabotage the American war effort.[60] During the next two years, racial tension among U.S. forces in Vietnam and West Germany rose sharply. There were serious clashes between black and white troops and violent defiance of white officers by black GIs. A concerned Pentagon was forced to prepare a program seeking to conciliate the grievances of blacks in uniform. In a special issue titled "Guerrilla War in the U.S.A.," *Scanlon's* editor estimated that there were tens of thousands of converted revolutionists in the army and that almost fifteen thousand were in military stockades.[61]

For Newton, the only way blacks would obtain the prosperity that had so long been denied to them was to have absolute control of their communities. In a 1970 prison interview, Newton proclaimed that "whites must work in their own communities. Blacks and whites will form coalitions on specific issues that affect both communities, but blacks have to control their own communities. We can't leave decisions regarding our lives to white people any longer. We have been betrayed too many times."[62]

From the very beginning, blacks have been in the best position to understand the basis of the American political economy. No group in American society has been as subjected to the extremes of economic exploitation as blacks.[63] Generation after generation of blacks have been told that if you work hard you will succeed. However, as Stokely Carmichael has noted, "if that were true blacks would own America lock, stock and barrel."[64] Nevertheless, blacks have worked hard and have seen others enjoy most of the fruits of their labor while they have muddled through the squalor of poverty and deprivation, clinging only to the hope that their lot will one day get better. Understandably, black people's understanding has advanced over time as they moved from rural chattel slavery in an agrarian economy through peonage and wage slavery in developing capitalism to becoming mainstays of the three principal sectors of the working and lower class: the industrial proletariat, particularly in the auto, steel, and food-packing industries; the service proletariat, ranging from janitors and housekeepers to security guards to mass transportation workers in large metropolitan areas like New York, Washington, D.C., and Chicago; and the vast and growing number of the permanent and chronically unemployed and underemployed, which forms a distinctive feature of decaying monopoly capitalism and provides the main population of the jails and prisons.[65] Each change in blacks' relationship to the economic system has mainly represented a shift from one form of extreme economic subjugation to another. Newton was not far off when he intimated that while this system of government may make the society function at a higher level of technological efficiency, it is nevertheless an illegitimate system, since "it rests upon the suffering of humans who are certainly as worthy and as dignified as those who oppress them."[66]

Political scientist Robert C. Smith says the white Establishment has continued to reject the idea that the federal government has a role to play in dealing with the problems of poor blacks, contending that blacks are to blame for their own conditions.[67] Despite the increase in the number of black politicians, they have been unable (for the most part) to deliver on promises and programs designed to improve conditions for blacks. Although over three hundred blacks hold mayoral seats, for a number of reasons black representation has not been converted into significantly improved conditions for the black community as a whole. Black mayors have often been faced with a number of limitations. First, many of them have been weak mayors in council-manager forms of government. Second, the reform movement has stripped them of most of the patronage their white predecessors enjoyed. And third, because many of the more affluent whites have fled to the suburbs, taking their tax base with them, many of the cities where blacks have been elected mayor are for the most part financially impoverished.[68] Consequently, black officeholders have not been able to lower black unemployment, increase the availability of decent housing, upgrade the schools, end de facto segregation, or mitigate crime in their cities. Police brutality continues to be a problem for blacks everywhere, as witnessed by the beating of Rodney King, the sodomization of Abner Louima, and the killing of Amadou Diallo, former pro football player Demetrius DuBose, Malice Green, and others in the past ten years. Suffice to say, the benefits that sprung from the efforts of the Civil Rights movement have yet to impact significantly upon the lives of the dispossessed.[69]

That blacks have not made monumental gains since the founding of the Black Panther Party is disturbing but not surprising. Alexis de Tocqueville did not believe that blacks would ever experience equality in America. He saw blacks' plight to be inherent in American democracy: "I do not imagine that the white and black races will ever live in any country upon an equal footing. But I believe the difficulty to be still greater in the United States than elsewhere. . . . A despot who should subject the Americans and their former slaves to the same yoke, might perhaps succeed in commingling the races; but as long as the American democracy remains at the head of affairs, no one will undertake so difficult a task; and it may be foreseen that the freer the white population of the United States becomes, the more isolated will it remain."[70] More than 160 years after Tocqueville's observation, one is hard pressed to find fault with his analysis.

Although initially Newton viewed race as the key issue, he would come to see the importance of class. Newton's interpretation of black people's position and role in the American political system is insightful and thought provoking. Many of the observations that Newton made still hold true today. Former Panther Earl Anthony wrote years later, "I was impressed with Newton's theories . . . , however I was to see another side of the complex revolutionary theorist; that of the worldly black street brother."[71]

Huey Newton is the baddest mutherfucker ever to step foot inside of history.

—Eldridge Cleaver

All the "bad niggers" are either dead or in jail.

—Unknown

The origins of the phrase "bad nigger" and the use of the word "bad" by blacks as a term of endearment or admiration can be traced back to slavery. John Little, a fugitive slave who escaped to Canada, once recalled that Southern whites seeing a black man in shackles would often say, "Boy, what have you got that on for? . . . if you weren't such a bad nigger you wouldn't have them on."[1] "Bad niggers" were viewed by white slaveholders and those who supported the institution of slavery as slaves who were dangerous and difficult to control. However, for blacks, the individual in question was one who refused to submit and was willing to fight the system. Hence, other slaves generally admired these individuals. To be perceived as a "bad nigger," then as well as now, is nothing less than a badge of honor in the black community.[2] When one is referring to a "ba-ad" nigger, the more one prolongs the "a," the greater is the homage. Given the status that "bad niggers" enjoy in the black community, it is not surprising that most "bad niggers" are legends. Stackolee, John Hardy, Harry Duncan, and Devil Winston were just a few of the "bad niggers" to capture the imagination of blacks during the last decade of the nineteenth century. Whenever one seeks to disentangle a legend, one must begin by distinguishing the actual person from the stories woven around the legend. Huey P. Newton was no exception.

Huey P. Newton was his own man; he refused to allow anyone, especially the white Establishment, to determine his place in society. Eldridge Cleaver once said, "Huey P. Newton is the baddest mutherfucker to step foot inside of history."[3] At the time, who could argue with Cleaver? After all, Newton may have been one of few black men ever to kill a white police officer (in self-defense or otherwise) and to live to talk about it without having to spend the bulk of his life behind bars. The police officer as an omnipresent figure is captured by H. C. Brearley. He says that "the policeman represents the supreme test of daring. Here is a white man, armed, the embodiment of authority. Whoever gets the better of him has reached the highest goal of the bad nigger."[4] Perhaps the most famous of all "bad niggers" is Railroad Bill, about whose career dozens of ballads have been composed. Railroad Bill shot a police officer and escaped on a freight train. When a sheriff set out to bring him in, he met the same fate. Eventually Railroad Bill was captured and killed. That Newton allegedly shot and killed a young officer, John Frey, who had developed a reputation as being one of the most brutal and racist of Oakland's police officers only enhanced Newton's stature within the black community. Cleaver's description of Newton resembles the sentiment expressed by Samuel M. Strong: "The Bad Nigger refuses to accept the place given to Negroes."[5]

The "bad nigger" tradition is characterized by the absolute rejection of white authority figures. In Newton's case, this was never more evident than when he refused to be assigned a prison job and instead chose to serve out a large portion of his prison sentence in solitary confinement. He refused to work unless he was paid a legal minimum wage instead of the prison wage of twelve cents an hour. In Newton's words, "I refuse to work for slave wages."[6] As punishment, twenty-one hours of Newton's days were spent in solitary confinement. The severity of Newton's punishment for refusing to abide by prison rules is not uncommon. John Roberts writes that "the criminal punishment of blacks in the late nineteenth century had as a primary function the 'breaking' of recalcitrant 'bad niggers'—individuals who refused to submit to white authority and control in society."[7]

Newton's reputation as a "bad nigger" was to some extent forged during his childhood years. He spent the better part of his youth in constant conflict with both teachers and administrators. One such incident occurred when Newton was a student at Lafayette Elementary School. He recalled: "The school had a rule that you could dump the sand out of your shoes after a recess, just before you sat down. One day I was sitting on the floor, dumping the sand from each shoe. I had quite a bit of sand, and dumping it took time, too much for the teacher, who came up behind me and slapped me across the ear with a book, accusing me of deliberately delaying the class. Without thinking, I threw the shoe at her. She headed for the door at a good clip and made it through just in front of my other one."[8] Newton was sent to the principal's office for his act of insubordination, but he gained a great deal of prestige and respect from his peers for defying authority.

The actions of the "bad nigger" often enable other blacks to live their lives vicariously through them. John Roberts underscores this point when he says that black singers, storytellers, and audiences might temporarily and vicariously live through the exploits of their "bad nigger" heroes.[9] It allows them, if only for a fleeting moment, the metaphysical experience of leaving their inferior position. Moreover, the "bad nigger's" action is always carried out with great "style." Newton's personality sounds like Lawrence Levine's definition of the strong, self-contained hero who violated neither the laws nor the moral code but rather the stereotyped roles set aside for blacks.[10] L. D. Reddick's description of the "bad nigger" is also quite indicative of Newton. This personality type, he writes, fights all the way—violently protecting self and family against white racists. "Bad niggers" have little or no respect for laws that are not made by people like them or that do not serve their best interests. They expect no justice from the courts. And the police are their natural enemies.[11] In another sense, Newton's personality sounds somewhat like Roger D. Abraham's definition of the "hard-hero" in the black community, who is "openly rebelling as a man against the emasculating factors in his life."[12] Abraham cites John Henry as an example of the "hard-hero." This characterization does not fit Newton as well as Levine's strong, self-contained hero or Reddick's and Strong's "bad nigger" do because Abraham contends that "hard-heroes" are frustrated in their attempts to strike back at white society and, as a result, turn their anger on themselves and other blacks. However, both the "bad nigger" and the "hard-hero" welcomed and often instigated direct confrontations with white society's stereotype of the black person's role and place in American life. This type of defiance serves a need that prudence has normally forbidden people to indulge: to compensate for the pervasive insults and humiliations of past and present by letting "the white man know where to go and what to do."[13] Newton did this by picking up the gun and confronting white police about their proclivity for brutalizing blacks. His posture was the antithesis of the shuffling and timid white stereotype of blacks.

Both Newton and the figures just described were fearless characters. A clear example of Newton's courage can be found in one particular story told by another Panther:

> One night at a party, Huey accidentally stepped on some brother's shoes, and Huey stepped back and said, "Excuse me, brother." The brother—he was bad, one of those bad dudes' he said, "Motherfucker, scuse me, don't reshine my shoes." When the dude dropped his arm slightly behind his back, Huey saw this. He knew this was the time to fire, next thing you knew, Huey fired on him and decked him, and all the other bad dudes at the party who were this dude's friends wanted to know who this cat thinks he is. And so they jumped up and said that Huey needs his ass kicked, and Huey told them, "I'll fight all of you one at a time or all of you at the same time and you won't wait outside for me, I'll be waiting outside for you." And then he walked outside and waited and dared them to come outside.[14]

Perhaps the best example of fearlessness in Newton's life was his utter disregard for death and danger. As a youngster, Newton would flirt with disaster by driving onto a railroad crossing and waiting for an oncoming train. As the train approached, Newton would stand pat, only to speed off at the last possible moment, leaving his passengers stricken with terror and angry that Newton would pull such a stunt. Because Newton always emerged from these encounters unscathed, he soon began to believe that he could outmaneuver anything and anybody, and thus he never passed up a chance to try. Said Newton, "I never feared death. I thought I was invincible."[15] As a result of this belief, Newton concluded that he could not be killed. He would hold on to the idea that he was immune to death for a long time. Ironically, it may have been Newton's disregard for death that led to his tragic demise. As one former Panther explained, "If someone pulled a gun on you or me, we'd get real polite. But Huey would be the kind of guy to say 'OK, shoot me.' His ego would not allow him to back down. He would push the confrontation. Finding him dead on a street corner is consistent with his character." His ego and sense of bravado simply would not allow him to back down from anybody or anything.[16]

This disposition is present not only in the way Newton lived his life but also in the way he conducted himself as leader of the Black Panther Party. There are similar accounts in African American folklore where this disregard for death is evident. Defiant heroism is represented by the plantation folklore of the "bad niggers" or the "crazy niggers" who, pushed beyond their tolerance limits, retaliated with violence even if doing so guaranteed their own death. The spirit of defiance in the face of death is given electric expression in a poem by Claude McKay:

> If we must die, let it not be like hogs hunted and penned in an
> inglorious spot, While round us bark the mad and hungry dogs,
> mocking their mock at our accursed lot. If we must die—oh,
> let us nobly die, so that our precious blood may not be shed
> in vain; then even the monster we defy shall be constrained to
> honor us though dead![17]

Newton's demeanor as well as the positions that he took toward the white Establishment proved to be of symbolic import to the black community. Much like the first group of black elected officials, the "bad nigger" or "hard-hero" can also play an important symbolic role. Until the early years of the Black Power movement, many whites regarded blacks as innately childlike, nonviolent, Bible-quoting figures striving to be recognized as full-fledged human beings. When brutal opposition to black progress persisted from people like Bull Connor and black children were being dynamited to death in church, many white Americans expected verbal outrage by blacks but noth-ing more.[18] Newton's status as the "bad nigger" or "hard-hero" was part of what enabled him to be an effective revolutionary leader. Eldridge Cleaver is eloquent on this point:

> To see Huey Newton step forward and confront murderous, brutal, vicious gestapo pigs and to see him do this fearlessly and to hear him articulate the grievances of his people and to hear him hurl forth an implacable demand for alleviation of those grievances, it was a thing that has to be seen in a certain per-spective and in a certain context. If you can understand that then you can understand why and how Huey P. Newton was able to get other Black men and women to pick up the gun and stand with him in defense of our people.[19]

Because of Newton's stature and actions, his presence proved to be important symbolically in several ways. First, he was viewed as a role model for many in and outside the black community. In light of this, what is missing from Strong's, Levine's, and Abraham's depiction of the "bad nigger" is that the "bad nigger" is also good, which explains why so many people revere the "bad nigger." In Newton's case, that he had killed a white police officer proved how bad he was; at the same time, that he had not meant to kill the police officer proved how good he was. The reverence that Newton enjoyed was clearly evident the day he was released from prison. Hugh Pearson writes that on August 5, 1970, Newton emerged from prison to be greeted by ten thousand people of all colors, as if he were God.[20] One Panther explained that there was a tendency "to look upon Huey as being above and beyond others, to view Huey as being different from every-body else." He added, "It happens more and more to black people who have an understanding about Huey, and who know a little about his leadership."[21]

Newton also had all the characteristics of a charismatic leader. Robert Tucker writes that charismatic leaders are not merely leaders who are idolized and freely followed for their extraordinary leadership qualities but those who demonstrate such qualities in the process of summoning people to join in a movement for change and in leading such a movement.[22] Over time, Newton developed what some have argued is needed by a charismatic leader: a keen understanding of the political, social, and economic relations that governed the lives of ordinary citizens, coupled with the ability to express their grievances in national terms and to exploit a personal relationship with them to build a mass movement.[23] In addition, Max Weber points out that charismatic leaders are natural leaders "in time of psychological, physical, economic, political distress" and that charisma inspires its followers with "a devotion born of distress and enthusiasm." In short, the key to the followers' response to the charismatic leader lies in the distress that the followers experience.[24] The followers respond to the charismatic leader with passionate loyalty because the salvation, or promise of it, that the leader appears to embody represents the fulfillment of urgently felt needs. Virtually all black people who speak about their condition look forward to some undefined future when the veil of oppression and suffering will be lifted. For some blacks, Newton represented a light at the end of that tunnel.

In *A Taste of Power*, Elaine Brown wrote that it was an amazing thing to see Newton walking the streets of Oakland. He drew large crowds of eager children, teary-eyed women with flowers, and men reaching out to shake his hand.[25] At a time when some blacks were reluctant to stand up to the oppressor and demand that their people be treated fairly because they feared being beaten, maimed, or killed by the local authorities, Newton not only stood firm but did so with gun in hand and dared the police to draw first. This is especially noteworthy because, as Leon F. Litwack observes, whites viewed and made the object of their most violent and organized aggressive actions those "bad niggers" who took on leadership roles in the black community.[26] The following is a condensed version of Seale's description of a scene where Newton stood down the police in front of the Party's headquarters in "bad nigger" fashion:

> This nigger is telling pigs, "If you draw your gun, I'll shoot you." Anything that happens, this nigger's the baddest nigger

you ever seen. Because this nigger is telling ten pigs, "I don't give a damn what you do." I'm exercising my constitutional right. The nigger told the pigs that if they act wrong or get down wrong I'm going to kill you. I'll defend myself! So what do you do? You say, this nigger is bad. This nigger is crazy. But I like this crazy nigger. I like him because he's good. He doesn't take bullshit.[27]

One of the most talked about showdowns involving Newton and the police occurred on the day the Panthers escorted Betty Shabazz, Malcolm X's widow, from the San Francisco airport fully armed. Close to thirty police officers arrived outside the offices where Shabazz had been taken to be interviewed by Eldridge Cleaver. The police surrounded the building, creating conditions for a standoff with the Panthers inside. When the Panthers finally ushered Shabazz from the building, an altercation ensued between Newton and an officer. According to Cleaver, who witnessed the exchange from the steps of the building, Newton brought up the rear as the Panthers were exiting the building and was blocked by a police officer who ordered Newton to stop pointing his gun. At this time, Newton, ignoring pleas to keep cool, stepped up to the police officer and said, "What's the matter got an itchy finger?" When the officer did not answer, Newton reportedly taunted him saying, "You want to draw your gun?" According to Cleaver, the other officers were pleading with this officer to back off. As Cleaver notes, the officer was staring into Newton's eyes, measuring him up. "O.K.," Newton said. "You big fat racist pig, draw your gun." When there was no move, Newton pumped a round of ammunition into the chamber of the shotgun and sneered, "Draw it, you cowardly dog! I'm waiting."[28] After several moments, the police officer lowered his head, and Newton walked off triumphantly.

Few people have taken such an aggressive stance in the face of intense adversity over such a long period of time. As Cleaver put it, Newton and the Black Panther Party told whites, "We will no longer tolerate the inferior position to which you have consigned us, we will have our manhood we will have it now or the earth will be leveled by our attempts to gain it."[29] Newton's rhetoric resembled that of a young Malcolm X, and his gun toting was shared by Robert Williams, the North Carolina militant. However, unlike both of those men, Newton did not display a fiery demeanor when confronting the authorities; rather, Newton almost always appeared calm and cerebral, willing to engage in an intellectual sparring match even under the most extreme duress. Newton's verbal chess games could be seen as a type of boasting. His style made others boast about him, too. Elaine Brown describes a meeting between Newton and Nation of Islam leader Louis Farrakhan:

Brown: Farrakhan had been travelling around Northern California saying, we in the Nation say that a man is what he eats. . . . Now, some people, denounce others as pigs, yet they themselves eat the pig. . . . We say that if a man eats the pig, He must be the pig! Upon hearing this Newton invited Farrakhan to his home to get clarification on the matter. Farrakhan arrived with twenty members of the FOI, the Nation's infamous security force; the Fruit of Islam. They were all searched for weapons by Panthers waiting in the lobby. Only five would be allowed entrance to the penthouse. The scene had been set perfectly by Huey. Panthers in full blue and black uniforms, including berets, were standing strategically at attention. They were all holding shotguns, noticeable even in the dimly lit apartment. Huey showed Farrakhan to a chair at one end of this massive table. Huey sat at the opposite end.

Huey: My Brother, I appreciate the time you've taken to meet with us.

Farrakhan: We welcome the opportunity to speak with our good Brother in struggle.

Huey: We in the Black Panther Party have always appreciated the teachings of the Honorable Elijah Muhammad. At the same time, my Brother, we identify completely with the principles taught by Malcolm X.

Brown: That was when I thought the FOI seated at the table would jump up and initiate the inevitable battle.

Huey: Indeed, that was why I personally took charge of Sister Betty Shabazz's security when she came to speak here in the Bay Area some time ago after Malcolm's murder.

Brown: Out of the corner of my eye, I saw a shotgun jump when he said that. The dangerous FOI at the table sat up, dangerous men, not merely because they were "true believers," men pledged to be ready at any time to meet Allah in Paradise for their beliefs. And I knew Huey was prepared to send them there that night.

Farrakhan: Yes, Brother Malcolm was an interesting man, though misguided. He lost faith, though, and . . .

Huey: Yes, well anyway excuse me, my Brother, but I actually did not ask you here to speak about the dead past. . . . I wanted to talk to you about a little matter, which has given me great concern, my Brother.

Farrakhan: Speak on it, Brother.

Huey: First, I want to be sure I have understood you correctly. . . . I believe you say that a man is what he eats, is that correct—my Brother?

Farrakhan: That is what we say, Brother.

Huey: You have also said that if a man eats the pig, he must be the pig. Is that also correct, Brother?

Farrakhan: Yes, that is so. You see, we in the Nation believe the pig is a dirty animal, and to eat any part of it is a sin against Allah.

Huey: I understand, my Brother. I accept what you say, and I appreciate you saying it. I have, however, another question. Are you a man?

Brown: Huey threw back his head in anticipation of triumph. Everyone seemed puzzled, including Farrakhan.

Farrakhan: Why, of course, is that your question, Brother?

Huey: Yes . . . well, not quite. Here is my question: if a man is what he eats and you are a man, what part of the man do you eat?!

Brown: With that, Huey dramatically slid to the edge of his chair, leaning forward to look directly into Farrakhan eyes, waiting for an answer. Farrakhan fell back in his chair, threw his head back, and laughed heartily.

Farrakhan: That's a good one, Brother. You got me there. I understood you completely, my Brother. And I assure you, we'll be more careful in our references . . .

Brown: That night the brothers could not have been more proud of their hero.[10]

The admiration Brown displays in recounting this story gives merit to H. C. Brearley's point that black woman give the "bad nigger" his full share of praise.[31] What made Newton different from other "bad niggers" is that he had both "street smarts" and "book smarts." Newton not only stood on street corners and engaged in fistfights and other behavior in which street-corner blacks partake, but he also was formally educated—a college graduate. One could argue that Newton was the street tough's "bad nigger" as well as the learned person's "bad nigger," a rare combination indeed.

Newton's defiance when confronting the police was clearly psychologically gratifying and symbolically important to many people who had been intimidated by the police. Erik Erikson put the Black Panther Party's practice of armed self-defense into perspective when he said:

> When you faced down those policemen—not threatening them with your guns or indicating with gestures that you would shoot first, but daring them to shoot first. That was a very important psychological condition you created there. You gave them the initiative and said, "OK, you shoot first." You made something very revolutionary out of it when you made it clear that you didn't come to shoot them, but if they had come to shoot you then you should come with it. You paralyzed them morally, don't you think?[32]

For decades the white police were the most immediate physical and symbolic representative of white oppression for many in the black community. To have black men and women willing to risk death by defying such white symbols was extremely important. Newton risked his life on numerous occasions over a long period of time, mostly in defense of the black community. In a *Playboy* interview, Newton said, "We wanted to show that we didn't have to tolerate police abuse, that the black community would provide its own security, following the local laws and ordinances and the California Penal Code."[33]

Newton and the Black Panther Party also showed blacks that they did not have to rely on government assistance or white handouts, that blacks could be self-reliant. Instead of putting oneself through the often humiliating experience of applying for welfare or other public assistance, blacks could turn to the Black Panther Party for food, clothing, medical assistance, and transportation. While the Black Panther Party obviously did not have the government's wealth or resources, the Party was still able to provide services to hundreds of thousands of black residents over the years. Indeed, the Black Panther Party's free grocery giveaway preceded the Meals on Wheels program that later became popular.

Newton demonstrated that blacks could lead, organize, and strategize just as effectively as whites. A good example of Newton's leadership qualities and his ability to get things done occurred in early 1967, when he and others set out to get a streetlight installed at a dangerous intersection in Oakland where several school-aged children had been killed. Newton, along with others, filed a petition with the city of Oakland to get a traffic light installed and were told that the light would be up late the next year. When Newton threatened that the Black Panther Party would direct traffic in the interim, the Oakland City Council saw to it that the light was installed shortly thereafter.[34] Seeing Newton in a position of authority seemed to enable other oppressed people to conceive what was once thought to be impossible. Two years after Newton and Seale founded the Panthers, Richard and Milton Henry formed the Republic of New Africa in Detroit, also a black militant group. In New Zealand, activists founded the Polynesian Panther Party and staged a sit-in against the government.[35] Soon after, "Black Panthers" in Israel pressed for better treatment of non-Western Jews. Back home, members of the Afro-American Society (AAS) at Cornell University, after having taken over a campus building in an effort to pressure the school into creating a black studies program, marched out in military formation with their weapons in a manner that imitated the famous Black Panther march into the California state capitol in 1967.[36] Indeed, the AAS minister of defense, one of the first students out of the door, wore (for effect) a bandolier of bullets across his chest in much the same way that Newton had.

Newton's symbolic impact on the black community, white community, and oppressed communities at large is immeasurable. An attempt to assess Newton's impact on the psyche and self-esteem of blacks across the country was made by Cleaver, who said, "For four hundred years black people have been wanting to do exactly what Huey Newton did, that is, to stand up in front of the most deadly tentacle of the white racist power structure, and to defy that deadly tentacle, and to tell that tentacle that he will not accept the aggression and the brutality, and that if he is moved against, he will retaliate in kind."[37] Newton called upon all black Americans to become conscious and proud of their race, to avoid dependent relationships with whites that foster self-doubt in one's abilities, and to exhibit pride in identifying with Africans as well as other people of color throughout the world. One could call Newton a hero. Abraham defines a hero as a man whose deeds epitomize the masculine attributes most highly valued within a community. Certainly during Newton's lifetime, as well as now, one of the major characteristics of manhood within the black community is the courage to stand up to whites in words and actions. Newton's life-long, valiant struggle against the Establishment and those individuals who sought to force blacks into an inferior place contributed to the many legendary stories that surround him.

Charles P. Henry argues that both the myth and the reality of the "bad nigger" constitute a continuing historical source of revolutionary vision.[38] At the same time, he argues that for the most part, none of the "bad niggers" has represented a transforming political leadership.[39] He points out that the potential for the transforming leadership of the "bad nigger" is perhaps best illustrated by the life of Malcolm X. Henry says it was Malcolm's style, his refusal to back down despite the odds rather than his ideology or organization, that attracted his followers. When one looks at Newton, however, one finds more than just style. Like Malcolm, he displayed courage, but he was also a member of an organization that was unmatched in popularity and impact by any other Black Power group, an organization that was guided by a dynamic figure. Given that, Newton was a transforming political leader.

Huey was a brilliant guy. He was one of the four or five real geniuses I've met in my lifetime.

—Bob Trivors

A genuine intellectual possesses at least two characteristics—the desire to tell the truth and the courage to do so. Consequently, this individual is inevitably considered a "troublemaker" and a "nuisance" by the ruling class seeking to preserve the status quo. Others accuse the intellectual of being utopian or metaphysical at best, subversive or seditious at worst.[1] Similarly Karl Marx said the function of a philosopher is two-fold: to help explain change—that is, to be a thinker—and to help bring about change—that is, to be an activist.[2] Newton embodied these criteria.

Sociologist J. Herman Blake saw Newton as "the quintessential teacher—in the sense that his approach was to provide people with processes by which they can arrive at answers rather than give them the answers themselves. That is what you are doing when you talk about states of change, internal contradictions, processes of development and transformations."[3] Much like Marx, Newton sought to understand the world in order to change it and to shape and to realize the individual's destiny in it. Newton was fond of saying, "If I can move one grain of sand from one spot to another, then the world will never be exactly the same."[4] Over time, Newton evolved into a sophisticated thinker and tactician. He had vision: as the world changed, his ideology did the same to keep pace. The ideology with which Newton helped lead the Black Panther Party evolved through several phases, each of which was accompanied by fissures, fractures, and defections.

In the beginning, Newton characterized the Black Panther Party as black nationalists because he thought that nationhood was the answer to imperialism. He assumed that black people could solve a number of their problems by becoming a nation, but he soon realized that this analysis showed his lack of understanding of the world's dialectical development. In

Newton's words, "Our mistake was to assume that the conditions under which people had become nations in the past still existed. To be a nation, one must satisfy certain essential conditions, and if these things do not exist or cannot be created, then it is impossible to be a nation."[5] Later, he argued that what was really needed was revolutionary socialism. After a more rigorous analysis of U.S. and global conditions, he found socialism only was not enough. Socialism would bring about a more equitable distribution of America's resources, but it would not bring about freedom for the oppressed. He reasoned that in order to liberate the oppressed, the ruling elite would have to be deposed. The only way to make this happen was to unite with other oppressed peoples of the world and move en masse against the established order. When the Panthers sought solidarity with other oppressed groups, it marked the internationalist stage of their development. Newton recognized that people of color were under siege all over the world by the same forces. The main difference between what was happening to black Americans and others was the degree to which blacks were being oppressed. In addition, it can be argued that during this phase of the organization's ideological development, Newton was moving toward a more humanistic outlook. At the outset, black people's salvation was Newton's principal concern—some might say only concern; later, Newton would come to believe that human differences must be encouraged and understood rather than denied and feared. This is rather evident, as Newton reached out to a number of groups, including gays and lesbians as well as other marginalized peoples in and outside of the United States. In fact, Newton was an early champion of gay and lesbian rights.[6] In many ways, the inability of other black activists to deal with people's differences prevented them from seeing the increasing importance of global coalition politics.

Upon further study, Newton realized that with the advent of sophisticated technology, the United States had grown into an empire. Because of its might, the United States was able to wield its influence over nations, dominating their institutions to such an extent that these countries were stripped of their nationhood status, thus making them more like communities. Newton argued that since internationalism was an interrelationship among a group of nations, it was impossible for the Panthers to be internationalists. As a result of these transformations and developments, Newton decided that Intercommunalism was the most appropriate characterization of the world situation. For Newton, this term best described the ever-changing political, economic, cultural, and social relationships among people and nations in the world. Intercommunalism would serve as the basis for seizing the wealth and resources from the ruling circle and distributing them in an equitable and proportional fashion throughout the communities of the world.

As a leader, Newton remained attuned to the pulse of the people, so much so that he made a conscious decision to de-emphasize the gun as part of the Black Panther Party's program when it appeared to him that such a show of force frightened some blacks who otherwise might have been sympathetic to the Panthers' cause. His decision to put aside the gun drew the ire of numerous left-wing activists as well as the anger of some Panthers. This decision would lead to a split within the Black Panther Party from which the organization would never fully recover.[7] It was rumored that the Symbionese Liberation Army targeted Newton for death because of his decision to de-emphasize the gun.[8] One could criticize Newton for not making this decision earlier. On the other hand, had he done so, it might have rendered Panther patrols of police ineffective. Others have argued that the Party's early emphasis on the gun was a tactical error because it invited police harassment and other forms of governmental repression of Black Panther Party chapters throughout the country. Consequently, Panthers became the victims of manhunts, political trials, and outright killings—a search and destroy mission probably unprecedented in America for its scope and systematic ferocity.[9] Between 1968 and 1971, local police stormed into and wrecked Black Panther offices in more than ten cities, stealing thousands of dollars in funds and arresting, beating, and shooting the occupants in well-planned, unprovoked attacks. According to Michael Parenti, during this period, more than 40 Panthers were killed by local police.[10] In 1969 alone, law enforcement officers arrested 348 Panthers, many of whom were jailed for long periods of time without bail.[11] By 1978, there were at least 24 Black Panthers still in prison.[12] Newton argued that black activists were being "sent to prison for what they did, but they are kept in prison for what they believe."[13] In spite of all this, Newton argued that the Party's gun-toting posture was "historically necessary and valid" as a building block in creating a revolutionary consciousness among dispirited blacks, just as the survival programs were yet another step and ideological comprehension another. Still, one cannot help but wonder if Newton naively underestimated the lengths that the state would go in its attempt to annihilate a militant organization. That the Panthers were black fueled the state's determination even more.

Yohuru R. Williams submits that while many of the pronouncements of the Black Panther Party certainly warranted investigation, the take-no-prisoners attitude at all levels of government resulted in a web of violence and disinformation that totally disregarded the Constitution.[14] Indeed, to say that the Panthers represented a clear and present danger is to say that conditions were so deplorable and so miserable that people in ghettoes and barrios were prepared to adopt the Party's proposals and launch a revolution. If conditions were that bad, logic would dictate that those in power would concern themselves with eliminating such conditions and not those who brought them to the public's attention. The harassment of the Black Panther Party was due in part to the fear of those in positions of political and economic power that their way of life would end if black discontent resulted in the realization of black advancement.

Newton was also criticized for forging relationships with white groups. Stokely Carmichael warned Newton that whites would destroy the movement, alienate blacks, and weaken the Party's effectiveness in the community.[15] Bayard Rustin said of the white Left, "These people are really saying, 'You sic em, nigger Panthers. You bring about a revolution for us while we go on living our nice little jolly lives. You niggers do it. We'll be right behind you—at a considerable distance.'"[16] Rustin's point was not farfetched. As a case in point, in 1969, Tom Hayden, cofounder of SDS, talked about the need to wage an assault on the Oakland Alameda County Sheriff's department. White radicals and counterculturalists couldn't do it, he said; they weren't ready. The only ones who could bring off "armed resistance" were the Panthers, according to Hayden. Because Cleaver, Newton, and Seale were all either in jail or on the run at the time, Hayden went to David Hilliard to discuss the possibility of trying to shoot down an Alameda sheriff's helicopter. Hilliard is said to have looked at Hayden with disdain and responded: "Just like you, Tom. Get a nigger to pull the trigger."[17] Still, Newton thought that there were many white radicals who were "sincere about trying to realign themselves with mankind and to make a reality out of the high moral standards that their fathers and forefathers merely expressed."[18] He pointed out white opposition to and criticism of U.S. involvement in Vietnam and the Dominican Republic as examples of their sincerity. Newton later acknowledged that although Carmichael was wrong in principle, he was right in terms of what happened to the Black Panther Party. Newton admitted that as a result of coalitions with whites, "the Black Panther Party found itself lured into the free speech movement, the psychedelic scene, and experimentation with drugs."[19] Not only were these causes irrelevant and counterproductive to the Party's program, they weakened the organization's infrastructure. Newton found this impact to be most pronounced during his three years in jail. Upon Newton's release, much of his time was spent rebuilding the organization.

In addition to underestimating the adverse impact of forming alliances with whites, Newton underestimated the potential of Pan-Africanism and culture as a cohesive force for people of African descent. Many have contended that while black Americans were faced with economic and political crises, the crisis of culture was the greatest impediment to African American progress. They maintain that before blacks could move forward politically, they had to free themselves culturally.[20] Whether Newton's repudiation of Pan-Africanism as a unifying cultural force was due to a lack of foresight and vision on his part or stemmed from a feud with Carmichael and Karenga that colored his judgment is difficult to discern. Errol Henderson writes that "none of the successful revolutions that the BPP evoked were explicable unless one appreciated the role by which leaders utilized their indigenous culture as a means of mobilization and transformation."[21] One could argue that culture is very important in the fight for liberation because nations have fought against their oppressors yet maintained the culture of their slave masters. If one is fighting for a revolution, one is talking not only about changing the centers of power but also about changing the value and belief system.[22]

Despite his tendency to be egocentric and shortsighted, Newton was able to put theory into practice. As Marx and Lenin said, theory becomes aimless if it is not connected with revolutionary practice, just as practice "gropes in the dark if its path is not illuminated by revolutionary theory." For Newton, theory came about as a result of observing and analyzing reality. He argued, "Instead of trying to fit reality into theory, one must derive theory from reality. After one gathers and collects a set of facts, then one can set up a program to deal with the problems at hand."[23] In addition, Newton asserted that "theory should only be accepted as valid if it delivers a true understanding of the phenomena that affect the lives of people."[24] He also recognized that neither theory nor practice could afford to be rigid, and, as a consequence, there was room for both admission of error and redefinition of the situation based on changing conditions and the evolution of consciousness. Drawing upon the works of Marx, Fanon, Mao, Malcolm X, and Nietzsche, Newton was able to construct a mode of thought that he used to deal with problems that oppressed people faced, particularly black people. Eldridge Cleaver characterized Newton this way: "Newton is motivated by a deep and burning preoccupation and concern with the plight of black people, who is seeking solutions to the problems of black people, and who recognizes that it is going to take a very fundamental action on a revolutionary level to cut into the oppression and to motivate people, black people, to take a revolutionary stance against the decadent racist system that is oppressing them."[25]

While few questioned Newton's commitment to black

uplift, some questioned his choice of revolutionary role models, arguing that the work carried out by Third World revolutionaries was anything but similar to the tasks that lay before black militants in America. Political scientist Matthew Holden claims that from a strictly technical standpoint, neither Mao nor Giap nor Che provides any clues for warfare on behalf of a large minority population in an industrial society. Furthermore, Holden says, "No matter how carefully would-be American revolutionaries study the *Battle of Algiers* [which was required viewing for Panthers] there is a basic military fact. Algiers was surrounded by a friendly hinterland, but the urban ghettoes are enclaves surrounded by a hostile countryside."[26] In an interview, one Panther exclaimed, "I couldn't understand why Mao Tse Tung was so important to Huey. If anything, the Black Panther Party should have been looking toward Africa for answers, not Asia."[27] Contrary to what Holden may believe, Newton was not ignorant of that fact. In the late 1960s, Newton admitted in an interview that "we (black revolutionaries) can't do the same things that were done in Cuba because Cuba is Cuba and the U.S. is the U.S. Cuba has many different terrains to protect the guerrilla. This country is mainly urban. We have to work out new solutions to offset the power of the country's technology and communication; its ability to communicate very rapidly by telephone and teletype and so forth. We do have solutions to these problems and they will be put into effect. I wouldn't want to go into the ways and means of this, but we will educate through action."[28]

What Holden and others fail to realize is that, dialectically speaking, Newton was a pragmatist. He was adept at extracting concepts, theories, and paradigms from the works and experiences of others that he deemed applicable to the black experience in America while discarding that which was irrelevant. For instance, in *Guerrilla Warfare*, Che Guevara wrote that the Cuban Revolution offered three guiding principles for revolution in the Americas : popular forces can win a war against the army; it is not necessary to wait until all conditions for making revolution exists; and in underdeveloped America the countryside is the basic area for armed fighting.[29] While Newton believed (rightly so) that the third point could be not applied in the United States, he saw a great deal of value in the other two. Another example of Newton's pragmatism involves his reading of Marx. Newton did not believe in some of Marx's conclusions, especially concerning the lumpenproletariat, but he recognized Marx as one of the great contributors in the area of dialectical materialism. In fact, he would use Marx's mode of thought (dialectical materialism) to help develop his own philosophy. Newton noted that in every discipline and walk of life there are people who have distorted visions or personal idiosyncrasies but who nonetheless produce ideas worth considering. For Newton, whether a revolutionary's or scholar's experience or writings corresponded neatly to the way things worked in the United States was to some degree irrelevant and immaterial to whether that person developed a system of thinking or strategy that helped develop truths about the processes in the material world.

Newton had an uncanny ability to critically analyze and synthesize complex theories. He encouraged criticism of his ideas because he thought that criticism was a necessary component in the process of intellectual growth. Mao said that "the mistakes of the past must be exposed without sparing anyone's sensibilities; it is necessary to analyze and criticize what was bad in the past with a scientific attitude so that work in the future will be done more carefully and done better."[30] Newton implemented this principle by subjecting his writings and theories to scrutiny with the intention of soliciting feedback that would help him strengthen his ideas about how the world works. In Newton's words, "Once you think you can't be corrected, once you think you can't lose an argument, then you're a fool. And I don't want to be the fool."[31] In 1974, Newton was able to formulate a stronger position paper on the notion of Intercommunalism as a result of the 1971 Yale colloquium where he was invited to present his work. Although the work still appears somewhat abstract (which some argue ultimately alienated some members of the Party who were unable to grasp the complexity of the concept), others deem it to be a valuable theoretical construct.

Nikhil Pal Singh writes that Newton's thinking is important for three reasons: it acknowledged "the world-ordering" power of the U.S. during that period; it attempted to theorize a relationship between intra- and international conflict and struggle; and it argued that an effective "anti-imperialism" must be based on the understanding that the global power and domestic hegemony of the American state are integrally linked.[32] In contrast, one frustrated Panther recalled, "It was too much for the average Party member, so how could we explain it to the community? Intercommunalism was fine for Erik Erikson or the Yale students but not for the grass-roots community."[33] Said another Panther, "In many ways Intercommunalism was a very convoluted concept, incomprehensible at times."[34] Hayes and Kiene support this point, suggesting that in some respects Newton's rapidly advanced thinking was not accompanied by sufficient political education so that rank-and-file Panthers could fully comprehend the new set of ideas and thus convey them in a coherent manner to the community.[35] Newton was not totally unaware of this problem. In a 1974 paper, he wrote that his biggest problem was trying to simplify ideology for the masses. "So far I haven't been able to do it well enough to keep from being booed off the stage," Newton wrote.[36] Still, Intercommunalism is an important and original contribution to revolutionary political theory; it is a counterideology, the core of which is an unyielding commitment to break loose from the chains of U.S. imperialism, the end result of centuries of slavery, and from other forms of domination suffered at the hands of the white oppressor. Newton's call for a worldwide revolution was derived from a careful and elaborate analysis of the global political order, as well as from an elucidation of the glaring discrepancy between the so-called American Dream and the dismal political, economic, social, and psychological realities that people of color and oppressed people in general experience on a daily basis.

Credit should also be given to Newton for his work with the black lumpenproletariat. He tapped into a segment of the population that society had written off as incorrigible and transformed them into a revolutionary force. In the words of

Alprentice (Bunchy) Carter, "Huey Newton was able to go down, and take the nigger on the street, niggers who had been bad and relate to him, understand what was going on inside him, what he was thinking, and then implement that into an organization, into a Program and a Platform."[37]

Newton also dealt with the gender question as well as any leader of an organization dominated by males. This is not to say that contradictions on this issue did not exist within the Black Panther Party. Indeed, the autobiographies of Assata Shakur and Elaine Brown as well as the accounts of other Panther women indicate that while the Party publicly proclaimed its support for the equality of women, its practice was a bit more ambiguous.[38] Newton was concerned with purging male chauvinism from the Black Panther Party, yet paradoxically he was guilty of it himself. It seems though that he realized that it was absurd to talk about changing relations between classes or races until issues regarding male-female relations were dealt with. Like Malcolm X, Newton realized that the revolution pivoted on the political consciousness and social development of women. The degree to which he remained sensitive to this issue is revealed in the number of men reprimanded by and expelled from the organization because of their inappropriate or oppressive behavior toward their female comrades as well as the number of women who rose to leadership and other prominent positions within the Black Panther Party. Al Amour and Robert Collier maintain that much of the Party's success was due in large part to the pivotal role played by Panther women.[39] Fanon pointed to the importance of women in the politics of collective struggle by the oppressed when he wrote: "[We] must guard against the danger of perpetuating the feudal tradition which holds sacred the superiority of the masculine element over the feminine."[40] Newton's writings indicate that he believed that the gender question was inextricably linked to broader sociopolitical issues. Indeed, low-paying menial jobs, unemployment, and welfare regulations all have powerful, predictable consequences for personal relationships between women and men.

Karl Marx is given credit with developing the most complete revolutionary ideology, yet Marx's revolution consisted mainly of two principal actors—the bourgeoisie and the workers. He also failed to deal adequately with the questions of race and gender. In the Gramscian tradition, Newton challenged Marx's analysis. Antonio Gramsci, the Italian Communist, argued that there are many groups that do not belong to the bourgeoisie or to the proletariat. According to Gramsci, a revolutionary ideology would seek out, mobilize, and organize these groups.[41] Unlike other Black Power and civil rights organizations whose membership could be considered homogeneous in composition, the Black Panther Party was varied in its makeup. Members were recruited from all walks of life.[42] And few can deny that Newton's work with the lumpenproletariat was unprecedented in the United States. Some have maintained that Newton's refusal to screen new members on the basis of prior arrest records put the organization at risk. Indeed, some of these individuals displayed a penchant for criminal activity, indiscriminate violence, and a lack of discipline, which played into the hands of the media and law enforcement.[43] That some Panthers engaged in a variety of what mainstream society considers illegalities may be explained in part by examining the Panthers' unorthodox definition of crime. As one Panther explained, "I refer to crime as being the exploitation of poor people by filthy rich, money avaricious capitalist pigs."[44] This outlook coincides with an observation made by sociologist Robert Staples, who pointed out that "many blacks do not consider America to be a fair and just society, hence feel little obligation to obey its laws."[45] Indeed, the Panthers' position on the role of blacks in relation to the white Establishment implies just that when they say that "there are no laws that the oppressor makes that the oppressed are bound to respect."

The historical relationship of blacks and whites to the American legal system has always been radically different. It is important to understand that for whites, the law has been the means by which their life and property are protected and their freedom guaranteed. For blacks, the law has been used at one time to enslave them and later to restrict their freedom in many different ways. African slaves arrived on the North American continent under conditions that placed them outside of the law. Under slavery, blacks literally had no legal rights; they could not look to the law for protection of rights or redress of grievances. In post-Civil War America, African Americans hardly had the opportunity to develop a positive view of the law because the legal rights granted them upon emancipation were rapidly usurped by new laws designed to limit and deny them their basic human and civic rights. Throughout this nation's history, African Americans have seen a double standard of justice in which whites are less likely to be convicted if arrested and less likely to receive severe punishment if convicted. They have seen the testimony of whites accepted when in conflict with the testimony of blacks. They have witnessed blacks arrested and convicted for minor infractions when more serious crimes committed by whites go unpunished. They wonder why American society reacted so strongly to the killings of white students at Kent State University in 1970 but was unmoved by the slaughter of blacks at historically black South Carolina State and Jackson State universities. Is it any wonder that some Party members would hold the law in such contempt?

Be that as it may, media coverage of Panther infractions reinforced many whites' misperceptions; for other whites, it confirmed what they had always heard, and it served to turn off some blacks who considered themselves law-abiding citizens. While it is true that a small cadre of Party members engaged in counterproductive behavior, the fact remains that Newton tapped into a sector of the population that society had deemed to be beyond rehabilitation and transformed them into productive social-change agents. As an alternative to falling victim to gangs, prostitution, and other crimes, Newton encouraged young blacks to organize for justice and community development. History and oppression had taught Newton that it was not enough for oppressed people to be angry about the inferior position to which they had been relegated. The supreme task was to organize, unite, and channel that anger in a way that achieved productive revolutionary ends. Newton also formed alliances that transcended racial, class, and gender lines. Given all that, one could argue that Newton's understanding of revolution was more inclusive and nuanced than Marx's. Seale once said that "Marx would probably turn over in his grave if he could see lumpenproletariat Afro-Americans putting together the ideology of the Black Panther Party. Marx used to say that the lumpenproletariat wouldn't do nothing for the revolution."[46]

Newton recognized that one had to use different tactics at different times in history because everything is in a constant state of change. His observation apparently eluded other political activists. One member of the Communist Party inexplicably opined that "the problem with the Panthers' approach to politics, in both its early and later stages, was that they were always substituting themselves for someone. When their emphasis was on military confrontation, they were substituting themselves for mass revolutionary activity, and when their emphasis was on free handouts, they were substituting themselves for the welfare departments."[47] That this activist could not see the merit in organizational adaptation to meet the needs and wants of a disadvantaged community at different phases in time is hard to understand.

Early on, Newton discounted the ability of black politicians to influence government policy. Over time he came to see conventional politics as a viable supplement to protest politics. Upon making this turnabout he urged Seale to run for mayor of Oakland. In doing so, he ordered the Party to close most of its chapters and reassigned Panthers and their resources to Oakland to work on Seale's campaign. There are indications that Newton began to view electoral politics in a different light as early as 1972. That year he publicly called for "every black, poor, and progressive human being" to support the presidential candidacy of Shirley Chisholm, the first African American woman elected to Congress and the first to run for president.[48] This shift in thinking represented a sharp departure from the Party's previous militant stance; nonetheless, it met the approval of the Bay Area's black community. One *Ramparts* writer described the euphoria that permeated the Oakland Auditorium the night Seale announced his candidacy: "The hat Bobby tossed into the ring was no gangster Borsalino or soft brown fedora but one of those big, broad-brimmed, bad ass jobs, and the people received it with class."[49] No one was more excited about Seale's electoral chances than Newton. Said Newton: "Upon this victory we shall move to implement, in concrete ways, a people's program for the people of this city, and then in other cities and counties and states. We shall build upon this firm foundation, and go from victory to victory across this entire nation, until the principles of freedom and justice for all shall be delivered to all by the power of all, the power of the people."[50] Later that same year, when Tom Bradley was elected mayor of Los Angeles, making him the first and only black to hold that office in that city, Newton congratulated him on his historic achievement, despite the fact that Bradley had repudiated Newton during the mayoral campaign. "We hope that you, Mr. Bradley, will bring us all closer to true freedom and justice in Los Angeles and elsewhere in America," Newton is quoted as saying.[51]

Newton's about-face on the issue of electoral politics can be explained in part when he says that he came to realize that "to enlighten the masses the contradictions in the system had to be 'heightened,' and at times electoral politics may be the most legitimate way to do this."[52] Seale emerged from the primary, only to lose a runoff election to John Reading, the eventual winner. However, because of Seale's strong showing, the Panthers were able to win a seat on the Oakland Board of Education and several seats on a city-wide community board responsible for the allocation of federal poverty funds.[53] According to Newton, the Party's purpose for launching a mayoral campaign was to acquaint the grass-roots black community with a new image of the Panthers and to create a viable network that could be used for other community efforts. His ultimate goal was not to take over Oakland but "to elect effective representation of our poor and black community in every governmental institution that's supposed to be serving us."[54] Ollie A. Johnson argues that Newton believed that if Seale was elected mayor the Party could promote an economic development plan that included turning Oakland's port into a highly profitable state-of-the-art facility, promoting local black businesses and implementing new human capital endeavors. Newton also wanted to keep pressure on black politicians to be more responsive. Seale's mayoral race enabled the Black Panther Party to organize a large voter registration drive that would later serve as the foundation for the election of several minority candidates in the mid to late 1970s. In 1973, a coalition of liberal whites and minorities was successful in electing the first Latino council member. And in 1977, Oakland elected Lionel Wilson, a moderate judge, as its first black mayor and the first Democrat elected since World War II. The Black Panther Party was responsible for registering more than ninety thousand black Democrats during the 1977 mayoral race.[55] Black electoral mobilization continued in 1979 with the election of Wilson Riles Jr. to the city council.[56] By the mid 1980s five of the nine members on Oakland's city council were black, as were the city manager and the city's director of economic development. By this time, black political mobilization had long been transformed from a movement outside the system to electoral politics within the system. Reginald Major points out that until the Panthers became involved in electoral politics, Oakland blacks had been incapable of electing to office individuals who identified with their interests.[57]

Manning Marable says that "by the late 1960s, the Black Panther Party had become the most influential revolutionary nationalist organization in the United States."[58] Enrique Cha Cha Jimenez, head of the Young Lords, concurred with this assessment, stating, "We see and recognize the Black Panther Party as a vanguard party, a vanguard revolutionary party. And we feel that as revolutionaries we should follow the vanguard party. This is why we follow them."[59] Newton's perception of the Black Panther Party as the vanguard for revolutionary change is similar to that of a chosen people. In other words, he saw the Black Panther Party as a chosen people and himself as a sort of black jeremiad who issues warnings to racist white America concerning the judgment that would come from the sin of slavery and the continued practice of denigration and subjugation.[60] Although Newton does not say so, it appeared that, for him, the Black Panther Party had sort of a messianic role in achieving not only black people's but all oppressed people's redemption. He once said, "The Black Panther Party was formed to oppose evils in society. We thought of ourselves as the vanguard of the people."[61] One could argue that Newton's perception of the Black Panther Party as the vanguard was buttressed by a belief in black people's capacity to endure and survive. The African slave trade and the nonviolent Civil Rights movement were testimonials to the belief that blacks could endure and outlast the worst pain and violence that white racists could inflict. Support for this argument is found in a William Brink and Louis Harris survey that reported that blacks believe that in a contest of violence, black performance would be superior to that of whites.[62] This belief is an important clue to the willingness of blacks to risk death in the face of insurmountable odds.

While Newton held fast to the belief that blacks would lead the revolution, he never clearly or comprehensively answered the following all-important questions: What does it take to actually overthrow the United States government by force of arms? What was the Black Panther Party's strategy for waging such a revolutionary war? And what is required to get the oppressed masses to see revolution as the only viable option? Matthew Holden argued that talk of a revolution in the U.S. was unrealistic. He asserted that anyone who advocated armed rebellion on a large scale was either hopelessly naive in believing that retribution would not be severe in the extreme or was sunk in despair and advocating a kind of kamikaze politics.[63] Furthermore, he believed that both the technical and the political requirements for armed rebellion were absent, and likely to remain absent, in the United States—so that such an enterprise would be an invitation to the genocide that some advocates of armed rebellion foresaw and an exercise in self-confirming prophecy. Others were not as morbid in their assessment for a potential black-led revolution. Lieutenant Colonel William R. Corson, staff secretary to President Johnson's special group on counterinsurgency, researched the possibilities of a revolutionary movement in the United States. He even acquired a professorship at Howard University in Washington, D.C., to get close to black students to study them. In stark contrast to Holden's perspective, Corson concluded that "without the students, black extremists cannot mount their revolution; with them they may be able to."[64]

Although Newton and the Black Panther Party clearly did not bring about a revolution, they left behind a rich legacy of resistance and service that has arguably gone unmatched by any other organization, black or white, since its demise. Not only did Newton and the Black Panther Party protect blacks from police brutality, they also provided basic staples like food, clothing, and health care to those in need. The Black Panther Party's attempt to "meet the needs of the people" should not be considered palliative or reformist. Newton and the Panthers were nurturing and cultivating the development of a potential revolutionary juggernaut.[65] He kept the organization's social service programs in perspective. The Black Panther Party would not, said Newton, regard the survival programs as a definitive answer to the problem of black oppression. However, since "the people and only the people make revolutions, the goals of the revolution could be achieved only if the people were kept from perishing from lack of care and sustenance."[66]

Throughout the 1970s and early 1980s, Newton and the Black Panther Party continued to work for reform of the courts, juries, and prisons, which included opposing the death penalty. Newton continued to hope for socialism in the United States.[67] The Party also continued to speak out against police brutality and mounted campaigns against the Bakke and Weber decisions, U.S. Supreme Court cases that tested "reverse discrimination" in university admission programs and in employment opportunities.[68] Their support of other disenfranchised groups never wavered. "As long as there is oppression in this society, I will continue to speak out against it," said Newton in a 1980 interview.[69] When hundreds of persons with disabilities staged a twenty-six-day sit-in at the Department of Health, Education and Welfare in San Francisco in 1977, demanding federal action on their behalf, the Panthers immediately sprung into action, declaring their support and providing the demonstrators with food and other essentials.[70] When the Black Veterans Association came under attack by the Oakland police, Newton publicly denounced the police department's actions.[71] As present-day grassroots community service organizations continue to grapple with problems such as increases in homelessness, unemployment, incarceration, and insufficient health care, these organizations need look no further than Huey P. Newton and the Black Panther Party (with all its flaws) for an inspirational model on which to build for a better future.

All criticism is an autobiography.

—Unknown

Most followers of 1960s radicalism, either those who lived it or read about it, are aware of Huey P. Newton's revolutionary exploits. Few, however, are familiar with Newton's political writings. With the exception of Stokely Carmichael and Maulana Karenga, few activists of the Black Power era amassed the portfolio of Newton. Newton's writings appear to serve five basic purposes: (1) to provide an autobiographical account of his childhood and journey to political maturity; (2) to provide insight into the beginnings, history, and inner workings of the Black Panther Party; (3) to inform the public concerning what he thought about and where he stood on the pressing issues of the day; (4) to debunk and unravel misunderstandings about the Black Panther Party, the most misunderstood organization of that era; and (5) to help raise the consciousness of the masses.

In addition to his many papers, essays, and articles, Newton is also the author or coauthor of five thought-provoking books. Because of Newton's stature as a controversial and national figure, his books drew attention from scholarly and literary circles.[1] Reviews of Newton's books are a mixed bag of favorable assessments, backhanded compliments, and stinging and sometimes unwarranted criticism. A number of the critiques are filtered with comments that border on the personal, petty, and frivolous. These particular reviewers treat Newton as a sideshow and his writings as bumbling declarations in an attempt to convince others, as well as themselves, that as a theorist Newton was a bush leaguer—an amateur who should not be paid much attention to by those who consider themselves serious students of political theory. This kind of thinking coincides with what philosopher Lewis R. Gordon talks about in his article "Racist Ideology." Gordon submits that the most dominant feature of supremacist ideology is the extent to which it is premised upon a spirit of evasion and dismissal.[2]

While favorable appraisals of Newton's work do exist, they are few and far between. One reviewer of *To Die for the People* commented, "[He] is an excellent polemicist, and his arguments are well worth reading."[3] Another critic of the same work opined: "[This collection] reveals the Black Panther leader to be intelligent and articulate. He discusses movingly the needs of his people, the oppressed people of the United States, and indeed of other nations as well. The work also shows, however that Newton has many simplistic notions about the nature of America. He makes constant references to Marxist analogies. The doctrine of the oppressed and the oppressors becomes an all-consuming concept with him. . . . However Newton should be read because he is intelligent [and] because he does represent one point of view that is important today."[4] By contrast, another reviewer of this same work (with an apparent ax to grind) wrote in the *Saturday Review*, "[This is] a badly written Marxist interpretation of Afro-American life that few readers will want to finish. . . . [The author] is disappointing as a speaker—many of these political writings were delivered as speeches and, as a theoretician, he is worse."[5] The most objective yet critical assessment of *To Die for the People* was published in the *Nation*. In it, the author points out that Newton's mind runs along didactic and tactical rather than scholarly lines.[6] This point is not without merit, since Newton's ideas on a number of foreign and domestic issues are insightful, but he doesn't draw from or build on the writings of other intellectuals on similar subjects the way in which Stokely Carmichael does in his much celebrated book, *Black Power*.

Assessments of *Revolutionary Suicide*, Newton's second book, were equally harsh. One writer alleges that Newton's revolutionary rhetoric and faulty logic stand in the way of a reader's full understanding of the Black Power movement.[7] Along the same lines, another reviewer commented: "*Revolutionary Suicide* is a rather carefully thought-out apologia for the Black Panthers; the anti-white ideology is played down in an apparent effort to represent the party as a legitimate and respectable political organization. Unfortunately, Newton feels compelled to discuss philosophical theory—without much success."[8] The reviewer ends with a back-handed compliment, saying, "However, he writes well, and his book will be most useful to those interested in the Black Panther's gradual move into the political mainstream."[9]

In Search of Common Ground is a work coauthored with Erik Erikson, the renowned Harvard psychiatrist. Before proceeding with a discussion concerning the book's reception, it would be useful to talk briefly about the way in which this project came to fruition. This book was derived from discussions between Newton and Erikson that took place over three meetings. The venue for the first two meetings was a formal colloquium set on the campus of Yale University in 1971. What the promoters of this seminar, and indeed many of those in attendance, had hoped for was a scenario where Newton was going to show up in full Panther regalia with shotgun in tow and shouting such familiar slogans as "Off the Pig," "Power to the People," and "Down with the Power Structure." On the other hand, Erikson was expected to be cerebral and psychoanalytic, which would make for a combustible yet lively production. However, the students were disappointed because the meeting never developed into the confrontational type of episode they had hoped it would. Students tried to lure Newton into being the militant activist they had come to know over the years. Nonetheless, Newton would not sway from his original intention, which was to discuss matters of an intellectual nature. By contrast, Erikson was slated to be the pensive clinician and professor. The idea that Newton, adorned with gold horned-rimmed glasses, would come to these meetings with the purpose of presenting ideas in a careful and well-thought-out manner was unfathomable for many of the Ivy Leaguers. Hence, when Newton ventured into such heady territory as dialectical materialism; the philosophical ideas of Hegel, Kant, and Peirce; and the psychoanalytical theories of Freud, Jung, James, and Erikson, many were taken aback with disappointment. Radicals were disappointed because they wanted sterner words from the revolutionary they had come to idolize, moderates because they were anticipating another kind of entertainment, and conservatives because the sheer temperateness of Newton's demeanor deflated the indignation they were ready to exude.

In the following pages I will review a number of more concrete and specific criticisms of Newton's work and assess them for accuracy, relevance, strength of argument, and overall merit. Recall that the first reviewer of *To Die for the People*, remarked that Newton has many simplistic notions about the nature of America and about the nature of the American people. To support this point, the reviewer contends that for Newton, "the oppressor is the white man who has the money and the guns. And this is the man blacks should fight."[10] A close reading of this book shows that Newton's perception of the oppressor evolved over time. Early on in Newton's political development, he, like Malcolm X, viewed all whites as the oppressor, although Newton never went so far as to believe that all whites were devils as Malcolm did. But, like Malcolm, as Newton matured intellectually, he began to abstain from making blanket condemnation statements about whites. Indeed, Newton's evolution on this issue took considerably less time than Malcolm's, whose egalitarian outlook did not crystallize until one or two years before his death. Not long after the founding of the Black Panther Party, Newton began to make a distinction between the oppressor—that is, the white ruling class and its agents of oppression—and the white proletariat, which, like the black working class, is also oppressed. For Newton, the oppressor was, to use Panther rhetoric, the avaricious capitalist, black or white, whose wealth was derived from keeping others subjugated. The enemy, as Eldridge Cleaver always put it, is a three-tiered oppressor: the big-time tycooning avaricious businesspersons, the lying demagogic tricky politicians, and the fascist pig cops, militia, and agents who work for the avaricious, demagogic ruling class.[11] Newton realized that if blacks were to wage an unyielding and successful revolutionary struggle against these agents of oppression, it would be in the best interest of blacks to ally with others (including whites) whose own self-interest is to seek a world free of injustice.

Later on in this essay, the reviewer states that "Newton has really lost sight of the contemporary black situation."[12] He goes on to assert that despite what Newton says, the United States is finally making progress in race relations. The reviewer incredibly cites his position as executive director of Community Progress Council of York County, Pennsylvania, as evidence that race relations were improving in this country: "In my current position, I work with numerous blacks. My Board of Directors is led by the black leadership of York County, Pennsylvania, and I, a white man, take direction from that Board. It was they who selected me for my current position and it is they who, in determining policy and personnel changes at the highest levels, have never thought in terms of color but merely of getting a job done."[13]

What this reviewer fails to realize is that there has always been some black tokenism within the white Establishment. The racial makeup of the Board of Directors of York County, Pennsylvania, was not and may never be representative of the racial configuration of boards of directors across the country. Second, that the black leadership of York County, Pennsylvania, selected a white to be the executive director does not indicate an improvement in race relations. Historically, whites have always enjoyed a degree of equity when blacks are in charge; the issue is and always has been that blacks have received an unequal portion of America's bounty when whites are in charge. Simply put, whites have never supported blacks at the rate that blacks have supported whites. The reviewer closes by saying inexplicably, "It would be much better for Newton and his followers if they would put aside their excessive reliance on doctrine and theory and come to grips with the ever changing reality that is contemporary America."[14]

Another critique of Newton's work that deserves mentioning is one where the writer concludes that Newton's pronouncements on doctrinal matters "are not of much interest; when he has an intriguing idea he lacks the ability to develop it or place it in an appropriate theoretical context."[15] Missing from this review are examples that show Newton's analysis to be lacking in substance and context. One could argue that when Newton writes about the correct handling of a revolution he places it in its proper context when he references the writings of Ho Chi Min, Mao Zedong, and Kim Il Sung and draws parallels to the revolutions that occurred in Cuba, China, Kenya, and Algeria. Although the political, social, and economic terrain in the United States may be different from those countries in a number of ways, Newton controls for this by extrapolating from these historic events what he deems applicable to the liberation of oppressed peoples in the United States while discarding that which has little relevance. Other examples of Newton's ability to develop ideas and place in them in their proper context can be found in the chapters on black capitalism, prisons, and the relevance of the church.

A more recent critique of *To Die for the People* reiterates almost the same criticism—that Newton lacks the ability to develop or explain his ideas fully. Unlike the reviewer discussed previously, this writer tries to support his claims with relevant examples. In *Black Power Ideologies*, political scientist John McCartney writes that Newton argues that a prerequisite for mastering nature is the use of the scientific method, which Newton defines as the exercise of "disinterest" while examining, measuring, and analyzing nature and society. McCartney goes on to say that Newton never clearly distinguishes between "uninterest," which he says means a total lack of interest in a scientific method, and "disinterest," which he sees as essential for successfully practicing the scientific method.[16] In other words, from McCartney's standpoint, Newton never clearly explains how an attitude of disinterest can be exercised toward a problem or process one is "interested" in investigating. "He simply leaves this intriguing paradox unexplained."[17]

Again, a careful reading of that passage reveals that Newton does defines what he means by "uninterest" and "disinterest." He argues that in order to understand a particular phenomenon, science developed what is called the scientific method. One of the characteristics of this method is "disinterest." Disinterest does not mean that the researcher is devoid of any interest in the study. Disinterest means that the researcher has no preplanned investment in the study's outcome. In other words, the researcher does not promote an outcome but simply collects the data and analyzes it. In so doing, the researcher begins with a basic premise. After the researcher agrees on the premise or hypothesis and collects the data, logic, impartiality, and consistency are all that is required to test that hypothesis.

McCartney's second point—that Newton falsely identifies Marx as the founder of dialectical materialism because, according to Newton, Marx successfully integrated Immanuel Kant's theory of pure reason with the rules of the scientific method—is partly accurate. McCartney is correct when he says that nowhere does Marx incorporate Kant's theory of pure reason.[18] Kant believed in strict separation between mind and body and that the notion that everything we know comes through our senses cannot be true. What we know does not come from our senses but rather from our minds. Kant says the senses are disorganized, the mind then comes in and organizes them. Marx says senses are already organized because the world is orderly. Organization is a product of development, not a snapshot with an eternal form.

McCartney's final point is that Newton's claim that Marx was the first great ideologist of dialectical materialism is wrong because Marx's first statement about "dialectical materialism" was made between 1844 and 1848, under the stimulus of Feuerbach's materialist interpretation of Hegel, which was done in the late 1830s to early 1840s.[19] McCartney is again correct—Marx did not precede Feuerbach on the question of dialectical materialism, but Marx went further in his analysis. In other words, Feuerbach did not make the final step, whereas Marx did; Marx said that we are material beings in a material world, which develops dialectically. Because Marx made this final step one could make the argument, as Newton did, that Marx was indeed the grandfather of dialectical materialism.

Reviews of *Revolutionary Suicide* were less substantive than McCartney's critique. Several reviews of the book were of a petty and sarcastic nature. One review begins by critiquing *Revolutionary Suicide* as an appropriate title for the book. The reviewer states, "The author devotes a considerable amount of effort, in the first part of this work, to differentiating 'revolutionary suicide,' a title more in keeping with its content might have been: Poverty, Policemen, Courts, Schools and Prisons."[20] Furthermore, the writer asserts, "In developing programs and political strategy to deal with the political and economic needs of the poor, Newton would have done well to have consulted with such blacks as Carl Stokes, former mayor of Cleveland; Mayor Richard Hatcher of Gary, Indiana, and newly elected Mayor [Tom] Bradley of Los Angeles."[21] The writer maintains that these men have demonstrated their astuteness in interpreting the mood, needs, and aspirations of black people. Interestingly, Bradley's legacy includes accusations by many in the black community that his administration neglected inner-city black communities. Moreover, given the numerous awards, certificates, and citations that the Black Panther Party received in recognition of the programs and services the organization provided disadvantaged communities throughout the country, one might wonder why Stokes, Hatcher, and Bradley did not consult the Black Panthers. In addition, the reviewer says that when "Newton confines his remarks and explanations to domestic problems and institutions with which he is familiar, his style and the substance of his arguments is [sic] at times informative and persuasive. However, his arguments in relation to international politics are shallow and his sweeping unsubstantiated generalizations are unimpressive."[22] Here again the author fails to substantiate his charges with examples that support his argument, thereby being guilty of the very weakness with which he charges Newton. Two other separate writers went so far as to express some doubt as to how much of this book was written by Newton. One reviewer points out that the first page says it was written "with the assistance of another author, so it is difficult to tell where Newton leaves off and the other author begins."[23] "Having seen Newton recently on [the television show] *Firing Line* where he philosophized incomprehensibly, I've some doubts as to how much of this quite cogent book is Newton's own," said another reviewer.[24] At the same time, this same reviewer incorrectly identifies Newton as the Panthers' information minister rather than the correct title of minister of defense. The critique ends with "the back cover has

Newton barechested and pensive, suggesting a future career should he abandon white baiting: Harry Belafonte II. But can he sing as well as he shoots?"[25] The glaring mistake about Newton's title and the silly fashion in which the reviewer closes his essay make one wonder just how seriously this critique should be taken.

The same reviewer who implied that much of the book was written by someone other than Newton seemed determined to paint Newton as a hatemonger and separatist. The writer repeatedly uses the word "hate" when referring to Newton. He says that Newton has a violent hatred for the Establishment. Later the reviewer states that Newton displays a fanatical hatred of the police and law enforcement. The writer also says that "at a time when the nation is trying to enforce good civil rights laws with sensible integration of schools and public facilities, Newton is pushing actively for segregation rather than integration."[26] This criticism is puzzling since it was levied at a time when Newton began to view conventional politics as an avenue for black uplift. At the end of the article, the author refers to the Black Panther Party as a "hate army." A mere cursory reading of Newton's writings reveals that Newton was not one to harbor hate against individuals or things. Rather, what Newton hated was the reality that historically blacks have been awarded fewer jobs, received an inferior education, given fewer rights under the law, and had less power to make and enforce public policy. Simply put, what Newton hates is the inferior position to which whites have strategically consigned blacks. That this writer would charge Newton with being consumed with hatred is perplexing, for in James Baldwin's essay, "On Being 'White' . . . and Other Lies," Baldwin wrote, "Antiblack racism is America's longest hatred."[27]

Like most books, Newton's works are clearly not without weaknesses. While some of the criticisms were relevant and well founded, many of the criticisms were ill informed and misguided. It is important for a reviewer to describe a book in balanced terms so that the reader can make an independent judgment of it. In addition, attacking a work because one disagrees with the author's politics, even though the author's politics have nothing to do with the work at hand, is unacceptable. In nearly every write-up the reviewer was guilty of (intentionally and unintentionally) the second and negligent in executing the first. On a number of occasions the reviewer seemed to focus more on Newton and his organization instead of critiquing Newton's words. A perfect example of this can be found in a review of *Revolutionary Suicide* titled "Power to Whom?," an obvious play on the phrase "Power to the People" commonly associated with the Panthers. In his assessment of the book, Colin Wilson compared Newton to a deranged serial killer. Wilson recalled: "A few weeks ago I was reading one of the most terrifying books I have ever read; *Killer*, by Thomas Gaddis and James Long, the journal of a mass murderer named Panzram who killed 21 people out of sheer hatred of society and its justice. It is frightening because Panzram was *also* [my emphasis] basically decent and intelligent, and you can see the logic of his life long 'act of revenge' against society. After the sickening atmosphere of that book, *Revolutionary Suicide* is like a breath of fresh air. Newton is basically as illogical as Panzram; but at least he has developed his intelligence and learned to express himself."[28]

Whether done intentionally or unintentionally, the indulgence in character assassination, petty fault-finding, and the subjectivity in which most of the reviews/critiques were written help to undermine Newton's credibility as a serious student of politics. Granted, for the most part Newton's books are not scholarly, but they show him to be an evolving theorist who was constantly wrestling with complex theoretical issues—some of which had been ignored in part or gone unnoticed by many in the Black Power movement. In addition, Newton's books are an indispensable resource for understanding his thought processes and the Black Panther Party's aims, struggles, and evolution, as well as the hatred that the government harbors against those it considers a threat to the tranquility of the American democratic social order.

What We Want/What We Believe: Black Panther Party Platform and Program

1. We want freedom. We want power to determine the destiny of our Black Community.

We believe that Black people will not be free until we are able to determine our destiny.

2. We want full employment for our people.

We believe that the federal government is responsible and obligated to give every man employment or a guaranteed income. We believe that if the white American business will not give full employment, then the means of production should be taken from the businessmen and placed in the community so that the people of the community can organize and employ all of its people and give a high standard of living.

3. We want an end to the robbery by the capitalist of our Black Community.

We believe that this racist government has robbed us and now we are demanding the overdue debt of forty acres and two mules. Forty acres and two mules was promised 100 years ago as restitution for slave labor and mass murder of Black people. We will accept the payment in currency which will be distributed to our many communities. The Germans are now aiding the Jews in Israel for the genocide of the Jewish people. The Germans murdered six million Jews. The American racist has taken part in the slaughter of over fifty million Black people: therefore we feel that this is a modest demand that we make.

4. We want decent housing, fit for shelter of human beings.

We believe that if the white landlords will not give decent housing to our Black community, then the housing and the land should be made into cooperatives so that our community, with government aid, can build and make decent housing for its people.

5. We want education for our people that exposes the true nature of this decadent American society. We want education that teaches us our true history and our role in the present-day society.

We believe in an educational system that will give to our people a knowledge of self. If a man does not have knowledge of himself and his position in society and the world, then he has little chance to relate to anything else.

6. We want all Black men to be exempt from military service.

We believe that Black people should not be forced to fight in the military service to defend a racist government that does not protect us. We will not fight and kill other people of color in the world who, like Black people, are being victimized by the white racist government of America. We will protect ourselves from the forces and violence of the racist police and the racist military, by whatever means necessary.

7. We want an immediate end to Police Brutality and Murder of Black people.

We believe we can end police brutally in our Black community by organizing Black self-defense groups that are dedicated to defending our Black community from racist police oppression and brutality. The Second Amendment to the Constitution of the United States gives a right to bear arms. We therefore believe that all Black people should arm themselves for self-defense.

8. We want freedom for all Black men held in federal, state, county and city prisons and jails.

We believe that all Black people should be released from the many jails and prisons because they have not received a fair and impartial trial.

9. We want all Black people when brought to trial to be tried in court by a jury of their peer group or people from their Black communities, as defined by the Constitution of the United States.

We believe that the courts should follow the United States Constitution so that Black people will receive fair trials. The 14th Amendment of the U.S. Constitution gives a man a right to be tried by his peer group. A peer is a person from a similar economic, social, religious, geographical, environmental, historical and racial background. To do this the court will be forced to select a jury from the Black community from which the Black defendant came. We have been, and are being tried by all-white juries that have no understanding of the "average reasoning man" of the Black community.

10. We want land, bread, housing, education, clothing, justice and peace. And as our major political objective, a United Nations-supervised plebiscite to be held throughout the Black colony in which only Black colonial subjects will be allowed to participate, for the purpose of determining the will of Black people as to their national destiny.

When, in the course of human events, it becomes necessary for one people to dissolve the political bands which have connected them with another, and to assume, among the powers of the earth, the separate and equal station to which the laws of nature and natures God entitle them, a decent respect to the opinions of mankind requires that they should declare the causes which impel them to the separation.

We hold these truths to be self-evident, that all men are created equal: that they are endowed by their Creator with certain unalienable rights; that among these are life, liberty, and the pursuit of happiness. That, to secure these rights, governments are instituted among men, deriving their just powers from the consent of the governed; that, whenever any form of government becomes destructive of these ends. it is the right of the people to alter or to abolish it, and to institute a new government, laying its foundation on such principles, and organizing its powers in such form, as to them shall seem most likely to effect their safety and happiness. Prudence, indeed, will dictate that governments long established should not be changed for light and transient causes; and, accordingly, all experience hath shown, that mankind are more disposed to suffer, while evils are sufferable, than to right themselves by abolishing the forms to which they are accustomed. But, when a long train of abuses and usurpations, pursuing invariably the same object, evinces a design to reduce them under absolute despotism, it is their right, it is their duty, to throw off such government, and to provide new guards for their future security.

Preface

1. Charles Evers, "The Black American and the Press," in *The Black Politician: His Struggle for Power*, ed. Mervyn Dymally (Belmont, Calif.: Duxbury Press, 1971), 72.

2. Hanes Walton Jr. and Robert C. Smith, *American Politics and the African American Quest for Universal Freedom* (New York: Addison-Wesley Longman, 2000), 106.

3. Eldridge Cleaver, interview by Charles E. Jones, Virginia Beach, Va., March 24, 1995.

4. John T. McCartney, *Black Power Ideologies: An Essay in African-American Thought* (Philadelphia: Temple University Press, 1992), 133.

5. "Huey in Scandinavia," *Black Panther*, March 31, 1973, 11.

6. Huey P. Newton, *Revolutionary Suicide* (New York: Harcourt Brace Janovich, 1973), 180–81.

7. "I Cannot Be Intimidated Because I Have Given My Life to the People," *Black Panther*, 1978.

8. Michael E. Jennings Jr., "Social Theory and Transformation in the Pedagogy of Dr. Huey P. Newton," *Educational Foundations* (winter 1999): 79–96.

9. Cornish Rogers, "Demythologizing Huey Newton," *Christian Century*, August 15–22, 1973, 795.

10. The most widely known transgressions include the alleged shooting and murder of a seventeen-year-old prostitute and assault with a deadly weapon in connection with the pistol-whipping of his tailor. Both of these events transpired in 1974.

11. Georg Wilhelm Friedrich Hegel, *Introduction to the Philosophy of History*, trans. John Sibree (New York: Dover, 1956), 91–99.

12. Jan N. Pieterse, *White on Black: Images of Africa and Blacks in Western Popular Culture* (New Haven, Conn.: Yale University Press, 1992), 34.

13. David Hume, "Of National Characters," in *The Philosophical Works*, ed. Thomas Hill Green and Thomas Hodge Grose, vol. 3 (Aalen: Scientia Verlag), 252 n.1.

14. Emmanuel C. Eze, "The Color of Reason: The Idea of 'Race' in Kant's Anthropology," in *Post Colonial African Philosophy: A Critical Reader*, ed. Emmanuel Eze (London: Blackwell, 1997), 130.

15. Maria Mootry, "Confronting Racialized Bioethics: New Contract on Black America," *Western Journal of Black Studies* 24 (spring 2000): 2.

16. Richard J. Herrnstein and Charles Murray, *The Bell Curve: Intelligence and Class Structure in American Life* (New York: Free Press, 1994).

17. Charles W. Mills, *The Racial Contract* (Ithaca, N.Y.: Cornell University Press, 1997), 96.

18. Hugh Pearson, *The Shadow of the Panther* (Reading, Mass.: Addison Wesley, 1994).

Introduction

1. Louis G. Heath, ed., *Off the Pigs! The History and Literature of the Black Panther Party* (Metuchen, N.J.: Scarecrow Press, 1976), ix.

2. Lori Olszewski and Rick DelVecchio, "Huey Newton Shot to Death in West Oakland," *San Francisco Chronicle*, August 23, 1989.

3. William Brand and Larry Spears, "Friends and Foes Remember Newton: Visionary, Thug," *Oakland Tribune*, August 23, 1989.

4. "The Black Panthers' Two Paths," *New York Times*, August 24, 1989.

5. Stanley Crouch, "Huey P. Newton: RIP," *New Republic* (September 18–25, 1989), 10.

6. Pearson, *Shadow of a Panther*, 8.

7. Bob Avakian, *Bob Avakian Talks about Huey Newton and the Panthers* (Chicago: The Revolutionary Worker, 1991), 6.

8. T. Harry Williams, "The Gentleman from Louisiana: Demagogue or Democrat?" *Journal of Southern History* 26 (February 1960): 3–21; T. Harry Williams, *Huey Long* (New York: Vintage, 1969).

9. Williams, "The Gentleman from Louisiana," 3–21; Williams, *Huey Long*.

10. Aldon Morris, *The Origins of the Civil Rights Movement* (New York: Free Press, 1984), 1.

11. Digby Diehl, "The Black Panther Party Is Not a Separatist Party," *Washington Post*, August 16, 1972.

12. "We Have to Attend to Our People: An Interview with Comrade Huey P. Newton," *Black Panther*, September 2, 1972, 12.

13. Newton, *Revolutionary Suicide*, 20.

14. Newton, "We Have to Attend to Our People."

15. Gene Marine, *The Black Panthers* (New York: Signet, 1969), 15.

16. Newton, *Revolutionary Suicide*.

17. Ibid., 67–70.

18. Ibid., 29.

19. Malcolm X with Alex Haley, *The Autobiography of Malcolm X* (New York: Grove Press, 1964), 179.

20. Marine, *Black Panthers*, 16.

21. Newton, *Revolutionary Suicide*, 50.

22. Ibid.

23. Ibid., 78.

24. Pearson, *Shadow of the Panther*, 284.

25. Huey P. Newton, "The Dialectics of Nature," unpublished manuscript, 1974.

26. Huey P. Newton, "The Historical Origins of Existentialism and the Common Denominators of Existential Philosophy," unpublished manuscript, 1979.

Out of the Ashes of Despair Rises a Militant Phoenix: The Birth of the Black Panther Party

1. *Seale on Ice: An Exclusive, Uncensored Interview with the Black Panther Leader*, 59 min., Center for Cassette Studies, 1970–71.

2. Huey P. Newton, *To Die for the People* (New York: Random House, 1972), 63.

3. The Philadelphia-based Revolutionary Action Movement (RAM) was founded by Maxwell Stanford in the early 1960s. One of the arguments RAM put forth was that in order for conditions to improve for the black masses, certain conservative black leaders as well as oppressive and racist white leaders would have to be killed.

4. Newton, "Historical Origins of Existentialism," 77–78.

5. Newton, *Revolutionary Suicide*, 80.

6. Ibid., 71.

7. Huey P. Newton, *War Against the Panthers: A Study of Repression in America* (New York: Harlem River Press, 1996), 27.

8. Eldridge Cleaver, "On Cleaver," *Ramparts*, December 14–28, 1968, 10.

9. Gerard J. DeGroot, *Student Protest: The Sixties and After* (New York: Longman, 1998).

10. Paula Giddings, *When and Where I Enter* (New York: William Morrow, 1984.

11. "NAACP Claims Brutality by Police in L.A.," *Los Angeles Times*, February 19, 1962, in NAACP Papers Group 111, Folder: A243, Manuscript Division, Library of Congress; Yohuru R. Williams, *Black Politics/White Power* (Naugatuck, CT: Brandywine Press, 2000).

12. Ibid.

13. Ibid.

14. Brian T. Downes, "A Critical Re-examination of the Social and Political Characteristics of Riot Cities," *Social Science Quarterly* 51 (December 1970): 349–60.

15. In July 1967, President Lyndon B. Johnson set up this commission, headed by Governor Otto Kerner of Illinois, to investigate the origins and causes of the uprisings and to make recommendations to prevent or contain such disorders in the future.

16. Robert H. Brisbane, *Black Activism: Racial Revolution in the United States 1954–1970* (Valley Forge, Pa.: Judson Press, 1974), 171.

17. Martin Luther King Jr., *The Trumpet of Conscience* (New York: Harper & Row, 1968), 57.

18. Kay Boyle, *The Long Walk at San Francisco State* (New York: Grove Press, 1970), 102.

19. Ibid., 102–3.

20. Paul Takagi, "A Garrison State in 'Democratic' Society," *Crime and Social Justice* 1 (spring/summer 1974): 29.

21. Henry Hampton and Steve Fayer, eds., *Voices of Freedom* (New York: Bantam Books, 1990), 351.

22. Earl Anthony, *Spitting in the Wind: The True Story Behind the Legacy of the Black Panther Party* (Santa Monica, Calif.: Roundtable Publishing, 1990), 30.

23. Boyle, *Long Walk*, 101.

24. Malcolm X, *The Autobiography of Malcolm X*.

25. V. I. Lenin, "What Is to Be Done?," in *Lenin, Selected Works* (New York: International Publishers, 1936), 2.

26. Régis Debray, *Revolution in the Revolution?* (New York: MR Press, 1967).

27. Huey P. Newton, "A Newspaper Is the Voice of a Party," *Black Panther*, March 13, 1971, 15.

28. Jonina M. Abron, "Raising the Consciousness of the People: The Black Panther Intercommunal News Service, 1967–1980," in *Voices from the Underground: Insider Histories of the Vietnam Era Underground Press*, ed. Ken Wachsberger (Tempe, Az.: Mica Press, 1993).

29. Newton, *To Die for the People*, 60.

30. Roland Freeman, interview by author, Los Angeles, July 2, 1993.

31. According to the evidence of Jean Powell, former Black Panther Party national secretary, testifying before the Senate Permanent Investigations Sub-Committee in 1969, in the Spivack Report 4:4, June 30, 1969; Steve McCutheon, interview by Charles E. Jones and Judson L. Jeffries, Oakland, Calif., June 6, 1992; Freeman interview.

32. Lee Rainwater, "The Problems of Lower Class Culture," *Journal of Social Issues* 26 (spring 1970): 133.

33. F. H. Giddings, *Principles of Sociology* (New York: MacMillan, 1896).

34. Robert Ezra Parks and Ernest W. Burgess, *Introduction to the Science of Sociology* (Chicago: University of Chicago Press, 1921), 220.

35. Lee Rainwater, "Neighborhood Action and Lower-Class Style," in *Neighborhood Organization for Community Action*, ed. John B. Turner (New York: National Association of Social Workers, 1968), 10.

36. Karl Marx and Freidrich Engels, "Manifesto of the Communist Party," in *The Marx Engels Reader*, ed. Robert C. Tucker (New York: W. W. Norton, 1978), 474, 482.

37. Mao Tse Tung, *Quotations from Chairman Mao Tse Tung* (Peking: Foreign Languages Press, 1972).

38. CLR James, "The Revolutionary Answer to the Negro Problem in the U.S." (1948), in *The CLR James Reader*, ed. Anna Grimshaw (New York: Blackwell, 1992), 182–89.

39. H. Bruce Franklin, "The Lumpenproletariat and the Revolutionary Youth Movement," *Monthly Review* 21 (January 1970): 10–25.

40. Everett Cherrington Hughes and Helen MacGill Hughes, *Where Peoples Meet: Racial and Ethnic Frontiers* (Glencoe, Ill.: Free Press, 1952).

41. Manning Marable, *The Crisis of Color and Democracy* (Monroe, Maine: Common Courage Press, 1992), 205.

42. Maurice Cornforth, *Materialism and the Dialectical Method* (New York: International Publishers, 1971), 194.

43. "Odyssey of Huey Newton," *Time*, November 13, 1978, 38–39.

44. Floyd W. Hayes III, "Black Consciousness and the Black Student's Union," unpublished manuscript, 1968.

45. Robert F. Williams, *Negroes with Guns* (1962; reprint, Chicago: Third World Press, 1973). The idea of patrolling the police did not originate with the Black Panther Party. A group called the Community Action Program (CAP) in Los Angeles first started patrolling the police in 1965 but without the open use of guns. If they were armed, they did not let on that they were. It is also believed that the Deacons for Defense and Justice in Louisiana patrolled the police in the 1960s but with gun in hand.

46. Bobby Seale, interview by Charles E. Jones, Atlanta, October 24, 1996.

47. Newton, *Revolutionary Suicide*, 166–67.

48. Anita Frankel, " 'New Panthers' Face Old Problems," *Ramparts*, February 24, 1978, 6; William Lee Brent, *Long Time Gone: A Black Panther's True-Life Story of His Hijacking and Twenty-five Years in Cuba* (New York: Times Books, 1996).

49. "An Interview with Bobby Seale," Black Panther Party, Community Information Center, Maryland State Chapter, n.d.

Distortions, Misrepresentations, and Outright Lies: Setting the Record Straight

1. William L. Van DeBurg, *A New Day in Babylon* (Chicago: University of Chicago Press, 1992).

2. Bobby G. Seale, "Free Huey," in *Rhetoric of Black Revolution*, ed. Arthur L. Smith (Boston: Allyn and Bacon, 1969), 180–81.

3. Benjamin Muse, *The American Negro Revolution: From Nonviolence to Black Power* (New York: Citadel Press, 1970), 242.

4. Ibid.

5. Robert Blauner, "Internal Colonialism and Ghetto Revolt," *Social Problems* 16 (fall 1969): 393–408.

6. Joel D. Aberbach and Jack L. Walker, "The Meanings of Black Power: A Comparison of White and Black Interpretations of a Political Slogan," *American Political Science Review* 64 (June 1970): 367–88.

7. William Van DeBurg, *A New Day in Babylon* (Madison: University of Wisconsin Press, 1992), 18.

8. Harold Cruse, *The Crisis of the Negro Intellectual* (New York: Quill, 1967), 555.

9. Erik H. Erikson and Huey P. Newton, *In Search of Common Ground* (New York: W. W. Norton, 1973), 136.

10. Ibid., 62.

11. Joe Blum and Dave Wellman, "A Prison Interview with Huey Newton," summer 1968.

12. Oliver C. Cox, *Caste, Class and Race: A Study in Social Dynamics* (New York: Doubleday, 1948).

13. Bernadine Dohrn, "White Mother Country Radicals," *New Left Notes*, July 29, 1968.

14. Ibid., 136

15. Philip Foner, ed., *The Black Panther Speaks* (New York: Lippincott, 1970), 57.

16. Todd Gitlin, *The Sixties: Years of Hope, Days of Rage* (New York: Bantam Books, 1987), 349.

17. Huey P. Newton, "To the RNA," *Black Panther*, December 6, 1969.

18. Newton, *Revolutionary Suicide*.

19. Newton, "To the RNA."

20. *The Late 60's in Review I*, 60 min., Education Research Group, 1969.

21. J. F. Rice, *Up on Madison Down on 75th Street* (Evanston, Ill.: The Committee, 1983), 17.

22. Ibid.

23. Clayborne Carson, *In Struggle: SNCC and the Black Awakening of the 1960s* (Cambridge: Harvard University Press, 1981); H. Rap Brown, interview by author, Binghamton, N.Y., November 1991. Said Brown: "The Black Panther Party concluded that I had outlived my usefulness."

24. Helen Stewart, "Buffering: The Leadership Style of Huey P. Newton, Co-Founder of the Black Panther Party" (master's thesis, Brandeis University, 1980), 66; Willie Ricks, interview by author, Los Angeles, May 10, 1998; Emory Douglas, interview by author, San Francisco, June 15, 1992.

25. Stokely Carmichael, *Stokely Speaks: Black Power Back to Pan-Africanism* (New York: Random House, 1971), 195.

26. Phil Hutchings, "What Program for Black Liberation Movement," *Radical Forum*, June 19, 1974.

27. Ricks interview; George M. Fredrickson, *Black Liberation* (New York:

Oxford University Press, 1995), 296; Stewart, "Buffering," 66; Heath, *Off the Pigs!*, 53.

28. Stokely Carmichael and Charles V. Hamilton, *Black Power: The Politics of Liberation* (New York: Vintage, 1992).

29. Lawrence Lader, *Power on the Left* (New York: W. W. Norton, 1979), 269.

30. Michael Newton, *Bitter Grain* (Los Angeles: Holloway House, 1980), 103.

31. Donald Freed, interview by author, July 20, 1993.

32. Brent, *Long Time Gone.*

33. Seale, *Seize the Time*, 208.

34. Floyd Hayes III and Francis A. Kiene III, " 'All Power to the People': The Political Thought of Huey P. Newton and the Black Panther Party," in *The Black Panther Party Reconsidered*, ed. Charles E. Jones (Baltimore: Black Classic Press, 1998), 166.

35. David Horowitz, Lecture, "The 1960s," University of Southern California at Los Angeles, April 22, 1997.

36. Charles E. Jones and Judson L. Jeffries, "Don't Believe the Hype: Debunking the Panther Mythology," in Jones, *Black Panther Party Reconsidered*, 35.

37. Alphonso Pinkney, *Red, Black and Green: Black Nationalism in the United States* (New York: Cambridge University Press), 176; Richard Parker, interview by author, Cambridge, Mass., May 24, 1995.

38. Ibid., 120. This point does not take away from the extraordinary job that Eldridge Cleaver did in publicizing Newton's situation.

39. *Black Panther*, August 30, 1969, 13.

40. Lader, *Power on the Left*, 333.

41. Ibid., 334.

42. George Katsiaficas, *The Imagination of the New Left: A Global Analysis of 1968* (Boston: South End Press, 1987), 77.

43. Erikson and Newton, *In Search of Common Ground*, 43.

44. Lader, *Power on the New Left*, 269.

45. Newton, *To Die for the People*, 152–55.

46. Pinkney, *Red, Black and Green*, 121.

47. Lader, *Power on the Left*, 269.

48. *Black Panther*, October 11, 1969.

49. Pinkney, *Red, Black and Green*, 122.

50. Gilbert Moore, *A Special Rage: A Black Reporter's Encounter with Huey P. Newton's Murder Trial, the Black Panthers and His Own Destiny* (New York: Harper & Row, 1971), 42.

51. Foner, *Black Panthers Speak*, xxvii.

52. Ibid.

53. According to a September 1984 definition offered by the Department of State, Bureau of Public Affairs.

54. Moore, *Special Rage*, 258.

55. Huey P. Newton, "The Black Panther Party," in *Racial Conflict: Tension and Change in American Society*, ed. Gary T. Marx (New York: Little Brown, 1971), 200.

56. Rogers, "Demythologizing Huey Newton."

57. Pinkney, *Red, Black and Green*, 99.

58. Rogers, "Demythologizing Huey Newton."

59. Jerome H. Skolnick, *The Politics of Protest: A Task Force Report Submitted to the National Commission on the Causes and Prevention of Violence* (New York: Simon and Schuster, 1969), 153.

60. "Prelude to a Revolution," interview with Huey P. Newton by John Evans, 76 min., Xenon Entertainment Group, 1988.

61. Newton, *Bitter Grain*, 108; Ron Jacobs, *The Way the Wind Blew: A History of the Weather Underground* (New York: Verso, 1997).

62. Hannah Arendt, *On Violence* (New York: Harcourt Brace and World, 1970), 5.

63. Edward Keating, *Free Huey* (New York: Dell, 1971), 1.

64. Newton, "Black Panther Party," 7.

65. Erikson and Newton, *In Search of Common Ground*, 63.

66. Ibid., 64.

67. Frederick Douglass, *The Life and Times of Frederick Douglass* (New York: Collier, 1962), 104–5.

68. Newton, *Revolutionary Suicide*, 246.

69. Erikson and Newton, *In Search of Common Ground*, 62.

70. Daniel James, *The Complete Bolivian Diaries of Che Guevara and Other Captured Documents* (London, 1968), 312, 551.

71. "Interview with Huey P. Newton," *Guardian* 5:22 (1970), 7.

72. Newton, "Black Panther Party," 7.

73. Herbert Marcuse, *A Critique of Pure Tolerance* (Boston: Beacon Press, 1966), 103.

74. Newton, *Revolutionary Suicide*, 111.

75. Ibid., 7.

76. The original statement said "We want an end to the robbery by the white man of our Black Community." This was later changed to "capitalist."

77. Pearson, *Shadow of the Panther*, 112.

78. Louis G. Heath, ed., *The Black Panther Leaders Speak* (Metuchen, N.J.: Scarecrow Press, 1976), 220–21.

79. Erikson and Newton, *In Search of Common Ground*, 89.

80. Newton, *Revolutionary Suicide*, 297.

81. "Huey Newton Interviewed," *Alameda (California) Times-Star*, January 31, 1972.

82. Newton, *To Die for the People*, 47.

83. Robert Allen, *Black Awakening in Capitalist America* (Garden City, N.Y.: Doubleday, 1969), 87.

84. Newton, *To Die for the People*, 47.

85. Newton, "Black Panther Party," 8.

86. Newton, *To Die for the People*, 102–3.

87. James Boggs, "Black Seventies," in *The Black Seventies*, ed. Floyd B. Barbour (Boston: Porter Sargent, 1970), 182–83.

88. Newton, *Revolutionary Suicide*, 330.

89. Newton, *To Die for the People*, 16–17, 44–45.

90. Erikson and Newton, *In Search of Common Ground*, 69.

91. Ibid.

92. Ibid., 70.

93. Huey P. Newton, "Huey P. Newton Talks to the Movement" (Chicago: The Movement, 1968).

94. Newton, *To Die for the People*, 14–15.

95. Ibid., 17.

96. Newton, *War Against the Panthers*, 94.

97. Joseph Stalin, *Foundations of Leninism*, vol. 10, *Selected Works* (New York: International Publishers, 1939), 136.

98. "Interview with Huey P. Newton," 7.

99. Newton, *To Die for the People*, xxi.

100. Huey P. Newton, "The Correct Handling of a Revolution," *Black Panther*, May 18, 1968.

Newton's View of People and the State

1. Erikson and Newton, *In Search of Common Ground*, 75.

2. Lester G. Crocker, *Rousseau's Social Contract* (Cleveland: Case Western Reserve University, 1968).

3. Newton, *Revolutionary Suicide*, 4.

4. Herbert Hendin, *Black Suicide* (New York: Basic Books, 1969).

5. Ibid., 4.

6. Fyodor Dostoevsky, *Crime and Punishment*, trans. Constance Garnett (New York: Heritage Club, 1938).

7. Newton, *Revolutionary Suicide*.

8. Newton, *To Die for the People*, 22.

9. Mao Tse Tung, *Quotations*.

10. Erikson and Newton, *In Search of Common Ground*, 116.

11. Elaine Brown, *A Taste of Power: A Black Woman's Story* (New York: Pantheon, 1992), 252.

12. Thomas Hobbes, *Leviathan* (New York: E. P. Dutton, 1914).

13. Huey P. Newton, "In Defense of Self-Defense," *Black Panther*, June 20, 1967.

14. Ibid.; Erikson and Newton, *In Search of Common Ground*.

15. Brown, *Taste of Power*, 252.

16. Newton, *Revolutionary Suicide*, 166.

17. Ibid., 165.

18. Ibid.

19. Newton, *To Die for the People*, 221.

20. Erikson and Newton, *In Search of Common Ground*, 141.

21. David Hilliard and Lewis Cole, *This Side of Glory* (Boston: Little Brown, 1992), 121.

22. "I Cannot Be Intimidated."

23. Ibid.

24. Jack Slater, "Huey Newton Speaks Out," *Los Angeles Times*, August 25, 1977.

25. "I Cannot Be Intimidated."

26. Judith N. Shklar, *American Citizenship: The Quest for Inclusion* (Cambridge: Harvard University Press, 1991), 85–86, 63–65, 91–94.

27. Newton, "In Defense of Self-Defense."

28. Ibid., 364.

29. Newton, *To Die for the People*, 17.

Critiquing Newton's Critique of Pan-Africanism

1. Immanuel Geiss, *The Pan-African Movement: A History of Pan-Africanism in America, Europe, and Africa*, trans. A. Keep (New York: Africana Publishing, 1974), 177.

2. Ibid., 190.

3. W. E. B. Dubois, *The World and Africa* (New York: International Publishers, 1965), 7.

4. Rayford Logan, "The Historical Aspects of Pan-Africanism, 1900–1945," in *Pan-Africanism Reconsidered*, ed. American Society of African Culture (Berkeley: University of California Press, 1962), 37–38.

5. Locksley Edmondson, "The Internationalization of Black Power: Historical and Contemporary Perspectives," *Mawazo* 1 (December 1968): 16–29.

6. Robert Allen, *Reluctant Reformers* (Washington, D.C.: Howard University Press, 1983), 239.

7. Adolph Reed, *W. E. B. DuBois and American Political Thought* (New York: Oxford University Press, 1997), 79.

8. Huey P. Newton, "On Pan-Africanism or Communism," unpublished manuscript, 1972.

9. Ibid.

10. Maulana Karenga, *Introduction to Black Studies* (Los Angeles: Sankore Press, 1993).

11. Blum and Wellman, "Prison Interview with Huey Newton."

12. Newton, "On Pan-Africanism or Communism."

13. DuBois, *World and Africa.*

14. Karenga, *Introduction to Black Studies.*

15. Newton, "On Pan-Africanism or Communism."

16. Frantz Fanon, *The Wretched of the Earth* (New York: Grove Press, 1963).

17. Malcolm X, *By Any Means Necessary* (New York: Grove Press, 1970).

18. Ibid.

19. Ibid., 50

20. Huey P. Newton, "On Pan-Africanism or Communism."

21. Stokely Carmichael, "A Declaration of War," transcript of speech, February 17, 1968, in Oakland, Calif., in *Running Man*, 1:1 (May–June 1968), 17–21.

22. Carmichael, *Stokely Speaks*, 202.

23. W. E. B. DuBois, "The Future of Africa—A Platform," in DuBois, *DuBois Speaks*, vol. 1, 649.

24. Reed, *W. E. B. DuBois*, 83.

25. Kwame Nkrumah, *Africa Must Unite* (New York: Frederick A. Praeger, 1963), 119.

26. Press Conference, "Huey Calls Stokely Carmichael a CIA Agent," August 26, 1970.

27. Elliot M. Rudwick, "DuBois versus Garvey: Race Propagandists at War," *Journal of Negro History* 28 (1959): 423, 426.

28. Kwame Nkrumah, *Neo-Colonialism: The Last Stage of Imperialism* (London: Nelson, 1965).

29. Huey P. Newton, "Uniting Against the Common Enemy," *Black Panther*, October 23, 1971.

30. Horace Campbell, "Pan-Africanism in the Twenty-First Century," in *Pan-Africanism: Politics, Economy and Social Change in the Twenty-First Century*, ed. Tajudeen Abdul-Raheem (New York: New York University Press, 1996), 216.

31. Yuri Smerten, *Kwame Nkrumah* (New York: International Publishers, 1987), 84.

32. Arthur S. Gakwandi, "Towards a New Political Map of Africa," in Abdul-Raheem, *Pan-Africanism*, 185.

33. Kwame Nkrumah, *Class Struggle in Africa* (New York: International Publishers, 1970), 25.

34. David E. Cronon, *Black Moses: The Story of Marcus Garvey and the*

Universal Negro Improvement Association (Madison: University of Wisconsin Press, 1955).

35. Nkrumah, *Class Struggle*, 26.

36. Rhett S. Jones, "Why Pan-Africanism Failed: Blackness and International Relations," *Griot* 14 (spring 1995): 58–69.

37. Rupert Emerson, "Pan-Africanism," *International Organization* 16 (spring 1962): 282.

The Party Line: The Ideological Development of the Black Panther Party

1. Martin R. Delany, "A Project for an Expedition of Adventure to the Eastern Coast of Africa," in *Black Brotherhood: Afro-Americans and African*, ed. Okon Edet (Lexington, Mass.: D. C. Heath, 1971), 71.

2. McCartney, *Black Power Ideologies*, 15.

3. Karenga, *Introduction to Black Studies*.

4. Walt Thompson, "What's Left of the Black Left?," *Ramparts*, June 1973, 53.

5. Ibid., 179.

6. Maulana Karenga, *Kawaida Theory: An Introductory Outline* (Inglewood, Calif.: Kawaidi Publications, 1980), 15.

7. David Pitney-Howard, *The Afro-American Jeremiad* (Philadelphia: Temple University Press), 12.

8. Erikson and Newton, *In Search of Common Ground*, 27–28.

9. "Interview with Huey P. Newton," 7.

10. Newton, "On Pan-Africanism or Communism," 4.

11. Brisbane, *Black Activism*, 177.

12. "Interview with Huey P. Newton," 7.

13. Sol Stern, "America's Black Guerrillas," *Ramparts*, September 2, 1967, 26.

14. Ibid., 180.

15. Ibid., 7; Robert Blauner, *Racial Oppression in America* (New York: Harper & Row, 1972).

16. Newton, *Bitter Grain*, 105.

17. McCartney, *Black Power Ideologies*, 31.

18. Newton, *To Die For The People*, 37.

19. Jimmy Mori, "The Ideological Development of the Black Panther Party," *Cornell Journal of Social Relations* 12 (spring 1977): 137–55.

20. Boyle, *Long Walk*, 135.

21. Mori, "Ideological Development," 137–55.

22. Allen, *Reluctant Reformers*, 324.

23. Jon Frappier, "Chase Goes to Harlem: Financing Black Capitalism," *Freedomways* 28 (April 1977): 23.

24. James Boggs, "The Myth and Irrationality of Capitalism." *Review of Black Political Economy* 1 (spring/summer 1970): 27–35.

25. "Newton Calls Constitution Outdated, Urges Socialism," *San Francisco Examiner and Chronicle*, September 6, 1970.

26. Ibid.

27. Jules Archer, *Revolution in Our Time* (New York: Julian Messner, 1971).

28. Foner, *Black Panthers Speak*, 51.

29. Ibid., 5.

30. Lader, *Power on the Left*, 270.

31. Foner, *Black Panthers Speak*, 229.

32. Archer, *Revolution in Our Time*, 51.

33. Lader, *Power on the Left*, 267–69.

34. "Newton Calls Constitution Outdated."

35. Ibid.

36. "Interview with Huey Newton," 7.

37. Lader, *Power on the Left*, 323.

38. Robert Rhodes, "Internationalism and Social Consciousness in the Black Community," *Freedomways* 12 (third quarter, 1972): 230.

39. *The Observer* (London), August 6, 1967; "Black Power in Britain," *Life* (October 16, 1967), 8–17; *East African Standard* (Nairobi), April 30, 1968; "The Black Man in Search of Power," *The Times New Team*; Charles Perkins, "Black Power," *Union Recorder* (published by Sydney University Students Union), June 13, 1968, 110–13 (Perkins, who is part aboriginal, was regarded by many as the Australian Martin Luther King). See also "Black Power May Emerge in Australia," *Nationalist* (Dar Es Salaam), August 23, 1968; Murray Barnard, "For Negroes in Halifax, Black Power v. Ping Pong," *Macleans* (Toronto), November 1967, 1.

40. Newton, *To Die for the People*, 31.

41. Heath, *Black Panther Leaders Speak*, 219.

42. Rhodes, "Internationalism," 230.

43. Newton, "Black Panther Party," 8.

44. Lader, *Power on the Left*, 271.

45. "Huey Calls Stokely Carmichael a CIA Agent."

46. *Ibid.*, 38.

47. Newton, *To Die for the People*, 199.

48. Foner, *Black Panthers Speak*, 145.

49. Newton, *To Die for the People*, 31.

50. Ibid., 178.

51. Heath, *Off the Pigs!*, 218.

52. Newton, *Bitter Grain*, 118.

53. Newton, *Revolutionary Suicide*, 324.

54. Newton, *To Die for the People*, 322.
55. Newton, "Intercommunalism: A Higher Level of Consciousness," unpublished manuscript, 7.
56. Erikson and Newton, *In Search Of Common Ground*, 31.
57. Ibid., 32.
58. Newton, *War Against the Panthers*, 28.
59. Erikson and Newton, *In Search Of Common Ground*, 25.
60. Jean-Jacque Rousseau, *Discourse on the Origins and Foundations of Inequality among Men*, trans. Maurice Cranston (London: Penguin, 1984).
61. Erikson and Newton, *In Search Of Common Ground*, 35.
62. Newton, "Intercommunalism."
63. Erikson and Newton, *In Search Of Common Ground*, 35.
64. Newton, *To Die for the People*, 37.

What Did He Do to Be So Black and Blue?: Blacks and the American Political, Economic, and Social Order

1. Newton, *To Die for the People*.
2. Alexis de Tocqueville, *Democracy in America*, ed. Mayer Lerner and Max Lerner (1835; reprint, New York: Harper & Row, 1966),
3. Newton, *To Die for the People*, 157.
4. Huey P. Newton, "Eliminate the Presidency," unpublished manuscript, 1974.
5. Huey P. Newton, "Towards a New Constitution," *Black Panther*, November 28, 1970, 9.
6. Ibid.
7. Newton, *To Die for the People*.
8. James Conyers and Walter Wallace, *Black Elected Officials* (New York: Russell Sage Foundation, 1976), 6.
9. Oscar Handlin, *The Newcomers: Negroes and Puerto Ricans in a Changing Metropolis* (Cambridge: Harvard University Press, 1959).
10. Robert Collier, interview by author, Binghamton, N.Y., November 1991; Charles "Cappy" Pinderhughes, interview by author, Cambridge, Mass., August 1993.
11. Heath, *Off the Pigs!*, 22.
12. James M. Washington, ed., *Testament of Hope: The Essential Writings of Martin Luther King, Jr.* (San Francisco: Harper & Row, 1986), 308.
13. Ibid.
14. Michael B. Preston, "Black Elected Officials and Public Policy," *Policy Studies Journal* (winter 1978): 196–201.
15. Huey P. Newton, "Culture and Liberation," *Tricontinental* 11 (March–April 1969): 196–201.

16. Joe R. Feagin, *Racist America: Roots, Current Realities, and Future Reparations* (New York: Routledge, 2000), 242.

17. Heath, *Off the Pigs!*, 380.

18. Allen, *Black Awakening*, 26.

19. Bureau of Census, "Census Bureau Announces Number of Americans in Poverty Up for Fourth Year Although Poverty Rate Unchanged, Household Income and Health Care Coverage Drop," press release, October 6, 1994.

20. Randall Robinson, *The Debt: What America Owes to Blacks* (New York: Plume, 2000), 228.

21. Floyd W. Hayes III, "New Class Power: The Political Role of Black Policy Specialists," *Negro Educational Review* (2001).

22. H. Bruce Franklin, *The Victim As Criminal and Artist* (New York: Oxford University Press, 1978).

23. Frank McCoy, "Can Clinton's Urban Policies Really Work?," *Black Enterprise*, June 1994, 182.

24. Ellis Cose, *The Rage of a Privileged Class* (New York: Harper Collins, 1993).

25. Erikson and Newton, *In Search of Common Ground*, 107–8.

26. Kenneth B. Clark, *Dark Ghetto: Dilemmas of Social Problems* (New York: Harper & Row, 1965).

27. Newton, *Revolutionary Suicide*, 19.

28. Alvin F. Poussaint, "Education and Black Self-Image," *Freedomways* 8 (fall 1968): 335.

29. Ibid., 19.

30. Ibid., 185.

31. Ibid., 22.

32. Erikson and Newton, *In Search of Common Ground*, 108.

33. *Special Report to the Congress: Mandatory Minimal Penalties in the Federal Criminal Justice System* (Washington, D.C.: U.S. Sentencing Commission, August 1991).

34. Robin D. G. Kelly, *Yo Mama's Dysfunctional: Fighting the Culture Wars in Urban America* (Boston: Beacon Press, 1997).

35. Kelley, *Yo Mama's Dysfunctional*.

36. Ronald J. Ostrow, "U.S. Imprisons Black Men at 4 Times S. Africa Rate," *Los Angeles Times*, January 5, 1991; Samuel Walker, Cassia Spohn, and Miriam DeLone, *The Color of Justice* (Belmont, Calif.: Wadsworth, 2000), 268.

37. *Special Report to the Congress*.

38. John W. Roberts, *From Trickster to Badman: The Black Folk Hero in Slavery and Freedom* (Philadelphia: University of Pennsylvania Press, 1989).

39. Benjamin J. Brawley, *A Social History of the American Negro* (New York: Macmillan 1921), 291–93.

40. Anthony J. Lemelle Jr., *Black Male Deviance* (Westport, Conn.: Praeger, 1995), 97.

41. Manning Marable, "The Third Reconstruction: Black Nationalism and Race in a Revolutionary America," *Social Text* 4 (fall 1981): 1–27.

42. Robinson, *Debt*, 101. Whether the state of Washington can be considered a racist state is debatable—although it should be noted that in 1998 Washingtonians overwhelmingly approved a resolution banning "preferential treatment" based on race or gender to any group in the public sector.

43. "Huey P. Newton Urges Release of Georgia's Unjustly Imprisoned," *Black Panther*, May 4, 1974, 5.

44. Lynora Williams, "Jim Crow: What the Judges Do in Private," *Guardian*, October 10, 1979.

45. Walker, Spohn, and DeLone, *Color of Justice*.

46. Mills, *Racial Contract*.

47. Guy Johnson, "The Negro and Crime," *Annals of the American Academy* 217 (1941): 98.

48. Huey P. Newton, "War without Terms: The Death of George Jackson," unpublished manuscript, 1979.

49. "Statement by Huey P. Newton at the Chicago, Illinois Coliseum, February 21, 1971," *Black Panther*, April 10, 1971, 3.

50. Reginald Major, *A Panther Is a Black Cat* (New York: Morrow, 1974), 198.

51. Ibid.

52. Jessica Mitford, *Kind and Usual Punishment: The Prison Business* (New York: Vintage, 1974), 215, 209–10.

53. *Sourcebook of Criminal Justice Statistics—1975* (Albany, N.Y.: U.S. Department of Justice, Criminal Justice Research Center, 1976), 587, 614.

54. Huey P. Newton, "Prison, Where Is Thy Victory," *Black Panther*, July 22, 1969, 11.

55. Huey P. Newton, "A Citizen's Peace Force," unpublished manuscript, 36.

56. Ibid.; Lynn Cooper et al., *The Iron Fist and the Velvet Glove: An Analysis of the U.S. Police* (Berkeley, Calif.: Center for Research on Criminal Justice, 1975), 152.

57. Cooper et al., *Iron Fist*, 152.

58. Marcus Pohlman, *Black Politics in White Conservative America* (New York: Longman, 1998), 57.

59. Archer, *Revolution in Our Time*.

60. Kenneth O'Reilly, *Racial Matters* (New York: Free Press, 1989).

61. Ibid., 111.

62. Joy Johnson, "Huey Newton in Prison: An Interview," *Ramparts*, September 1970, 5.

63. Francis Fox Piven and Richard Cloward, *Poor People's Movements* (New York: Pantheon, 1977), 182.

64. Stokely Carmichael, *Black Power*, audiocassette, University of California at Berkeley, April 1966.

65. Franklin, *Victim as Criminal and Artist*, 248.

66. Newton, "Prison, Where Is Thy Victory," 11.

67. Robert C. Smith, *We Have No Leaders* (New York: SUNY Press, 1996).

68. Marcus D. Pohlman, *Governing the Postindustrial City* (New York: Longman, 1993); Pohlman, *Black Politics*.

69. Smith, *We Have No Leaders*.

70. Tocqueville, *Democracy in America*, 356.

71. Anthony, *Spitting in the Wind*; Earl Anthony, interview by author, Los Angeles, June 20, 1992.

The "Bad Nigger" Personified

1. Benjamin Drew, *A North Side View of Slavery. The Refugee: On the Narrative of Fugitive Slaves in Canada* (1856; reprint, New York: New York Times and Arno Press, 1968), 219–20.

2. William H. Wiggins, "Jack Johnson as Bad Nigger: The Folklore of His Life," in *Contemporary Black Thought*, ed. Robert Chrisman and Nathan Hare (New York: Bobbs-Merrill, 1973), 53–70.

3. Eldridge Cleaver, *Post-Prison Writings and Speeches* (New York: Random House, 1969), 41.

4. H. C. Brearley, "Ba-ad Nigger," *South Atlantic Quarterly* 38 (fall 1939): 75–81.

5. Samuel M. Strong, "Negro-White Relationships as Reflected in Social Types," *American Journal of Sociology* 52 (1946): 24.

6. Tim Findley, "Huey Newton Twenty-five Floors from the Street," *Rolling Stone*, August 3, 1972, 30–32.

7. Roberts, *From Trickster to Badman*, 175–78.

8. Newton, *Revolutionary Suicide*.

9. Roberts, *From Trickster to Badman*, 175–78.

10. Lawrence Levine, *Black Culture and Black Consciousness* (New York: Oxford University Press, 1977).

11. L. D. Reddick, "The Negro as Southerner and American," in *The Southerner as American*, ed. Charles G. Sellers (New York: E. P. Dutton, 1966), 133.

12. Roger D. Abraham, "Some Varieties of Heroes in America," *Journal of the Folklore Institute* 3 (1966): 36.

13. Matthew Holden, *The Politics of the Black Nation* (New York: Chandler Publishing, 1972), 18.

14. Seale, *Seize the Time*, 16.

15. Newton, *Revolutionary Suicide*, 48.

16. Pearson, *Shadow of the Black Panther*, 317; Landon Williams, interview by author, San Francisco, June 20, 1992.

17. Claude McKay, *A Long Way from Home* (New York: Lee Furman, 1937).

18. Bull Connor was the racist police commissioner in Birmingham, Alabama, during the heyday of the Civil Rights movement.

19. Eldridge Cleaver, "Huey's Standard," *Black Panther*, March 15, 1970, 3.

20. Pearson, *Shadow of the Panther*, 215; Paul Bullock, *Watts: The Aftermath* (New York: Grove Press, 1971).

21. Marine, *Black Panthers*, 12.

22. Robert C. Tucker, "The Theory of Charismatic Leadership," *Daedalus* 97 (summer 1968): 731–56; Robert C. Tucker, "Personality and Political Leadership," *Political Science Quarterly* 92 (fall 1977): 383–400.

23. A. W. Singham, *The Hero and the Crowd in a Colonial Polity* (New Haven, Conn.: Yale University Press, 1968).

24. Max Weber, *From Max Weber: Essays in Sociology*, ed. and trans. H. H. Gerth and C. Wright Mills (New York: Oxford University Press, 1968), 742.

25. Brown, *Taste of Power*, 25.

26. Leon F. Litwick, *Been in the Storm So Long* (New York: Alfred A. Knopf, 1979), 292–315.

27. Seale, *Seize the Time*, 92–93.

28. Cleaver, *Post-Prison Writings*, 35.

29. Dymally, *Black Politician*, 1.

30. Brown, *Taste of Power*, 286–90.

31. Brearley, "Ba-ad Nigger."

32. Erikson and Newton, *In Search of Common Ground*, 111–12.

33. "Huey Newton: A Candid Conversation with the Embattled Leader of the Black Panther Party," *Playboy*, May 1973, 73.

34. Seale, *Seize the Time*, 102.

35. "Polynesian Panther Party 7-Point Platform Serves the People," *Black Panther*, July 6, 1974, 4.

36. Donald A. Downs, *Cornell '69: Liberalism and the Crisis of the American University* (Ithaca, N.Y.: Cornell University Press, 1999), 1.

37. Cleaver, *Post-Prison Writings*, 41.

38. Charles P. Henry, "The Political Role of the 'Bad Nigger.'" *Journal of Black Studies* 2 (June 1981): 461–83.

39. Charles P. Henry, *Culture and African American Politics* (Bloomington: Indiana University Press, 1990), 98.

Conclusion: The Legacy of Huey P. Newton and the Black Panther Party

1. Paul A. Baran, *A Collective Portrait* (New York: Monthly Review Press, 1965); Jeffrey C. Goldfarb, *Civility and Subversion: The Intellectual in Democratic Life* (New York: Cambridge University Press, 1998).
2. Mostafa Rejai, *Comparative Political Ideologies* (New York: St. Martin's, 1984), 59.
3. Erikson and Newton, *In Search of Common Ground*, 142.
4. Bobby G. Seale, *A Lonely Rage* (New York: Times Books, 1978), 153.
5. Newton, "Intercommunalism."
6. Sarah Craig, "Panther Leader Newton Slain: Early Gay-Rights Supporter Gunned Down," *Windy City Times*, August 31, 1989, 6.
7. Wayne Pharr, interview by author, Los Angeles, June 1, 1993; Jimmy Slater, interview by Charles E. Jones and Judson L. Jeffries, Oakland, Calif., June 15, 1992. Contrary to popular belief, this split did not occur along geographical lines. In other words, there was no split between East Coast and West Coast Panthers, as some researchers have suggested. Instead, the split occurred irrespective of geographical location. There were some New York Panthers who sided with Cleaver and some who sided with Newton. Likewise, in Oakland, there were some who sided with Newton and some who sided with Cleaver. The same can be said for various other chapters across the United States.
8. "The Hearst Nightmare," *Time*, April 29, 1974, 12.
9. Michael Parenti, *Democracy for the Few* (New York: St. Martin's, 1995); "Evidence and Intimidation of Fascist Crimes by U.S.A.," *Black Panther*, February 21, 1970.
10. Ibid., 164–68; Robert J. Goldstein, *Political Repression in Modern America 1870 to the Present* (New York: Schenkman, 1978). This number has been disputed by some who claim that no more than thirty Panthers were killed by police throughout the country.
11. Kenneth O'Reilly, *Racial Matters* (New York: Free Press, 1989), 297.
12. Parenti, *Democracy for the Few*.
13. Newton, *Revolutionary Suicide*, 291.
14. Yohuru R. Williams, "In the Name of the Law: The 1967 Shooting of Huey Newton and Law Enforcement's Permissive Environment," *Negro History Bulletin* (April–June 1997): 6–18.
15. Huey P. Newton, *Revolutionary Suicide*, 195.
16. "The Panthers and the Law," *Newsweek*, February 23, 1970, 30.

17. Hilliard and Cole, *This Side of Glory*, 35; Boyle, *Long Walk*.

18. "Huey Newton Talks to the Movement About the Black Panther Party, Cultural Nationalism, SNCC, Liberals and White Revolutionaries," unpublished pamphlet by the Movement.

19. Newton, *Revolutionary Suicide*, 195.

20. Cruse, *Crisis of the Negro Intellectual*; Karenga, *Introduction to Black Studies*; Karenga, *Kawaida Theory*.

21. Errol Henderson, "The Lumpenproletariat as Vanguard?," *Journal of Black Studies* 28 (November 1997): 171–99.

22. Stokely Carmichael, "Pan-Africanism—Land and Power," in *Modern Black Nationalism: From Marcus Garvey to Louis Farrakhan*, ed. William L. Van DeBurg (New York: New York University Press, 1997), 205.

23. Johnson, "Huey Newton in Prison," 5.

24. Ibid.; Hilliard and Cole, *This Side of Glory*, 328.

25. Cleaver, *Post-Prison Writings*, 42.

26. Holden, *Politics*, 107.

27. Curtis Powell, interview by author, Queens, N.Y., January 1992.

28. "Interview with Huey P. Newton by the Movement 1970," in *The Movement, 1964–1970*, ed. Clayborne Carson (Westport, Conn.: Greenwood Press, 1993), 422.

29. Ernesto Guevara, *Guerilla Warfare* (New York: Vintage, 1961).

30. Tse Tung, "Quotations," 262.

31. Michael Rodgers, "Some Quiet Hours with Huey Newton," *Esquire* 1972, 156–58, 232.

32. Nikhil Pal Singh, "The Black Panthers and the Undeveloped Country of the Left," in Jones, *Black Panther Party Reconsidered*, 97.

33. Hilliard and Cole, *The Side of Glory*, 318–21.

34. Collier interview.

35. Hayes and, "'All Power to the People.'"

36. Newton, "Intercommunalism."

37. Alprentice (Bunchy) Carter, "The Genius of Huey Newton," *Black Panther*, March 3, 1969.

38. Deborah Bremond, interview by Charles E. Jones and Judson L. Jeffries, Oakland, Calif., June 17, 1992; Yvonne Jenkins, interview by Charles E. Jones and Judson L. Jeffries, Marin County, Calif., June 16, 1992.

39. Al Amour, interview by author, Los Angeles, April 3, 1993; Collier interview.

40. Fanon, *Wretched of the Earth*.

41. Roy C. Macridis, *Contemporary Political Ideologies* (Boston: Little Brown, 1983), 237.

42. Slater interview. The Black Panther Party consisted of a wide array of individuals. Among its members were college graduates and Ph.D's, laborers, clerks, teachers, and students.

43. Collier interview; Powell interview; Pinderhuges interview; Freeman interview.

44. Carter, "Genius of Huey Newton."

45. Robert Staples, "American Racism and High Crime Rates: The Inextricable Connection," *Western Journal of Black Studies* 8 (summer 1984): 62–72.

46. Seale, *Seize the Time*, 36.

47. Dorothy Healey and Maurice Isserman, *Dorothy Healey Remembers: A Life in the American Communist Party* (New York: Oxford University Press, 1990), 212.

48. "Huey Newton Backs Race by Mrs. Chisholm," *New York Times*, April 28, 1972.

49. Bo Burlingham, "Huey Newton's Revival Meeting in Oakland," *Ramparts* 1972, 10–11.

50. Huey P. Newton, "We Can Move Mountains and Turn the Tide of Reaction," *Black Panther*, May 19, 1973, 5.

51. Huey P. Newton, "Huey Newton Congratulates Bradley," *Black Panther*, June 9, 1973, 7.

52. Findley, "Huey Newton," 34.

53. Charles Hopkins, "The Deradicalization of the Black Panther Party" (Ph.D. diss., University of North Carolina, 1978), 142.

54. Marine, *Black Panthers*, 120.

55. Jim Haskins, *Power to the People: The Rise and Fall of the Black Panther Party* (New York: Simon and Schuster, 1997), 101.

56. Rufus Browning, Dale Marshall, and William Tabb, *Protest Is Not Enough* (Berkeley: University of California Press, 1984).

57. Major, *Panther Is a Black Cat*, 5.

58. Manning Marable, *Race, Reform and Rebellion: The Second Reconstruction in Black America* (Jackson: University Press of Mississippi, 1991), 110.

59. Heath, *Black Panther Leaders Speak*, 92.

60. Pitney-Howard, *Afro-American Jeremiad*.

61. "Newton Announces Changed Panther Program," *Drummer*, June 30, 1971, 1.

62. William Brink and Louis Harris, *Black and White: A Study of U.S. Racial Attitudes* (New York: Simon and Schuster, 1967).

63. Holden, *Politics*, 126.

64. William R. Corson, *Promise or Peril: The Black College Student in America* (New York: W. W. Norton, 1970), 1.

65. Art Goldberg, "The Panthers after the Trial," *Ramparts* 10, March 1972, 25.

66. Seale, *Seize the Time*, 415; Marine, *Black Panthers*, 73–74; Newton, *To Die for the People*, 21.

67. Les Ledbetter, "Violence Not Needed to Bring Socialism to U.S., Newton Says," *Oakland Tribune*, July 17, 1977.

68. Initially, Newton and the Panthers supported the Bakke decision, calling quotas decisive and labeling the University of California's special admissions program unconstitutional as practiced. When a shocked black community rejected the views of the Panthers, the organization modified its position. For more information see Morris Wright, "Panthers on Bakke: Call Quotas Divisive," *The Guardian*, October 12, 1977.

69. "B.P.P. Leader Discusses Strategy for 1980's," *Black Panther*, February 24, 1980.

70. Les Ledbetter, "Panthers Working within System in Oakland," *Oakland Tribune*, July 18, 1977.

71. "Huey Protests Attack on Black Vets," *Black Panther*, February 24, 1980, 5.

Postscript: Literary Criticisms of Newton's Work

1. As far as this writer can tell, *Insights and Poems* and *War Against the Panthers* did not elicit much attention.

2. Lewis Gordon, "Racist Ideology," *Social Text* 42 (1995): 40–45.

3. Norman Lederer, review of *To Die for the People*, by Huey P. Newton, *Library Journal* 97 (June 1972): 2170.

4. Fred Rotondara, review of *To Die for the People*, by Huey P. Newton, *Best Seller* 32 (June 1972): 139.

5. C. C. Ware, review of *To Die for the People*, by Huey P. Newton, *Saturday Review* 55 (July 1972), 52.

6. Bert Cochran, review of *To Die for the People*, by Huey P. Newton, *Nation*, June 1972, 822.

7. "Revolutionary Suicide," *Choice* 10 (July/August 1973), 862.

8. "Revolutionary Suicide," *Library Journal* 98 (March 1973), 855.

9. Ibid.

10. Rotondara, review of *To Die for the People*, 139.

11. "Radicals: The Divided Panthers." *Time*, February 22, 1971, 23; Eldridge Cleaver, "The California Governor's Election," audiocassette, University of California at Berkeley, 1968.

12. Rotondara, review of *To Die for the People*, 139.

13. Ibid.

14. Ibid.

15. Bert Cochran, "In the Grip of Egalitarian Passion," *Nation*, June 1972, 822.
16. McCartney, *Black Power Ideologies*, 137.
17. Ibid.
18. Ibid., 138.
19. Ibid.
20. Ernest M. Collins, review of *Revolutionary Suicide*, by Huey P. Newton, *Annals of the American Academy* 409 (September 1973): 211–12.
21. Ibid., 212.
22. Ibid.
23. Eugene A. Dooley, review of *Revolutionary Suicide*, by Huey P. Newton, *Best Seller* 33 (June 1973): 117.
24. D. J. C. Brudnoy, review of *Revolutionary Suicide*, by Huey P. Newton, *National Review*, September 14, 1973, 1009.
25. Ibid.
26. Dooley, review of *Revolutionary Suicide*, 116–17.
27. James A. Baldwin, "On Being White and Other Lies," *Essence*, December 1984, 72–73.
28. Colin Wilson, "Power to Whom?," *Spectator*, January 26, 1974, 110–11.

Archives and Libraries

Baltimore Cathedral Public Library, The Maryland Room

Eldridge Cleaver Papers, University of California at Berkeley Library

Georgia State University Library, Atlanta

Huey P. Newton Foundation, Black Panther Party Collection, Stanford University Library, Palo Alto, Calif.

Indiana University Library, Bloomington

Mississippi State Archive, Jackson

Oakland Public Library, File on the Black Panther Party, Oakland, Calif.

Ohio State University Library, Columbus

Purdue University Libraries, West Lafayette, Ind.

Schomburg Center for the Study of Black Culture, Black Panther Party Newspaper Clipping File, New York Public Library

Southern California Library for Social Studies and Research, Los Angeles

Transcripts of CBS interviews of Huey P. Newton, Harvard University Library, Cambridge

University of Michigan Library, Labadie Collection, Ann Arbor

University of Southern California Library, Los Angeles

URL, Civil Rights Movement Collection, University of California at Los Angeles Library

Books

Abdul-Raheem, Tajudeen, ed. 1996. *Pan-Africanism: Politics, Economy and Social Change in the Twenty-First Century.* New York: New York University Press.

Abron, Jonina M. 1993. "Raising the Consciousness of the People: The Black Panther Intercommunal News Service, 1967–1980." In *Voices From the Underground: Insider Histories of the Vietnam Era Underground Press,* ed. Ken Wachsberger. Tempe, Az.: Mica Press.

Allen, Robert. 1983. *Reluctant Reformers.* Washington, D.C.: Howard University Press.

———. 1969. *Black Awakening in Capitalist America.* Garden City, N.Y.: Double Day.

Anthony, Earl. 1990. *Spitting in the Wind: The True Story Behind the Violent Legacy of the Black Panther Party.* Santa Monica, Calif.: Roundtable Publishing.

———. 1970. *Picking Up The Gun.* New York: Pyramid Books.

Archer, Jules. 1971. *Revolution in Our Time.* New York: Julian Messner.

Arendt, Hannah. 1970. *On Violence*. New York: Harcourt Brace and World.

Baran, Paul A. 1965. *A Collective Portrait*. New York: Monthly Review Press.

Blauner, Robert. 1972. *Racial Oppression in America*. New York: Harper & Row.

Boggs, James. 1970. "Black Seventies." In *The Black Seventies*, ed. Floyd Barbour. Boston: Porter Sargent.

Boyle, Kay. 1970. *The Long Walk at San Francisco State*. New York: Grove Press.

Brawley, Benjamin J. 1921. *A Social History of the American Negro*. New York: Macmillan.

Brisbane, Robert H. 1974. *Black Activism: Racial Revolution in the United States 1954–1970*. Valley Forge: Judson Press.

Brent, William Lee. 1996. *Long Time Gone: A Black Panther's True-Life Story of His Hijacking and Twenty-five Years in Cuba*. New York: Times Books.

Brink, William, and Louis Harris. 1967. *Black and White: A Study of U.S. Racial Attitudes*. New York: Simon and Schuster.

Broderick, Francis S. 1959. *W. E. B. DuBois, Negro Leader in a Time of Crisis*. Stanford, Calif.: Stanford University Press.

Brown, Elaine. 1992. *A Taste of Power: A Black Woman's Story*. New York: Pantheon.

Browning, Rufus, Dale Marshall, and William Tabb. 1984. *Protest Is Not Enough*. Berkeley: University of California Press.

Bullock, Paul. 1971. *Watts: The Aftermath*. New York: Grove Press.

Campbell, Horace. 1996. "Pan-Africanism in the Twenty-First Century." In Abdul-Raheem, *Pan-Africanism*.

Carmichael, Stokely. 1997. "Pan-Africanism-Land and Power." In *Modern Black Nationalism: From Marcus Garvey to Louis Farrakhan*, ed. William L. Van DeBurg. New York: New York University Press.

———. 1971. *Stokely Speaks: Black Power Back to Pan-Africanism*. New York: Random House.

Carmichael, Stokely, and Charles V. Hamilton. 1992. *Black Power: The Politics of Liberation*. New York: Vintage.

Carson, Clayborne. 1981. *In Struggle: SNCC and the Black Awakening of the 1960s*. Cambridge: Harvard University Press.

Christian, R. M. 1971. *Ideologies and Modern Politics*. New York: Dodd, Mead.

Clark, Kenneth B. 1965. *Dark Ghetto: Dilemmas of Social Problems*. New York: Harper & Row.

Cleaver, Eldridge. 1969. *Post-Prison Writings and Speeches*. New York: Vintage.

Cleaver, Kathleen N. 1998. "Back to Africa: The Evolution of the International Section of the Black Panther Party 1969–1972." In Jones, *Black Panther Party Reconsidered*.

Conyers, James, and Walter Wallace. 1976. *Black Elected Officials*. New York: Russell Sage Foundation.

Cooper, Lynn, et al. 1975. *The Iron Fist and The Velvet Glove: An Analysis of the U.S. Police*. Berkeley, Calif.: Center for Research on Criminal Justice.

Cornforth, Maurice. 1971. *Materialism and the Dialectical Method*. New York: International Publishers.

Corson, William R. 1970. *Promise or Peril: The Black College Student in America*. New York: W. W. Norton.

Cose, Ellis. 1993. *The Rage of a Privileged Class*. New York: Harper Collins.

Cox, Oliver C. 1948. *Caste, Class and Race: A Study in Social Dynamics*. New York: Doubleday.

Crocker, Lester G. 1968. *Rousseau's Social Contract*. Cleveland: Case Western Reserve.

Cronon, David E. 1955. *Black Moses: The Story of Marcus Garvey and the Universal Negro Improvement Association*. Madison: University of Wisconsin Press.

Cruse, Harold. 1967. *The Crisis of the Negro Intellectual*. New York: Quill.

Debray, Régis. 1967. *Revolution in the Revolution?* New York: MR Press.

Delany, Martin R. 1971. "A Project for an Expedition of Adventure to the Eastern Coast of Africa." In *Black Brotherhood: Afro-Americans and African*, ed. Okon Edet. Lexington, Mass: D. C. Heath.

Dostoevsky, Fyodor. 1938. *Crime and Punishment*. Trans. Constance Garnett. New York: Heritage Club.

Douglas, Frederick. 1962. *The Life and Times of Frederick Douglass*. New York: Collier.

Downs, Donald A. 1999. *Cornell '69: Liberalism and the Crisis of the American University*. Ithaca, N.Y.: Cornell University Press.

Drew, Benjamin. 1968. *A North Side View of Slavery, the Refugee: On the Narrative of Fugitive Slaves in Canada*. 1856. Reprint. New York: New York Times and Arno Press.

DuBois, W. E. B. 1965. *The World and Africa*. New York: International Publishers.

———. 1940. *Dusk of Dawn: An Essay Toward an Autobiography of a Race Concept*. New York: Harcourt Brace.

———. 1919. "The Future of Africa—A Platform." In DuBois, *DuBois Speaks*, vol. 1.

Dymally, Mervyn M. 1971. *The Black Politician: His Struggle for Power*. Belmont, Calif.: Duxbury Press.

Erikson, Erik H., and Huey P. Newton 1973. *In Search of Common Ground*. New York: W. W. Norton.

Evers, Charles. 1971. "The Black American and the Press." In Dymally, *The Black Politician*.

Eze, Emmanuel C. 1997. "The Color of Reason: The Idea of 'Race' in Kant's Anthropology." In *Post Colonial African Philosophy: A Critical Reader,* ed. Emmanuel C. Eze. London: Blackwell.

Fanon, Frantz. 1963. *The Wretched of the Earth.* New York: Grove Press.

Feagin, Joe R. 2000. *Racist America: Roots, Current Realities, and Future Reparations.* New York: Routledge.

Foner, Philip S., ed. 1970. *The Black Panthers Speak.* Philadelphia: Lippincott.

Franklin, H. Bruce. 1978. *The Victim As Criminal and Artist.* New York: Oxford University Press.

Fredrickson, George M. 1995. *Black Liberation.* New York: Oxford University Press.

Gakwandi, Arthur S. 1996. "Towards a New Political Map of Africa in Pan-Africanism." In Abdul-Raheem, *Pan-Africanism.*

Geiss, Immanuel. 1974. *The Pan-African Movement: A History of Pan-Africanism in America, Europe, and Africa.* Trans. A. Keep. New York: Africana Publishing.

Giddings, F. H. 1896. *Principles of Sociology.* New York: Macmillan.

Giddings, Paula. 1984. *When and Where I Enter.* New York: William Morrow.

Gilmore, AL-Tony. 1975. *Bad Nigger!: The National Impact of Jack Johnson.* Port Washington, N.Y.: Kennikat Press.

Gitlin, Todd. 1987. *The Sixties: Years of Hope, Days of Rage.* New York: Bantam Books.

Goldfarb, Jeffrey C. 1998. *Civility and Subversion: The Intellectual in Democratic Life.* New York: Cambridge University Press.

Goldstein, Robert J. 1978. *Political Repression in Modern America 1870 to the Present.* New York: Schenkman.

Guevara, Ernesto. 1961. *Guerilla Warfare.* New York: Vintage.

Hampton, Henry, and Steve Fayer, eds. 1990. *Voices of Freedom.* New York: Bantam Books.

Handlin, Oscar. 1959. *The Newcomers: Negroes and Puerto Ricans in a Changing Metropolis.* Cambridge: Harvard University Press.

Haskins, Jim. 1997. *Power to the People: The Rise and Fall of the Black Panther Party.* New York: Simon and Schuster.

Hayes, Floyd W. III, and Francis A. Kiene III. 1998. "'All Power to the People': The Political Thought of Huey P. Newton and the Black Panther Party." In Jones, *Black Panther Party Reconsidered.*

Healey, Dorothy, and Maurice Isserman. 1990. *Dorothy Healey Remembers: A Life in the American Communist Party.* New York: Oxford University Press.

Heath, Louis G. 1976. *The Black Panther Leaders Speak.* Metuchen, N.J.: Scarecrow Press.

———., ed. 1976. *Off the Pigs! The History and Literature of the Black Panther Party.* Metuchen, N.J.: Scarecrow Press.

Hegel, Georg Wilhelm Friedrich. 1956. *Introduction to the Philosophy of History*. Trans. John Sibree. New York: Dover.

Hendin, Herbert. 1969. *Black Suicide*. New York: Basic Books.

Henry, Charles P. 1992. *Culture and African American Politics*. Bloomington: Indiana University Press.

Herrnstein, Richard J., and Charles Murray. 1994. *The Bell Curve: Intelligence and Class Structure in American Life*. New York: Free Press.

Hilliard, David, and Lewis Cole 1992. *This Side of Glory*. Boston: Little Brown.

Hobbes, Thomas. 1914. *Leviathan*. New York: E. P. Dutton.

Holden, Matthew. 1972. *The Politics of the Black Nation*. New York: Chandler Publishing.

Hughes, Everett Cherrington, and Helen MacGill Hughes. 1952. *Where Peoples Meet: Racial and Ethnic Frontiers*. Glencoe: Free Press.

Hume, David. 1992. "Of National Characters." In *The Philosophical Works*, ed. Thomas Hill Green and Thomas Hodge Grose. Aalen: Scientia Verlag.

"Interview with Huey P. Newton." 1971. In *Black Protest Thought in the Twentieth Century*, ed. August Meier, Elliott Rudwick, and Francis L. Broderick. New York: Bobbs-Merrill.

"Interview with Huey P. Newton by the Movement 1970." 1993. In *The Movement, 1964–1970*, ed. Clayborne Carson. Westport, Conn.: Greenwood Press.

Jacobs, Ron. 1997. *The Way the Wind Blew: A History of the Weather Underground*. New York: Verso.

James, CLR. 1992. "The Revolutionary Answer to the Negro Problem in the U.S." In *The CLR James Reader*, ed. Anna Grimshaw. 1948. Reprint. New York: Blackwell.

James, Daniel. 1968. *The Complete Bolivian Diaries of Che Guevara and Other Captured Documents*. New York: Stein and Day.

Johnson, Ollie A. 1998. "Explaining the Demise of the Black Panther Party: The Role of Internal Factors. In *Black Panther Party Reconsidered*, ed. Charles E. Jones. Baltimore: Black Classic Press.

Jones, Charles E. 1998. "Reconsidering Panther History: The Untold Story." in Jones, *Black Panther Party Reconsidered*.

———., ed. 1998. *The Black Panther Party Reconsidered*. Baltimore: Black Classic Press.

———., and Judson L. Jeffries. 1998. " 'Don't Believe the Hype': Debunking the Panther Mythology." In Jones, *Black Panther Party Reconsidered*.

Kant, Immanuel. 1960. *Observations on the Feeling of the Beautiful and Sublime*. Trans. John T. Goldthwait. Berkeley: University of California Press.

Katz, William Loren. 1995. *Eyewitness: A Living Documentary of the African American Contribution to American History*. New York: Simon and Schuster.

Karenga, Maulana. 1993. *Introduction to Black Studies*. Los Angeles: Sankore Press.

———. 1980. *Kawaida Theory: An Introductory Outline*. Inglewood, Calif.: Kawaidi Publications.

Katsiaficas, George. 1987. *The Imagination of the New Left: A Global Analysis of 1968*. Boston: South End Press.

Keating, Edward. 1971. *Free Huey*. New York: Dell.

Kelly, Robin D. G. 1997. *Yo Mama's Dysfunctional: Fighting the Culture Wars in Urban America*. Boston: Beacon Press.

King, Martin Luther, Jr., 1967. *The Trumpet of Conscience*. New York: Harper & Row.

Kohn, Hans. 1933. "Pan-Movements." In *Encyclopedia of the Social Sciences*. Vol. 11. New York.

Lader, Lawrence. 1979. *Power on the Left*. New York: W. W. Norton.

Lemelle, Anthony J. 1995. *Black Male Deviance*. Westport, Conn.: Praeger.

Lenin, V. I. 1936. "What Is to Be Done?" In *Lenin Selected Works*. New York: International Publishers.

Levine, Lawrence. 1977. *Black Culture and Black Consciousness*. New York: Oxford University Press.

Litwick, Leon F. 1979. *Been in the Storm So Long*. New York: Alfred A. Knopf.

Locke, John. 1956. *The Second Treatise of Government*. New York: Macmillan.

Logan, Rayford. 1962. "The Historical Aspects of Pan-Africanism, 1900–1945." In *Pan-Africanism Reconsidered*, ed. American Society of African Culture. Berkeley: University of California Press.

Macridis, Roy C. 1983. *Contemporary Political Ideologies*. Boston: Little Brown.

Major, Reginald. 1974. *A Panther Is a Black Cat*. New York: Morrow.

Malcolm X. 1970. *By Any Means Necessary*. New York: Grove Press.

———, with Alex Haley. 1964. *The Autobiography of Malcolm X*. New York: Grove Press.

Marable, Manning. 1992. *The Crisis of Color and Democracy*. Monroe, Maine: Common Courage Press.

———. 1991. *Race, Reform and Rebellion: The Second Reconstruction in Black America*. Jackson: University Press of Mississippi.

Marcuse, Herbert. 1966. *A Critique of Pure Tolerance*. Boston: Beacon Press.

Marine, Gene. 1969. *The Black Panthers*. New York: Signet.

Marx, Karl, and Freidrich Engels. 1978. "Manifesto of the Communist Party." In *The Marx-Engels Reader*, ed. Robert C. Tucker. New York: W. W. Norton.

McCartney, John T. 1992. *Black Power Ideologies: An Essay in African-American Political Thought*. Philadelphia: Temple University Press.

McKay, Claude. 1937. *A Long Way from Home*. New York: Lee Furman.

Memmi, Albert. 1967. *The Colonizer and the Colonized*. Trans. Howard Greenfield. Boston: Beacon Press.

Mills, Charles W. 1997. *The Racial Contract*. Ithaca, N.Y.: Cornell University Press.

Mitford, Jessica. 1974. *Kind and Usual Punishment: The Prison Business*. New York: Vintage.

Moore, Carlos. 1972. *Were Marx and Engels White Racists? The Prolet Aryan Outlook of Marx and Engels*. Chicago: Institute of Positive Education.

Moore, Gilbert. 1971. *A Special Rage: A Black Reporter's Encounter with Huey P. Newton's Murder Trial, the Black Panthers and His Own Destiny*. New York: Harper & Row.

Morris, Aldon. 1984. *The Origins of the Civil Rights Movement*. New York: Free Press.

Muse, Benjamin. 1970. *The American Negro Revolution: From Nonviolence to Black Power*. New York: Citadel Press.

Newton, Huey P. 1996. *War Against the Panthers: A Study of Repression in America*. New York: Harlem River Press.

———. 1973. *Revolutionary Suicide*. New York: Harcourt Brace Jovanovich.

———. 1972. *To Die for the People*. New York: Random House.

———. 1971. "The Black Panther Party." In *Racial Conflict: Tension and Change In American Society*, ed. Gary T. Marx. New York: Little Brown.

———., and Erica Huggins. 1975. *Insights & Poems*. San Francisco: City Light Books.

Newton, Michael. 1980. *Bitter Grain*. Los Angeles: Holloway House Publishing.

Nkrumah, Kwame. 1970. *Class Struggle in Africa*. New York: International Publishers.

———. 1965. *Neo-Colonialism: The Last Stage of Imperialism*. London: Nelson.

———. 1963. *Africa Must Unite*. New York: Frederick A. Praeger.

O'Reilly, Kenneth. 1989. *Racial Matters*. New York: Free Press.

Park, Robert Ezra, and Ernest W. Burgess. 1921. *Introduction to the Science of Sociology*. Chicago: University of Chicago Press.

Parenti, Michael. 1995. *Democracy for the Few*. New York: St. Martin's.

Pearson, Hugh. 1994. *The Shadow of the Panther*. Reading, Mass.: Addison-Wesley.

Pieterse, Jan N. 1992. *White on Black: Images of Africa and Black in Western Popular Culture*. New Haven, Conn.: Yale University Press.

Pinkney, Alphonso. 1976. *Red, Black and Green: Black Nationalism in the United States*. New York: Cambridge University Press.

Pitney-Howard, David. 1990. *The Afro-American Jeremiad*. Philadelphia: Temple University Press.

Piven, Francis Fox, and Richard Cloward. 1977. *Poor People's Movements*. New York: Pantheon.

Pohlman, Marcus. 1998. *Black Politics in White Conservative America*. New York: Longman.

———. 1993. *Governing the Postindustrial City*. New York: Longman.

Rainwater, Lee. 1968. "Neighborhood Action and Lower-Class Life Style." In *Neighborhood Organization for Community Action*, ed. John B. Turner. New York: National Associations of Social Workers.

Reddick. L. D. 1966. "The Negro as Southerner and American." In *The Southerner as American*, ed. Charles G. Sellers. New York: E. P. Dutton, 1996.

Reed, Adolph, Jr. 1997. *W. E. B. DuBois and American Political Thought*. New York: Oxford University Press.

Rejai, Mostafa. 1984. *Comparative Political Ideologies*. New York: St. Martin's.

Rice, J. F. 1983. *Up on Madison Down on 75th*. Evanston, Ill.: The Committee.

Roberts, John W. 1989. *From Trickster to Badman: The Black Folk Hero in Slavery and Freedom*. Philadelphia: University of Pennsylvania Press.

Robinson, Randall. 2000. *The Debt: What America Owes to Blacks*. New York: Plume.

Rousseau, Jean-Jacques. 1984. *Discourse on the Origins and Foundations of Inequality among Men*. Trans. Maurice Cranston. London: Penguin.

———. 1913. *The Social Contract and Discourses*. Trans. G. D. H. Cole. New York: E. P. Dutton.

Sabine, George H. 1973. *A History of Political Theory*. Hillsdale, Ill.: Dryden Press.

Seale, Bobby G. 1969. "Free Huey." In *Rhetoric of Black Revolution*, ed. Arthur L. Smith. Boston: Allyn and Bacon.

———. 1978. *A Lonely Rage*. New York: Times Books.

———. 1970. *Seize the Time*. New York: Random House.

Shklar, Judith N. 1991. *American Citizenship: The Quest for Inclusion*. Cambridge: Harvard University Press.

Singahm, A. W. 1968. *The Hero and the Crowd in a Colonial Polity*. New Haven, Conn.: Yale University Press.

Singh, Nikhil Pal. 1998. "The Black Panthers and the 'Undeveloped Country' of the Left." In Jones, *Black Panther Party Reconsidered*.

Skolnick, Jerome H. 1969. *The Politics of Protest: A Task Force Report Submitted to the National Commission on the Causes and Prevention of Violence*. New York: Simon and Schuster.

Smerten, Yuri. 1987. *Kwame Nkrumah*. New York: International Publishers.

Smith, Robert C. 1996. *We Have No Leaders*. New York: SUNY Press.

Stalin, Joseph. 1939. *Foundations of Leninism*. Vol. 10, *Selected Works*. New York: International Publishers.

Tocqueville, Alexis de. 1966. *Democracy in America.* Edited by Mayer Lerner and Max Lerner. 1835. Reprint. New York: Harper & Row.

Tse Tung, Mao. 1972. *Quotations from Chairman Mao Tse Tung.* Peking: Foreign Languages Press.

Van DeBurg, William L. 1992. *New Day in Babylon: The Black Power Movement and American Culture, 1965–1975.* Chicago: University of Chicago Press.

Walker, Samuel, Cassia Spohn, and Miriam DeLone. 2000. *The Color of Justice.* Belmont, Calif.: Wadsworth.

Walton, Hanes, Jr., and Robert C. Smith. 2000. *American Politics and the African-American Quest for Universal Freedom.* New York: Addison-Wesley Longman.

Washington, James M., ed. 1986. *Testament of Hope: The Essential Writings of Martin Luther King, Jr.* San Francisco: Harper & Row.

Weber, Max. 1968. *From Max Weber: Essays in Sociology.* Ed. and trans. by H. H. Gerth and C. Wright Mills. New York: Oxford University Press.

Wiggins, William H. 1973. "Jack Johnson as Bad Nigger: The Folklore of His Life." In *Contemporary Black Thought,* ed. Robert Chrisman and Nathan Hare. New York: Bobbs-Merrill.

Williams, Robert F. 1973. *Negroes with Guns.* 1962. Reprint. Chicago: Third World Press.

Williams, T. Harry. 1969. *Huey Long.* New York: Vintage.

Williams, Yohuru R. 2000. *Black Power/White Politics, Civil Rights, Black Power, and the Black Panthers in New Haven.* Naugatuck, Conn.: Brandywine Press.

Journal Articles

Abraham, Roger D. "Some Varieties of Heroes in America." *Journal of the Folklore Institute* 3 (1966): 3.

Aberbach, Joel D., and Jack L. Walker. "The Meanings of Black Power: A Comparison of White and Black Interpretations of a Political Slogan." *American Political Science Review* 64 (June 1970): 367–88.

Bernstein, Deborah. "Conflict and Protest in Israeli Society: The Case of the Black Panthers of Israel." *Youth and Society* 14 (December 1984): 129–51.

Blauner, Robert. "Internal Colonialism and Ghetto Revolt." *Social Problems* 16 (fall 1969): 393–408.

Boggs, James. "The Myth and Irrationality of Capitalism." *Review of Black Political Economy* 1 (spring/summer 1970): 27–35.

Brearley, H. C. "Ba-ad Nigger." *South Atlantic Quarterly* 38 (fall 1939): 75–81.

Downes, Brian T. "A Critical Re-examination of the Social and Political Characteristics of Riot Cities." *Social Science Quarterly* 51 (December 1970): 349–60.

Edmondson, Locksley. "The Internationalization of Black Power: Historical and Contemporary Perspectives." *Mawazo* 1 (December 1968): 16–29.

Emerson, Rupert. "Pan-Africanism." *International Organization* 16 (spring 1962): 282.

Franklin, H. Bruce. "The Lumpenproletariat and the Revolutionary Youth Movement." *Monthly Review* 21 (January 1970): 10–25.

Frappier, Jon. "Chase Goes to Harlem: Financing Black Capitalism." *Freedomways* 28 (April 1977): 23.

Gordon, Lewis. "Racist Ideology." *Social Text* 42 (spring 1995): 40–45.

Hayes, Floyd W., III. "New Class Power: The Political Role of Black Policy Specialists." *Negro Educational Review* (forthcoming).

Henderson, Errol. "The Lumpenproletariat as Vanguard?" *Journal of Black Studies* 28 (November 1997): 171–99.

Henry, Charles P. "The Political Role of the 'Bad Nigger.'" *Journal of Black Studies* 2 (June 1981): 461–83.

Jeffries, Judson L. "Black Radicalism and Political Oppression in Baltimore: The Case of the Black Panther Party." *Ethnic and Radical Studies* 24 (January 2002): 34–69.

Jennings, Michael E., Jr. "Social Theory and Transformation in the Pedagogy of Dr. Huey P. Newton." *Educational Foundations* (winter 1999): 79–96.

Johnson, Guy. "The Negro and Crime." *Annals of the American Academy* 217 (1941): 98.

Jones, Charles E. "The Political Repression of the Black Panther Party: The Case of the Bay Area 1966–1971." *Journal of Black Studies* 18 (June 1988): 415–34.

Jones, Rhett S. "Why Pan-Africanism Failed: Blackness and International Relations." *Griot* 14 (spring 1995): 58–69.

Marable, Manning. "The Third Reconstruction: Black Nationalism and Race in a Revolutionary America." *Social Text* 4 (fall 1981): 1–27.

Mootry, Maria. "Confronting Racialized Bioethics: New Contract on Black America." *Western Journal of Black Studies* 24 (spring 2000): 1–8.

Mori, Jimmy. "The Ideological Development of the Black Panther Party." *Cornell Journal of Social Relations* 12 (spring 1977): 137–55.

Newton, Huey P. "Culture and Liberation." *Tricontinental* 11 (March–April 1969): 196–201.

Poussaint, Alvin F. "Education and Black Self-Image." *Freedomways* (fall 1968): 335.

Preston, Michael B. "Black Elected Officials and Public Policy." *Policy Studies Journal* (winter 1978): 196–201.

Rainwater, Lee. "The Problems of Lower Class Culture." *Journal of Social Issues* 26 (spring 1970): 133.

Rhodes, Robert. "Internationalism and Social Consciousness in the Black Community." *Freedomways* 12 (third quarter 1972): 230.

Rudwick, Elliot M. "DuBois versus Garvey: Race Propagandists at War." *Journal of Negro History* 28 (1959): 423, 426.

Sharakiya, A. M. "Pan-Africanism: A Critical Reassessment." *Transafrica Forum* 8 (winter 1991–92): 50.

Staples, Robert. "American Racism and High Crime Rates: The Inextricable Connection." *Western Journal of Black Studies* 8 (summer 1984): 62–72.

Strong, Samuel M. "Negro-White Relationships as Reflected in Social Types." *American Journal of Sociology* 52 (July 1946): 23–30.

Takagi, Paul. "A Garrison State in 'Democratic' Society." *Crime and Social Justice* 1 (spring/summer 1974): 29.

Tucker, Robert. "Personality and Political Leadership." *Political Science Quarterly* 92 (fall 1977): 383–400.

———. "The Theory of Charismatic Leadership." *Daedalus* 97 (summer 1968): 731–56.

Williams, T. Harry. "The Gentleman from Louisiana: Demagogue or Democrat?" *Journal of Southern History* 26 (February 1960).

Williams, Yohuru R. "In the Name of the Law: The 1967 Shooting of Huey Newton and Law Enforcement's Permissive Environment." *Negro History Bulletin* 61 (April–June 1997): 6–18.

Book Reviews

Brudnoy, D. J. C. Review of *Revolutionary Suicide*, by Huey P. Newton. *National Review*, September 14, 1973, 1009.

Cochran, Bert. "In the Grip of Egalitarian Passion." *Nation*, June 26, 1972, 822.

Collins, Ernest. Review of *Revolutionary Suicide*, by Huey P. Newton. *Annals of the American Academy* 409 (September 1973): 211–12.

Dooley, Eugene A. Review of *Revolutionary Suicide*, by Huey P. Newton. *Best Seller* 33 (June 1973): 117.

Edmonds, A. O. Review of *In Search of Common Ground*, by Erik H. Erikson and Huey P. Newton. *Library Journal* 99 (January 1974): 148.

Lederer, Norman. Review of *To Die for the People*, by Huey P. Newton. *Library Journal* 97 (June 1972): 2170.

Review of *Revolutionary Suicide*, by Huey P. Newton. *Choice* 10 (July/August 1973): 862.

Review of *Revolutionary Suicide*, by Huey P. Newton. *Library Journal* 98 (March 1973): 855.

Rotondara, Fred. Review of *To Die for the People*, by Huey P. Newton. *Best Seller* 32 (June 1972): 139.

Ware, C. C. Review of *To Die for the People*, by Huey P. Newton. *Saturday Review* 55, 1972, 52.

Wilson, Colin. "Power to Whom?" *Spectator*, January 26, 1976, 110–11.

Mainstream Newspapers

"The Black Panthers' Two Paths." *New York Times,* August 24, 1989.

Brand, William, and Larry Spears. "Friends and Foes Remember Newton: 'Visionary, Thug.'" *Oakland Tribune,* August 23, 1989.

Diehl, Digby. "The Black Panther Party Is Not a Separatist Party." *Washington Post,* August 16, 1972.

"Huey Newton Backs Race by Mrs. Chisholm." *New York Times,* April 28, 1972.

Ledbetter, Les. "Panthers Working Within System in Oakland." *Oakland Tribune,* July 18, 1977.

———. "Violence Not Needed to Bring Socialism to U.S., Newton Says." *Oakland Tribune,* July 17, 1977.

"Newton Announces Changed Panther Program." *Drummer,* June 30, 1971.

"Newton Calls Constitution Outdated, Urges Socialism." *San Francisco Examiner & Chronicle,* September 6, 1970.

Olszewski, Lori, and Rick DelVecchio. "Huey Newton Shot to Death in West Oakland." *San Francisco Chronicle,* August 23, 1989.

Ostrow, Ronald J. "U.S. Imprisons Black Men at 4 Times S. African Rate." *Los Angeles Times,* January 5, 1991.

"Party Putting Guns Down: Huey Newton Interviewed." *Alameda (Calif.) Times-Star,* January 31, 1972.

Slater, Jack. "Huey Newton Speaks Out." *Los Angeles Times,* August 25, 1977.

The *Black Panther* Newspaper

Carter, Alprentice (Bunchy). "The Genius of Huey Newton." March 3, 1969.

Cleaver, Eldridge. "Huey's Standard." March 15, 1970.

"Evidence and Intimidation of Fascist Crimes by U.S.A." February 21, 1970.

"Huey in Scandinavia." March 31, 1973.

"Huey P. Newton Urges Release of Georgia's Unjustly Imprisoned." May 4, 1974.

"Huey Protests Attack on Black Vets." February 24, 1980.

"I Cannot Be Intimidated Because I Have Given My Life to the People." 1978.

Newton, Huey P. "Huey Newton Congratulates Bradley." June 9, 1973.

———. "We Can Move Mountains and Turn the Tide of Reaction." May 19, 1973.

———. "Uniting Against the Common Enemy." October 23, 1971.

———. "A Newspaper Is the Voice of a Party." March 13, 1971.

———. "Towards a New Constitution." November 28, 1970.

———. "To the Courageous Revolutionaries of the National Liberation Front and Provisional Revolutionary Government of South Vietnam We Send Greetings." August 21, 1970.

———. "To the RNA." December 6, 1969.

———. "The Black Panthers." August 23, 1969.

———. "Prison, Where Is Thy Victory." July 12, 1969.

———. "The Correct Handling of a Revolution." May 18, 1969.

———. "In Defense of Self-Defense." June 20, 1967.

"Polynesian Panther Party 7-Point Platform Serves the People." June 6, 1974.

"Puerto Rican Young Lords Support BPP." June 7, 1969.

Sinclair, John A. "White Panther Party Supports Black Panther Party." October 11, 1969. "A Spokesman for the People: Huey P. Newton Devastates Buckley on *Firing Line*." February 24, 1973.

"Statement by Huey P. Newton at the Chicago, Illinois Coliseum, February 21, 1971." April 10, 1971.

"We Have To Attend to Our People: An Interview with Comrade Huey P. Newton." September 2, 1972.

Left-wing and Mainstream Publications

Avakian, Bob. *Bob Avakian Talks about Huey Newton and the Panthers* (Chicago: The Revolutionary Worker, 1991).

Barnard, Murray. "For Negroes in Halifax, Black Power v. Ping Pong." *Macleans* (Toronto), November 1967, 1.

"Black Power May Emerge in Australia." *Nationalist* (Dar Es Salaam), August 23, 1968.

Burlingham, Bo. "Huey Newton's Revival Meeting in Oakland." *Ramparts*, 1972, 10–11.

Cleaver, Eldridge. "On Cleaver." *Ramparts*, December 14–28, 1968, 10.

Craig, Sarah. "Panther Leader Newton Slain: Early Gay-Rights Supporter Gunned Down." *Windy City Times*, August 31, 1989, 6.

Dohrn, Bernadine. "White Mother Country Radicals." *New Left Notes*, July 29, 1968, 136.

Frankel, Anita. "New Panther Faces Old Problems." *Ramparts*, February 24, 1978, 6.

"Huey Newton Speaks from Jail." *Motive*, October 1968, 8–16.

Hutchings, Phil. "What Program for Black Liberation Movement?" *Radical Forum*, June 19, 1974, 8, 19.

Johnson, Joy. "Huey Newton in Prison: An Interview." *Ramparts*, September 1970, 5.

Newton, Huey P. "Politics and the Gun." *Guardian*, June 16, 1971, 7–8.

———. "Interview with Huey Newton." *Guardian*, September 22, 1970, 7.

Perkins, Charles. "Black Power." *Union Recorder* (published by the Sydney University Students Union), June 13, 1968.

Stern, Sol. "America's Black Guerrillas." *Ramparts*, September 6, 1967, 26.

Thompson, Walt. "What's Left of the Black Left?" *Ramparts*, June 1973, 53.

Williams, Lynora. "Jim Crow: What the Judges Do in Private." *Guardian*, October 10, 1979.

Wright, Morris. "Panthers on Bakke: Call Quotas Divisive." *Guardian*, October 12, 1977.

Popular Magazines

Baldwin, James A. "On Being White and Other Lies." *Essence*, December 1984, 72–73.

"Black Power in Britain." *Life*, October 16, 1967, 8–17.

Crouch, Stanley. "Huey P. Newton: RIP." *New Republic*, September 18–25, 1989, 10.

Findley, Tim. "Huey Newton Twenty-five Floors from the Street." *Rolling Stone*, August 3, 1972, 34.

"The Hearst Nightmare." *Time*, April 29, 1974, 12.

"Huey Newton: A Candid Conversation with the Embattled Leader of the Black Panther Party." *Playboy*, May 1973, 78.

Jones, Robert A. *Nation*, August 11, 1969, 102.

McCoy, Frank. "Can Clinton's Urban Policies Really Work?" *Black Enterprise*, June 1994, 182

Newton, Huey P. "'I Found Freedom in Jail': Black Panther Leader Recalls Ordeal of Solitary Confinement." *Ebony*, May 1973, 54–62.

"Odyssey of Huey Newton." *Time*, November 13, 1978, 38–39.

"The Panthers and the Law." *Newsweek*, February 23, 1970, 30.

"Radicals: The Divided Panthers." *Time*, February 22, 1971, 23.

Rodgers, Michael. "Some Quiet Hours with Huey Newton." *Esquire*, 1972, 156–58, 232.

Rogers, Cornish. "Demythologizing Huey Newton." *Christian Century*, August 15–22, 1973, 795.

Dissertations, Theses, and Other Unpublished Works

Hayes, Floyd W., III. "Black Consciousness and the Black Student's Union." Unpublished manuscript, n.d.

Hopkins, Charles. "The Deradicalization of the Black Panther Party." Ph.D. diss., University of North Carolina, 1978.

Newton, Huey P. "War Against the Panthers: A Study of Repression in America." Ph.D. diss., University of California at Santa Cruz, 1980.

———. "The Historical Origins of Existentialism and the Common Denominators of Existential Philosophy." Unpublished manuscript, 1979.

———. "War without Terms: The Death of George Jackson." Unpublished manuscript, 1979.

———. "The Dialectics of Nature." Unpublished manuscript, 1974.

———. "Eliminate the Presidency." Unpublished manuscript, 1974

———. "Intercommunalism." Rev. ed. Unpublished manuscript, 1974.

———. "On Pan-Africanism or Communism." Unpublished manuscript, December 1972.

———. "Intercommunalism: A Higher Level of Consciousness." Unpublished manuscript, 1970.

———. "A Citizens Peace Force." Unpublished manuscript, 1972.

Stewart, Helen L. "Buffering: The Leadership Style of Huey P. Newton, Co-Founder of the Black Panther Party." Master's thesis, Brandeis University, 1980.

Lectures and Speeches

Carmichael, Stokely., "A Declaration of War." Transcript of speech, February 17, 1968, in Oakland, Calif. *The Running Man* 1:1 (May–June 1968): 17–21.

———. Lecture, "Black Power." 55 min. University of California at Berkeley, April 1966. Audiocassette.

Cleaver, Eldridge. Lecture, "The California Governor's Election." 55 min. University of California at Berkeley, October 1968. Audiocassette.

Horowitz, David. Lecture, "The 1960s." University of Southern California, April 22, 1997.

Memoranda, Government Documents, and Reports

Bureau of Census. "Census Bureau Announces Number of America in Poverty Up for Fourth Year Although Poverty Rate Unchanged, Household Income and Health Care Coverage Drop." Press release, October 6, 1994.

"NAACP Claims Brutality by Police in L.A." *Los Angeles Times*, February, 19, 1962. Contained in NAACP Papers Group 111, Folder A243, Manuscript Division, Library of Congress.

Sourcebook of Criminal Justice Statistics—1975. Albany, N.Y.: U.S. Department of Justice, Criminal Justice Research Center, 1976.

Special Report to the Congress: Mandatory Minimal Penalties in the Federal Criminal Justice System. Washington, D.C.: U.S. Sentencing Commission, August 1991.

Spivack Report 4:4, June 30, 1969.

Pamphlets

Newton, Huey P. " Huey P. Newton Talks to the Movement." Chicago: The Movement, 1968.

Interviews

Amour, Al. Interview by Judson L. Jeffries. Los Angeles, April 2, 1993.

Anthony, Earl. Interview by Charles E. Jones and Judson L. Jeffries. Los Angeles, June 20, 1992.

Bremond, Deborah. Interview by Charles E. Jones and Judson L. Jeffries. Oakland, Calif., June 17, 1992.

Brown, H. Rap. Interview by Judson L. Jeffries. Binghamton, N.Y., November 1991.

Cleaver, Eldridge. Interview by Charles E. Jones. Virginia Beach, Va., March 24, 1995.

Collier, Robert. Interview by Judson L. Jeffries. Binghamton, N.Y., November 1991.

Douglas, Emory. Interview by Judson L. Jeffries. San Francisco, June 15, 1992.

Freed, Donald. Interview by Judson L. Jeffries. Los Angeles, July 1993.

Freeman, Roland. Interview by Judson L. Jeffries, Los Angles, July 2, 1993.

Jenkins, Yvonne. Interview by Charles E. Jones and Judson L. Jeffries. Marin County, Calif., June 16, 1992.

McCutheon, Steve. Interview by Charles E. Jones and Judson L. Jeffries. Oakland, Calif., June 6, 1992.

Parker, Richard. Interview by Judson L. Jeffries. Cambridge, Mass., May 24, 1995.

Pharr, Wayne. Interview by Judson L. Jeffries. Los Angeles, June 1, 1993.

Pinderhughes, Charles "Cappy." Interview by Judson L. Jeffries. Cambridge, Mass., August 1993.

Powell, Curtis. Interview by Judson L. Jeffries. Queens, N.Y., January 1992.

Ricks, Willie. Interview by Judson L. Jeffries. Los Angeles, May 10, 1998.

Seale, Bobby G. Interview by Charles E. Jones. Atlanta, October 24, 1996.

Slater, Jimmy. Interview by Charles E. Jones and Judson L. Jeffries. Oakland, Calif., June 15, 1992.

Williams, Landon. Interview by Judson L. Jeffries. San Francisco, June 20, 1992.

Transcripts. Videos, and Audiocassettes of Interviews

Blum, Joe, and Dave Wellman. "A Prison Interview with Huey Newton." Summer 1968.

Goldberg, Bernard. "Interview with Huey P. Newton." *CBS Morning News*, July 4, 1977.

Huey Newton Speaks. Interview with Huey P. Newton by Mark Lane. 47 min. Pardon Records, 1971.

Interview of Huey Newton by KPFA-FM Radio, August 14, 1970.

An Interview with Bobby Seale, Black Panther Party, Community Information Center, Maryland State Chapter, n.d.

The Late 60's in Review I. 60 min. Education Research Group, 1969. Audio-cassette.

Prelude to a Revolution. Interview with Huey P. Newton by John Evans (in 1967). 76 min. Xenon Entertainment Group, 1998.

Press Conference. "Huey Calls Stokely Carmichael a CIA Agent." August 26, 1970.

Seale on Ice: An Extensive, Uncensored Interview with the Black Panther Party Leader. 59 min. Center for Cassette Studies, 1970–71.